T0358351

Endorsements

"At face value, if you're not familiar with or operating in the industry, a discussion on China's property market and its digital transformation would seem either too niche or too complicated. Yet the masterful narration and poignant insights penned by Paul, Dean, and Roman make this a compelling and important read for all. They map out the digitalization of property against the backdrop of China's increasingly dominant technological innovation."

Tan Yinglan
Founding Managing Partner
Insignia Ventures Partners, Singapore

"This book captures the fascinating stories of 'smart city initiatives' in China, where urbanization has been a major driver of national development. As tech is a key pillar of urban infrastructure for any smart city, Chinese tech companies from Alibaba and Tencent to some start-ups are playing unparalleled and unprecedented roles. Paul and his colleagues tell you all you need and should know about these developments."

Ben Shenglin
Professor & Dean
International Business School & Academy of Internet Finance
Zhejiang University, Hangzhou

"The business landscape in the past three decades has been driven by data and digitization in the virtual world. The next three decades will see an explosion of data and digitization in the physical world, where online and offline will blend together. In order to truly understand this dynamic, one needs to use a lens both from top-down and bottom-up perspectives. Paul's deep understanding of global economies, geo-politics, financial systems and the role of real estate combine to illuminate the drivers behind this exciting evolution."

Joshua Varghese
Founding Partner, Axia Real Assets, Toronto

"The melding of AI and IoT is an equally accessible opportunity for all countries in the world. As long as we are all willing to innovate and invest in them, everyone can all get very promising returns. This book introduces many successful cases. It is an inspiring read for those who are interested in cutting edge innovations in proptech."

He Wanyu
CEO, XKool, Shenzhen

"This comprehensive volume provides a panoramic analysis of China's ongoing digital transformations. This book is a must-read for entrepreneurs and scholars of China alike."

Yushih Liao
Executive Vice President of R&D, Christie's International, Taipei

"As revealed in *Innovation's Crouching Tiger*, the 'five-year plan' is an effective observation tool for tracking the development of China's innovation ecosystem. The authors of this book proficiently use this tool to analyze contemporary issues, exemplary cases, and interesting stories in connection with digital transformation of property in Greater China, providing a clear, organized panoramic perspective for readers who wish to gain insights on such rapid-changing frontier."

Jili Chung
MIT Sloan Fellow, JD, MBA, MS, and Ph.D., author of
Innovation's Crouching Tiger, Shanghai

"Paul and his co-authors offer a fresh and timely insight into the key technologies shaping China's digital strategy and the new breed of corporate behemoths emerging from the region."

Lawson Emanuel
Principal, Hedosophia, London

"To find 'comparative' advantage requires the broadest possible understanding of the history, present circumstances and future plans of a nation's competitors. This book offers readers detailed perspectives into China's past success, its plans and aspirations. It is not necessary to 'agree' with China's plans to succeed by developing and exploiting comparative advantages. It is, however, essential that we understand China. This book helps readers achieve that understanding."

Fred Feldkamp
Author of *Financial Stability: Fraud, Confidence
and the Wealth of Nations*, Michigan

"An intriguing masterpiece with in-depth analysis of China's roadmap to be the next proptech powerhouse along the lines of its FinTech mastery. This book shows how this will be achieved through heavy investments in 5G, IoT and Blockchain."

Chia Hock Lai
President, Singapore FinTech Association & Co-Chairman
of Blockchain Association, Singapore

"China will be taking a leadership role in driving the global landscape for both FinTech infrastructure as well as the future world of regulated digital assets such as buildings and logistics. This book gives a peek into the exciting digital finance ecosystem that is rapidly developing in China. The authors have put together many unique insights with their deep insider perspective into a world which is largely opaque to an international audience."

Michael Sung
Co-Director of the Fudan Fanhai FinTech Research Center,
Shanghai

"The authors offer a unique insider's view of the coming revolution in the digitization of property assets. In addition, it lays out many ways in which finance, insurance, healthcare and environmental science will be embedded into a multi-trillion-dollar asset class which has barely been touched by the digital economy."

Zain Jaffer
Partner, Blue Field Capital, San Francisco

"*The Digital Transformation of Property in Greater China* brilliantly weaves together the digitization of urban planning and property as well as the massive government buildout behind it. Whether you are optimistic or pessimistic about China, this book will give you a far clearer picture of modern China and her wildly ambitious plans to create the infrastructure of the 21st century."

Sean Moss-Pultz,
CEO, Bitmark, Taipei

"Paul Schulte's latest book (with his co-authors Shemakov and Sun) is called *The Digital Transformation of Property in Greater China* and describes the transformation of the asset class through the smart city initiative. In fact, the title doesn't do the book justice, as it explains the integration of traditional infrastructure with FinTech and also emerging technologies like blockchain. In so doing, it also lays bare how far China is ahead of the rest of the world in building a truly integrated digital economy."

Rob Jesudason
Founding Partner and CIO
Serendipity Capital, Singapore

"Blockchain and 5G technologies are at the center of China's latest drive to digitize its physical assets, particularly commercial and residential real estates. This effort has brought and will continue to bring sweeping change to China's economic and financial system, with significant implications for the world. Read this book and you will get an excellent understanding of China's policy vision for new technologies over the coming years and how private businesses have used their imagination, innovation and partnerships with the public sector to bring digital transformation to daily life in China."

Taiyang Zhang
Founder, Ren and Talo Systems, Singapore

"For years, the conversation around proptech has been full of speculation and imagination. *The Digital Transformation of Property in Greater China* finally brings that conversation to reality through a comprehensive analysis of the technologies and policies that have already begun to shape the future of real estate, especially in China. The authors provide a roadmap toward opportunity to those who choose to understand it and a warning to those who do not. This book raises the right questions at a critical moment."

Jordan Kostelac
Director, PropTech, JLL Asia, Hong Kong

"'Government policy doesn't intersect directly with cutting edge technology.' A dangerously naïve sentiment that is particularly wrongheaded when considering China. This book is vitally instructive in 'connecting the dots' in the digitization of the economy for Western investors, executives, policymakers and institutions. The book offers a framework to understand how government policy, macro trends, digitization and human behavior all intersect to drive economies and power humankind forward. I believe it can deepen understanding and support informed decision-making among all stakeholders."

Jason W. Best
Managing Partner, Vectr Fintech Partners, Hong Kong

"This book offers insight into a massive on-going digital transformation as well as a new war on monetizing data to enable an economy to exponentially thrive in an increasingly competitive world. It's not just about technology or data but how to combine these two elements into a digitally accelerating economy. China and its actions along the Silk Road are creating an economic superpower based on data. And it is monetizing this data via building blocks of modern economies: people, industries, cities, buildings, finance, planning and execution. This book brings the key elements at play via use cases to create an in-depth understanding of the digitalized power struggle vying for ecosystems that drive expansion and competitiveness in a highly polarized century."

Jorge Sebastiao
CEO
Global Blockchain Organization-GBO, Dubai

"Paul Schulte, Roman Shemakov and Dean Sun provide an original, engaging and considered narrative map of the birth of Greater China's re-imagining both cities and real estate in a digital age. The book offers clear signposts for Greater China's aims and its commanding role of emergent technologies. At the same time, it analyzes the philosophical foundations of this seismic VoE (Value of Everything) economic revolution. I could not stop reading it — neither will you."

Andrew Stanton
CEO & Founder, Proptech-PR, London

"The US and China are engaged in one of history's greatest competitions over urban technology and proptech. While the United States' role has received an outpour of coverage, China's role has remained in the shadows. This book is the first cohesive work to make sense of China's proptech industry. This will be an essential field guide for everyone looking to understand technology's impact on the built world and the future of cities."

John Thomey
Founder of Urban Tech, Los Angeles

An insider's guide giving you an in-depth view into China and the companies changing our world. Chinese companies are innovation powerhouses, understanding how they harness these key technologies will give you a glimpse of the future. A must-read.

Richard Turrin
Author of *Cashless: China's Digital Currency Revolution*
Shanghai

"Paul, Dean, and Roman have articulated what many in the West have feared. China has a commanding and expanding lead in the Fourth Industrial Revolution. This is a data-based societal transformation requiring a level of state involvement that the US is yet to embrace. Rather than rejecting market mechanisms, China's centralized embrace of Blockchain, AI, and other forms of digital infrastructure will see private Chinese firms continue to be global leaders in FinTech, 5G, AI, and, as the book explores, proptech. This book is a celebration of what China can achieve through public/private collaboration. It is also a warning to the US of the widening innovation gap between itself and China."

Paul Krake
Founder of US-China Series, Chicago

The Digital Transformation of Property in Greater China

Finance, 5G, AI, and Blockchain

Singapore University of Social Sciences - World Scientific Future Economy Series

ISSN: 2661-3905

Series Editor
David Lee Kuo Chuen *(Singapore University of Social Sciences, Singapore)*

Subject Editors
Guan Chong *(Singapore University of Social Sciences, Singapore)*
Ding Ding *(Singapore University of Social Sciences, Singapore)*

Singapore University of Social Sciences - World Scientific Future Economy Series introduces the new technology trends and challenges that businesses today face, financial management in the digital economy, blockchain technology, smart contract and cryptography. The authors describe current issues that the business leaders and finance professionals are facing, as well as developments in digitalisation. The series covers several increasingly important new areas such as the fourth industrial revolution, Internet of Things (IoT), blockchain technology, artificial intelligence (AI) and many other forces of disruption and breakthroughs that shape today's realities of the economy. A better understanding of the changing environment in the future economy can enable business professionals and leaders to recognise realities, embrace changes, and create new opportunities — locally and globally — in this inevitable digital age.

Published*

Vol. 6   *Financial Management in the Digital Economy*
            by David Lee Kuo Chuen, Ding Ding and Guan Chong

Vol. 5   *The Digital Transformation of Property in Greater China: Finance, 5G, AI, and Blockchain*
            by Paul Schulte, Dean Sun and Roman Shemakov

Vol. 4   *Blockchain and Smart Contracts: Design Thinking and Programming for FinTech*
            by Lo Swee Won, Wang Yu and David Lee Kuo Chuen

Vol. 3   *Artificial Intelligence, Data and Blockchain in a Digital Economy, First Edition*
            edited by David Lee Kuo Chuen, supported by Singapore University of
            Social Sciences and World Scientific, in support of Singapore Digital (SG:D)
            and in collaboration with Infocomm Media Development Authority

*More information on this series can also be found at
https://www.worldscientific.com/series/susswsfes*

(Continued at end of book)

Singapore University of Social Sciences - World Scientific
Future Economy Series : **5**

The Digital Transformation of Property in Greater China

Finance, 5G, AI, and Blockchain

Foreword by **David LEE**

Paul SCHULTE
Dean SUN
Roman SHEMAKOV
Schulte Research, Singapore

SINGAPORE UNIVERSITY
OF SOCIAL SCIENCES

World Scientific

Published by

World Scientific Publishing Co. Pte. Ltd.
5 Toh Tuck Link, Singapore 596224
USA office: 27 Warren Street, Suite 401-402, Hackensack, NJ 07601
UK office: 57 Shelton Street, Covent Garden, London WC2H 9HE

Library of Congress Control Number: 2021936471

British Library Cataloguing-in-Publication Data
A catalogue record for this book is available from the British Library.

Singapore University of Social Sciences - World Scientific Future Economy Series — Vol. 5
THE DIGITAL TRANSFORMATION OF PROPERTY IN GREATER CHINA
Finance, 5G, AI, and Blockchain

ISBN 978-981-123-379-1 (hardcover)
ISBN 978-981-123-563-4 (paperback)
ISBN 978-981-123-380-7 (ebook for institutions)
ISBN 978-981-123-381-4 (ebook for individuals)

For any available supplementary material, please visit
https://www.worldscientific.com/worldscibooks/10.1142/12194#t=suppl

Desk Editors: Aanand Jayaraman/Yulin Jiang

Typeset by Stallion Press
Email: enquiries@stallionpress.com

Printed in Singapore

To Eric Bushell, Tomonori Tani, Adam Levinson, Amit Rajpal, and Rob Citrone: World-class investors and, more importantly, all good friends for more than a decade. They have taught me so much about China.

Paul Schulte

To Xu Yuan, without whose companion and friendship I could not complete this book.

Dean Sun

To my mother, Olena, for the sacrifices she made for me and my sister.

Roman Shemakov

About the Authors

Paul Schulte is the founder and editor of Schulte Research, a company that conducts research on banks, financial technology, bank algorithms and credit algorithms. He has had a career in equity research spanning 27 years on both the buy and sell sides covering the Asian and emerging markets. He also has five years of government policy experience in emerging markets. He has been frequently ranked in top-five positions in *Euromoney*, *Asiamoney* and *Institutional Investor*. In *Institutional Investor*'s 2010 poll, he received top rankings in All-Asia Banks Team, Asia Equity Strategy Team and Asia Economics Team.

Mr. Schulte was most recently at China Construction Bank Intl as Global Head of Financial Strategy and Asia Banks Research and based in Hong Kong. Prior to that, he was Managing Director and Head of Multi-Strategy and Asia-Pacific Banks Research for Nomura International. Prior to that, he was Chief Equity Strategist, Asia ex-Japan, for Lehman Brothers. He served from 2001 to 2006 as Portfolio Manager and Head of Research for GEMS equities at Big Sky Capital, a US$350 million global macro fund (Tiger Cub) of the Wynn Family funds in Los Angeles, California. At the same time, he was also a lecturer at the Hilton School of Business at Loyola Marymount University.

Prior to his time in Los Angeles, Mr. Schulte was Chief Asian Strategist for ING Baring Securities in Hong Kong (1996–2000). He also served as Chief Asian Strategist for CS First Boston in Hong Kong (1992–1996). In the 1980s, Mr. Schulte served as an Economic Policy Advisor to Indonesia's central bank (Bank Indonesia) and before that as an Analyst with the National Security Council at the White House in Washington, DC.

Mr. Schulte graduated summa cum laude from The Catholic University of America in Washington, DC with a B.A. in Philosophy in 1985. He received a Master of Arts in Political Economy in 1986, also from Catholic University, and then went on to earn a Master of Arts in International Finance in 1988 from the Fletcher School of Law and Diplomacy, a joint program with Tufts University and Harvard University.

On top of his research publishing career, Paul has 15 years of experience in teaching graduate students in several programs. He was an adjunct lecturer at the Conrad Hilton School of Business at Loyola Marymount University in Los Angeles from 2000 to 2006. From 2008 to the present, he has been teaching in various graduate programs at the University of Science and Technology in Hong Kong. These include the M.Sc., Executive MBA, as well as joint venture MBA programs with the Northwestern Kellogg School and the NYU Stern School. He also taught a seminar at the UCLA Anderson School. Most recently, he was chosen to be a Senior Fellow at the Fletcher School of Law and Diplomacy at Tufts University, a joint venture program with the Harvard Business School. His course include capital markets, banking cycles, and behavioral finance.

Paul is a senior fellow at Tufts University, HKUST, and SUSS in Singapore. His clients include some of the largest hedge funds globally. He works with several banks and insurance companies in Asia as well as two of the sovereign wealth funds. He is an advisor to IOSCO, the HKMA, the Malaysian SFC, as well as the Thai SEC. He recently conducted a one-week seminar for 55 Asian regulators on financial technology through the Asian Development Bank. His latest book is *The Next Revolution in Our Credit-Driven Economy: The Advent of Financial Technology.* His upcoming book is *Cryptocurrency, FinTech, InsurTech, and Regulation,* in conjunction with SUSS. He focuses on research on the Internet of Things in China as well as Insurtech in China. Paul also has a credential in counseling (specializing in drug and alcohol addiction) from Loyola Marymount University. He completed his internship at the UCLA School of Family Medicine. He is an avid tennis player and his avocation is military history.

Dean Sun is finishing his studies at Zhejiang University and is a University Excellence Scholar. He is ranked #2 in his Applied Mathematics cohort. He has written extensively on Chinese equity market derivatives. He also studied at Imperial College in London. He is an Associate with Schulte Research.

Roman Shemakov is a Henry Luce Distinguished Scholar. He is a high honors graduate of Swarthmore College in Economics, History, and Russian. His thesis was published in the *Columbia Journal of History*. His other writings are in the *Harvard Classics Journal, Toronto Urban Journal, Tulane Journal of Political Economy, Tufts Journal of International Affairs*, and the *American Chamber of Commerce*. He edited Paul Schulte's last book, *The Race for 5G Supremacy*. He currently works at an urban planning and smart city development firm in Taipei. His research concerns the geopolitical economy of technological innovation, urban planning, and economic development.

Other Books by Paul Schulte

Finance

The Next Generation in Our Credit-Driven Economy: The Advent of Financial Technology.

Wiley & Sons. (2015).

Handbook of Blockchain, Digital Finance and Inclusion: ChinaTech, Mobile Security and Distributed Ledger. Volume 2. Chapter 13. Mobile Technology: The New Banking Model Connecting Lending to the Social Network. (Lee & Deng, editors).

Elsevier. (2018).

AI & Quantum Computing in Finance & Insurance: Fortunes and Challenges for China and America. (With David Lee).

World Scientific. (2019).

The Race for 5G Supremacy: Why China Is Surging, Where Millennials Struggle, & How America Can Prevail. (With Austin Groves).

World Scientific. (2020).

www.Schulte-research.com (303 published articles on financial services and fintech).

Mental Health

Cravings for Deliverance: How William James, Father of American Psychology, Inspired 12 Step Programs.

Lantern Press. (2014).

Paths to Recovery for Gay and Bisexual Drug Addicts: Healing Weary Hearts.

Rowman & Littlefield. (2015).

There is no map for where we are going. ...Billions of people around the world working and playing in the OASIS every day. ...They meet, fall in love, and get married without meeting. The lines of distinction between a person's real identity and their avatar blur. It is the dawn of a new era, one where most of the human race now spends all of their free time. (Their) items are nothing but ones and zeros stored on servers, but they were also status symbols. Most items only cost a few credits.

Ready Player One, *Ernst Cline*, 2011

Contents

Foreword

The Digital Transformation of Property in Greater China is a timely
publication as we are only at the dawn of the digitization of physical
assets, especially property. Paul Schulte, Dean Sun, and Roman
Shemakov have done very solid work blazing a new trail in what
is a new industry. They have carried out a deep exploration and
a thorough compilation of research that will bring everyone up to
date on what China is planning and doing in the digitization of
physical assets, particularly commercial and residential real estate!
They have presented their thoughts in such clarity that, even those
who lack familiarity with the Asia-Pacific, will see that China is
leading the Fourth Industrial Revolution. China will lead the creation
of new industries as physical property is digitized and monetized via
solid public policy, private sector entrepreneurs, and existing super
apps. These super apps such as DingTalk, WeChatPay, and Lark
(in conjunction with 5G) can put powerful tools into the hands of
millions of small and medium-sized enterprises (SMEs) not just in
China but also throughout the Silk Road.

This seems incredulous to Western ears for one simple reason.
China failed to take advantage of the first two industrial revolutions
in the 18th and 19th centuries, and its economy faltered miserably for
two centuries, only gaining global traction in the early 2000s. Why?
One of history's most important lessons is that, during profound
periods of division in a country's ideology and direction — civil strife,
social chaos, and radically conflicting views of the future — political

survival will always take precedence over economic development. Public policies designed to propel a country in a unitary, healthy direction take a backseat to brutal struggles between political factions. When a country misses the opportunity to be part of an industrial revolution due to either cold or hot civil war, the economy can deteriorate faster than anyone can imagine.

In the 19th and 20th century, China learned a painful lesson: any country that achieves a technological lead will inevitably become the political and economic leader. The Chinese have since decided on — and are steadfastly committed to — leading the Fourth Industrial Revolution. We have seen an increased emphasis on sustainable growth and a decreased emphasis on political maneuvering to satisfy the center. Social and political stability remains the top priority, but it cannot be guaranteed without economic growth. This growth is reliant on technological progress in the sciences through R&D. Indeed, this is the basis of Five-Year Plans for the past 20 years.

Sadly, I wonder if the US is going in the opposite direction, where selfish political aims are trumping shared technological, scientific, and industrial goals. We see a political class in control over the past four years which is going backward on its reliance on science and technology policy to create a shared vision. A clear understanding of the role of government in the pursuit of technological and scientific goals is also absent.

When Deng Xiaoping started to move toward the socialist market economy in the mid-1990s, the Internet was in its infancy. By combining Internet technology with the market mechanisms, the Chinese economy has grown faster than any other country, in the process lifting 800 million people out of poverty. The Inclusive FinTech strategy that China adopted in the early 2010s has made it a financial leader in super apps, which are used in more than 50 countries. However, these results could not have been achieved in such a short time without centralized policy support.

With 1.4 billion people, it takes more than a strong will to implement a policy that seems unpopular in the short term. However, China also unleashed a powerful entrepreneurial spirit, encouraged competition at all levels, and gently forced the state sector to shrink in size relative to the private sector. This was a risky move but it has paid off in the long term, with the contribution of the somewhat-visible hand of the market. Political stability has been maintained while preventing a politically voluble rust belt from forming. The combination of the two — strong public policy as articulated through Five-Year Plans all the while encouraging private sector entrepreneurship — has fostered a practically unmatched innovation regime.

No one would have thought that Satoshi Nakamoto, a name practically synonymous with rebellious and libertarian cypherpunks, would appear in China's official government documents, especially in a country run by self-proclaimed communists. The idea of a communist utopia is one where the physical world is all there is — a world of pure materiality. It is ironic to see that a self-professed Marxist/communist regime has taken capitalism's most fascinating abstraction (cryptocurrency) and made it omnipresent through the Blockchain Service Network (BSN) and the newly launched Central Bank Coin. China's entire financial and physical world is hopping onto a new set of digital rails faster than any other country globally. I submit that the BSN and cryptocurrency will accelerate the advancement of proptech in ways that are very difficult to achieve in the West. This book is about precisely this phenomenon.

Why is this happening now and so quickly in China? It is pragmatism and eclecticism that is driving change in China, which has long realized that governments need entrepreneurs and free markets as well as state-owned enterprises (SOEs). The Chinese approach is complex and needs more in-depth study and research, and the "digital transformation of the property market in greater China" will provide a framework to understand the underlying pathway of both the government and the market within the country.

The Chinese Communist Party (CCP) has a complicated relation-ship with individual property rights, and blanket statements about its theoretical commitments will inevitably get mired in ideology. This book looks at what is happening, not what foreigners wish was happening. The CCP has taken four steps: enabling, regulating, stabilizing, and legitimizing markets. Coordination among different regulators is not perfect, and there are still doubts about whether they can adapt to international governance standards. Nevertheless, considerable efforts have been taken at all levels to lead the Fourth Industrial Revolution! What is clear is that we are on the brink of the greatest comparative governance experiment in human history.

What I am describing above is a massive and unprecedented effort to combine centralized governance with distributed ledger technology to digitize virtually any physical asset — a city, port, building, or home. I call this the Value of Everything (VoE) economy in China. A VoE economy tokenizes people, activities, and things in order to include everyone in the financial and economic system. Blockchain technology is now the central tenet of the VoE economy. If we combine this centralized policy of intense R&D to digitize the physical world with the help of a digitized currency distributed by the central bank, we get a new set of powerful rails which gives China autonomy over its digital future vis a vis the US dollar.

However, this technology has potential built-in tensions, which include (1) a give and take between central and local government, especially regarding transparency in fiscal management and implementation of regulatory frameworks; and (2) libertarian cypherpunks who see blockchain as decentralized and perceive it as the opposite of a centralized tool. These cypherpunks (can we dare call them digital marxists, since they seek to raze the old monetary system to the ground?) infer that a misuse of blockchain leads to a concentration of power and information. In reality, however, I believe the technology itself is neutral but the implementation of it ought to inspire genuine discussion. Blockchain only guarantees transparency, traceability, and accountability. It need not be centralized.

This latest development in China requires closer international attention. To accelerate the growth of blockchain technology and industrial innovation, the Beijing government has taken several initiatives. Several powerful entities within the Beijing Municipal Government have made many efforts toward applying blockchain technology to government services, all of which have had significant breadth and scope. To that end, the Beijing Blockchain Professionals Working Group has compiled a 141-page Innovation Blueprint of

Blockchain Applications in Government Services (or The Blueprint). The report was only officially released a few months ago. It summarizes the developments of blockchain infrastructure construction in Beijing. The intention is clear: blockchain is considered a public infrastructure and we should conclude that the central government will "build" this infrastructure throughout the country. This new GovTech (i.e. the VoE discussed earlier) leads to transparency and traceability and ensures compliance with centralized directives in local government. This will go a long way in reducing corruption.

In late 2020 and early 2021, pilot testing of the eCNY, more commonly known as Digital Payment/ Electronic Payment (DCEP), will take place in several cities. It is an attempt to promulgate a central bank digital currency (CBDC), which *may* be a way to bypass the US$-centric SWIFT payment system and work hand-in-hand with the Digital Silk Road initiative (via Blockchain Service Network or BSN). Importantly, this BSN works on interoperability of all types of blockchain (including more than eight cryptocurrencies) and can certainly build a more diversified digital infrastructure along the Belt and Road Initiative (BRI). All these have significant implications for the global payments system and portend a potential fall from grace of the US dollar as a global reserve currency.

The full picture is apparent if we examine the following four initiatives in greater detail, much of which is concisely covered in this book:

(1) The People's Bank of China (PBOC) has been doing research on CBDC since 2014 and already started the DC/EP piloting.
(2) China's BSN, a joint initiative between State Information Center, China Mobile, China UnionPay, and Red Date Tech, is now officially available for global commercial use.
(3) The Cyberspace Administration of China has issued a total of 730 licenses to blockchain service providers.
(4) The Standing Committee at the 13th National People's Congress has passed the Cryptography Law of the People's Republic of China to regulate how cryptography is used and managed, which

will have major impacts on activities and projects involving cryptography, including blockchain and cryptocurrencies. This will aid in the digitization of assets and the way they can be tokenized and traded — including property!

As seen from many of these use-cases and plans in China, blockchain technology will empower public services and further strengthen SMEs. These initiatives enhance the cooperation between the public and private sectors, offering the potential for a more digitized, inclusive, and connected society in China — including the entire fabric of physical infrastructure of ports, buildings, and homes. While The Blueprint shows the promising development of blockchain in local government agencies, it reflects just part of the national blockchain strategy. More importantly for property, the wholesale accelerated flow of information and value-exchange also reflects the speed of tokenization. Digitization of physical assets relies on tokenization and vice versa. Underlying all of this is the way in which tokenized and digitized physical assets are given provenance in ways the modern financial system simply cannot offer.

"Data, Data, Data" will become the rallying cry of the VoE economy when it comes to proptech. It is no longer "location, location, location." Privacy protection is the mission of the cypherpunks, and it is not inconsistent with programmable governance as a centralized and digitized buildout of smart city infrastructure is developed. On one hand, governments will certainly be protective of individual and property rights as they are increasingly traded as tokenized assets. On the other hand, a programmable and tokenized "central government" exists at a much different level, especially if one imagines the emergence of a Skynet, an artificial general superintelligence system with self-awareness. That sounds far-fetched — for now. This risk merits considerable debate.

However, we need to discuss and debate about whether a digital or data dictatorship is fiction or not. We now see politicians in the US making claims that monopolies like Google are built on massive private data collection and analysis need to be broken up. Even Alibaba is under the antitrust microscope. Any massive collection of digitized data will inevitably be regulated, and China has already moved ahead of the curve with aggressive action toward Alibaba. Property (a physical body, an idea, or a building) is the foundation of the citizen. As all three of these are digitized, we should not be surprised that those who collect and store this tokenized property will face antitrust scrutiny. On the other hand, blockchain-based tokenization offers guarantees of provenance — and subsequent elimination of fraud — way beyond any kind of guarantees currently in place.

A few years ago, who would have thought that governments would so quickly harness the best in blockchain design to take the lead in interoperability and data privacy protection! COVID-19 has certainly accelerated a process which was already occurring. Three important trends have all converged in COVID-19:

(1) the interoperability of blockchains;
(2) the convergence of technology; and
(3) the sudden inclusion of an erstwhile excluded population,

which have all led to a push toward the Chinese VoE economy.

Through the tokenizing of fiat, assets, and activities previously excluded from the financial markets, technology has empowered society to serve the people and businesses in need of cash, working capital, and cheap long-term capital. Perhaps the most significant positive benefit that it has achieved — and which is something many thought was impossible — has been the change in mindset toward empowerment, complementarianism, and the inclusion of everything previously excluded from our economic system.

Many will argue that the end game is still unclear. Is the Chinese government here to serve rather than to rule? Can it complement rather than compete? Can it empower rather than manipulate? Can it peacefully continue to manage the shrinkage of SOEs in favor of private sector entrepreneurialism? Can it safely upgrade labor as technological change causes redundancy in traditional manufacturing? These are yet to be seen. Nevertheless, the Chinese government has clearly expressed and decisively acted on its ambition to lead the Fourth Industrial Revolution, and it is a force to be reckoned with. That is clear and more examples can be found in this very well-written book.

This book is the fifth in the series of SUSS-World Scientific, and I am very honored to have Paul Schulte, Dean Sun, and Roman Shemakov contributing to the series. I want to congratulate the great work that they have accomplished. In particular, Paul has been working with the SUSS FinTech and Blockchain Group since 2016 and has taught several courses solo and with me. These courses are in great demand. We have also written a 600-page book together comparing US and China in payments, e-commerce and AI that we use in our coursework at Singapore University of Social Sciences, National University of Singapore, Nanyang Technological University, Singapore Management University, Shanghai University of Finance and Economics, and many other executive courses. The Chartered FinTech Professionals qualification awarded by the Global FinTech Institute will include these materials in its syllabus. Paul Schulte has been one of the most respected experts in finance and FinTech circles. His writings and research are widely circulated and read by professional investors, CEOs, academics, researchers, and graduate students. This volume speaks highly of the quality and foresight of Paul and his co-authors.

David Lee, Ph.D.

Introduction

For the past few centuries, banks have thought that they sold only one product: loans. These banks set a price (interest rate) and you take it or leave it. And they would charge hidden fees for every transaction for business loans, mortgages and personal loans for every rite of passage — births, weddings, vacations, renovations, home purchases, college for kids, and death.

Fintech changed all that. Fintech offers cheaper or free services at the touch of a button without months of waiting and massive paperwork — or even a building. The same goes for insurance. (This proverbial Amazon moment arrived for the banks in about 2015 and for insurance in about 2018.)

The Amazon moment for property arrived in 2019–2020. Like banks, property companies thought they only sold one thing: space to live or work or trade. For a price. And that price was measured in square feet. They bought, sold, and managed this square footage for often exorbitant (and hidden) fees and commissions — just like banks. All that is about to change now with proptech in the same way fintech has disrupted banks over the past five years. And in the same way that bookstores, department stores, and movie theaters have been disrupted by upstarts.

The physical space where we work, live, and play is being transformed into a digitized omni-channel experience. This experience will be tokenized, counted, and traded both through cryptocoins and sovereign coins on new digital rails. Property developers are rushing to understand the kinds of value-added services they must now provide. They know this must happen or their business will disappear in front of their eyes. Proptech companies are growing by leaps and bounds. We will show in this book that China is definitively in the lead. The emergence of COVID-19 has only accelerated the trends in proptech noted above. What was *already* a broken model has now turned into a money-losing and crumbling model. Urgency is required.

So, we see right in front of us a profound move from a primacy of "location, location, location" to a primacy of data. This includes the digitization of people, places, and things as they circulate in malls and offices. This will manifest a smarter placement of stores within buildings, complexes, neighborhoods, and cities using a vast array of digitized data. It will look at payments data to see consumer trends within certain neighborhoods. It will use facial recognition to detect customer satisfaction. It will use data to find new talent for tenants within buildings. And it will rely on super apps to create omni-channels to make choices easier and offer a wide array of products as well as experiences. Smart property developers will use these tools to develop pop-up strategies. They will use artificial intelligence (AI) tools to reduce worker accidents during construction. They will use apps to reduce carbon emissions and reduce utility costs. One thing is for sure. Those who do not grasp these tools will die on the vine.

The monetary equation for buildings used to be easy. Raise rents. Reduce costs. Maximize yields. Or increase the asset value itself. Proptech will aid in all four of these in the following ways:

(1) analyze data,
(2) manage and maintain properties,
(3) transact and keep tenants, and
(4) design and build properties.

These four are made for residential, commercial, and logistical companies to become more efficient, reduce costs, and add value to tenants. This book shows the companies at work in China as they do just this. The ultimate goal is three things:

(1) digitize the function of homes, buildings, warehouses, and entertainment centers;
(2) analyze the data; and
(3) create new services.

We submit that the proptech scene in the US is behind that of China because the US model is a "bottom-up" private-sector B2B primitive view that is aimed at cutting costs, increasing "engagement," and becoming more competitive. What is missing in the narrative of the US is that the digitization of physical assets requires a new digital railroad system. This can only be done through public–private partnerships. It is too heavy a chore for a company like Amazon to transform a 60-year-old system based on checks and credit cards — with no super apps in sight! The Biden Administration may do more to create a digital infrastructure, but only time will tell.

In China, however, there has been a top-down strategy in place since 2015 to create 500 digitized smart cities. It is a national policy. And real estate is clearly PART of the overall picture of integrating seven pillars of its digitization strategy:

(1) physical infrastructure
(2) 5G
(3) telecom
(4) payments
(5) crime and terrorism prevention surveillance
(6) police and medical emergency services, and
(7) energy.

How does the public and private interact? The private sector participates in China's careful study of the Five-Year Plans, searches out the policy implications, and simultaneously rides the wave. The Five-Year Plans are set in stone and do not change in material ways over five years. Also in China, real estate owners, for better or worse, are diversified owners of property. (In the US, they tend to be specialized). This is an advantage because the best digitized data is always the most integrated. Chinese real estate owners have residential, commercial, entertainment, and even agricultural land bases. Digitized assets can be analyzed and cross-traded throughout sectors, resulting in a richer ecosystem.

The question that arises from this nascent digitization is what exactly is a tenant willing to pay for? What are the new digital tools that are expected by the landlord in addition to just selling or managing a property asset? How can the many companies in this book monetize these digitized or tokenized assets?

Examples: How must landlords become better at integrating, digitizing and interpreting tenant behavior and activity in order to:

(1) offer better amenities
(2) increase services
(3) create talent networks
(4) integrate technology
(5) process data, and
(6) be the point of the spear for AI interpretation of this data.

China has an automatic lead here because of the super apps like WeChat (Tencent), DingTalk (Alibaba), and Lark (ByteDance). We discuss these vitally important tools in the book as these will complement the BSN to create "train stations" in the new digital railroad. (Alibaba's Ding Talk easily dominates). These will offer a great ease of building new apps into existing smartphone technology. And they create huge and automatic productivity gains since integrated economies of scale are digitally connected to millions of SMEs and hundreds of millions of people.

If the US is looking at China for guidance, Washington DC must do three things. First, create a coherent policy. Second, fund and organize startups in an entrepreneurial way. Third, help with the technological infrastructure. Amazon and Google are quietly carrying out many ingenious initiatives in proptech. But the smash up in late 2020 between Jack Ma and the powers in Beijing is a taste of things to come when the US wakes up to find one company controlling all vital digital infrastructure which can hold the central government hostage.

China has two very simple anchor policies. We believe the US government is only now quietly rolling out similar projects, although without much fanfare. This is in order not to anger entities on the right who do not believe in the government's participation in the private sector.

(1) China has rolled out Internet plus. This is the idea of merging digital technology and traditional industry, i.e. digitizing homes, commercial office space, transportation, logistics, utilities, and smart cities with an eye on eliminating environmental damage, creating new industries and reducing accidents.
(2) Made in China 2025. This is aimed more at fully digitizing logistics networks (both local and international) in both hardware and in super apps. This is done through:

    (i) 5G and Huawei.
    (ii) IoT for smart cars, homes, office, logistics.
    (iii) Robust hardware; 5G relay stations and edge technology.
    (iv) Super apps like WeChat, Lark, DingTalk.
    (v) Cloud rollout with AliCloud.
    (vi) Big Data analysis through private companies.
    (vii) AI — facial recognition.
    (viii) Robotics for manufacturing and mobility.

Can real estate companies manage this transition by themselves? Absolutely not. This is the same for banks and insurance. They need separate digital units for one simple reason. They do not have enough cash flow to upgrade an entire analog network. A separate digital unit is vital.

Can property developers harness vast amounts of data, analyze, and monetize it? NO.

This requires a much different understanding of

(1) data
(2) new policies of R&D
(3) use of super apps, and
(4) a "mobile first" approach.

This is very risky for established property companies. How do you reduce risk? Akin to the development of the telephone, highway, and telecom systems in the US in the 1950s and 1960s. The government must help. Government can reduce risk through:

(1) Supportive, easy to understand, consistent, and coherent policies. China does this through its Five-Year Programs.
(2) Create new infrastructure. The PRC central bank coin is such an example.
(3) Help build new networks. Red Date's new technologies can offer the use of cryptocurrencies for trade.
(4) Create new telecom backbones. China encourages super apps from Alibaba, Tencent, and ByteDance.
(5) Offer help in working capital, funding and ease of payments on the international end. This is BSN's role.

China is doing all of this in front of our eyes — and it is doing this very quickly. In this book, we look at the people and companies carrying out this transformation. We look at what big companies like Alibaba, Tencent, Ping An, JD, Yitu, and Huawei are doing in proptech. We look at the up and coming firms like GISUNI, GeoHey, MyDream, and ZifiSense. We also look at the ingenious people who are building the infrastructure, such as Dr. Zhu Long, who received his Ph.D. in Statistics from UCLA and is a leader at Yitu; Li Zhuoqun from ZifiSense, who obtained his Ph.D from Imperial College in mobile networks; and He Wanyu, who received her advanced degrees in architecture in Holland and whose mentor received the Pritzker Prize.

Section One of the book outlines how the government speaks to its people and to the outside world. This basic language starts with the elaborate and well thought out Five-Year Plans. Recently, blockchain and 5G have become a core part of the evolution of the Chinese economic plan launched as early as October 2015, and reaffirmed in November 2020. This, in the government's eyes, is the infrastructure of the future. Building with cement and steel is finished. Now all building must be done with cloud computing. This is the foundation for proptech and is the central theme of this whole book. Blockchain and 5G — in conjunction with BSN — have created a powerful foundation for digitized assets. These same digitized assets can now be tokenized and traded next to and along with Central Bank Coins and crypto currency via the Red Date rails.

Section Two addresses the titans in technology that are reimagining the government's vision of a digitized China — Alibaba, Ping An, and Tencent, who have used their capital reserves and brain trust to expand their digital empires into physical space. They are collaborating closely with municipal governments across China and digitizing urban services to create new types of business such as energy efficiency, digital marketing, tokenized building assets, and many other types of industries.

Section Three touches on the challenges that are emerging to either take the nascent property industry in unforeseen directions (startups) or destroy it before it even takes root (major conflict with the US). We outline the ongoing challenges, the stakes, and potential spillovers for the 21st century.

This book is about the people and companies, large and small, who are transforming a physical world into a digitized world, which can be traded on new crypto rails and analyzed to create entirely new industries.

Section 1
The Foundation

Section 1 addresses China's planning programs, the construction of telecommunication infrastructure, and the integration of its financial technology to transform property. We argue that these are the integral foundations that have made China's urban revolution — rapid urbanization, property digitization, and digital inclusion — possible. In these three chapters lie the fundamental mechanism that separates China's governmentality from that of the US or Europe. We do not make any normative claims in this section. Rather, we take China's policies and assumptions seriously for what they are and what they strive to be. We avoid reductionism, fearmongering, and absolutism. It is admittedly impossible to acknowledge the full complexity of a system that governs 1.4 billion people. The process of articulating a technological future, interconnecting all national infrastructure and digitizing national finance, is an incredibly convoluted process, but it is also one that requires very clear directives. In this section, we attempt to come as close as possible to offering a clear perspective on what policies China's government has passed, how their articulated goals have changed, and, most importantly, what impact it has had on the life of the nation's citizens.

Chapter 1 dives deep into China's Five-Year Plans to understand the nation's articulated vision and mission. It touches on the increasing evolution from quantitative goals to qualitative ones, and the transition of the planning system from military decrees to economic incentives. It becomes clear that since the late 2000s, digitization and urbanization have become the driving focus of China's vision for the 21st century. The most recent plans emphasize the importance of locally grown talent, the need for entrepreneurship, the cataclysmic environmental dangers, and the centrality of technology to China's urban future.

Most importantly, we emphasize the evolving digitization of urban space and property. From currency, land, and human capital, the Chinese government is creating the structures to digitize the property that underlies all urban life. This can be understood in three ways:

(1) As a whole-scale reorganization of day-to-day logistics. Bringing every form of exchange and government service online considerably reduces the complexity and manual labor. This makes everything from taxation to surveillance easy.

(2) The spillover effects of technological integration produce a tech-savvy population capable of broader and deeper innovation.

(3) The digitization of property creates indelible, objective, and traceable ownership. The government permits private exchange in virtual space because it has built the infrastructure. It has been built with the express purpose of connecting civic ownership laws, legitimate trading, legal status of ownership, and provenance of property and ideas. Most importantly, China understood before many other countries that the digitization of physical assets was the key to creating tradeable and tokenized currencies for logistics, commercial office space, urban housing, and healthcare. History will be the judge if this is a Marxist utopia or an authoritarian dystopia, but this project has nonetheless pulled almost a billion people out of poverty in the last 40 years, and it is creating some of the most modern cities in the world.

Chapter 2 analyzes China's telecommunication, the importance of 5G for physical property, and its evolving global tensions. 5G has become the keystone in the US–China trade war, brought international infamy to Huawei, and quickly forced nations into a second Cold War. We paint the picture of why this has happened and what to expect. While 3G and 4G were vital for creating a virtual ecosystem of apps, services, and finance, 5G is designed primarily for physical infrastructure. Additionally, edge computer and network slicing allows very small and localized infrastructure to serve huge swathes of neighborhoods. Telephone poles and lines will soon seem as anachronistic as public phone booths and typewriters. The nations able to fully integrate will become leaders in proptech, urban technology, Internet of Things (IoT), and big data. On balance, 5G is the final link necessary for the seamless integration of the virtual and the physical.

Chapter 3 touches on China's national blockchain project and potential of its Central Bank Digital Coin. The Blockchain Service Network, launched amidst the COVID-19 pandemic, will integrate every blockchain on a single network and bring Decentralized Applications (DApps) to small- and medium-sized enterprises (SMEs) across China. Over the course of the year, it has become equivalent to the water and gas infrastructure and has the potential to transform SMEs across China. So does the Digital Currency/Electronic Payment system, which is working to digitize the national currency, potentially eliminating money laundering, tax avoidance, and fraud.

Section 1 sets the foundation for the rest of the book. It outlines how the government in China speaks, so the private firms and municipal institutions across the country can listen and actualize. The US government built the Internet in the second half of the 20th century, so firms like Facebook and Amazon can imagine a digital world atop it. In essence, the Silicon Valley is one of the most successful socialist endeavors in the history of the world. The US military built the Internet rails so private talent could benefit. To continue criticizing China for being "socialist" is hypocritical. The Chinese government is leapfrogging the US to build new and more advanced infrastructure for their private firms to transform the world.

Chapter 1

Five-Year Plans and China's Vision of the Future

In the past 20 years, China has redefined what means to be a capitalist, socialist, or technocratic government. The country's Five-Year Plans (FYP) do not tell the whole story, but they are as close to a genuine archive of the plans for the future as we can get. If you want to know what China will do with its economic structure, its social programs, and its healthcare, read the FYP. While the US was invading Iraq, China was building highways, hospitals, and schools; Alibaba, Tencent, Ping An, and Huawei were being created out of thin air; all while the biggest cities in the world popped up along the Greater Bay Area. China now has the largest and most digitally included urban population in the world.

As the third decade of the 2000s draws near, we are seeing before us a rapidly digitizing China. Firms like Ping An, ByteDance, and Red Date are leading the market in actualizing wholesale inter-connection. By combining the technology from finance, insurance, telecommunication, and urban integration, China is digitizing its cities. WeChat, Tao Bao, and TikTok planted the seeds in 2010s that are finally being integrated into the physical property landscape in both cities and urban areas and will change the way in which 1.4 billion people work, buy, create families, eat, live, and imagine.

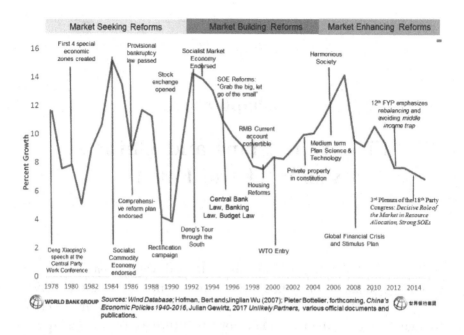

Figure 1.1. Forty years of reforms and GDP growth.
Source: Bert Hofman, "Reflections on Forty Years of China's Reforms," World Bank, February 1, 2018.

If we are to take a step back from either the overly optimistic or pessimistic view of planning, a clearer picture of modern China begins to emerge. There have been three distinct stages of development (Figure 1.1). First, an inward-looking and authoritarian collective decision-making characterizing the First through the Sixth FYPs that varied from understanding markets to shunning them (1953–1985).[1] Second, a consultation structured process for the Seventh to the Ninth FYPs that built and reformed markets (1986–2000).[2] The third stage is the dawn of the brainstorming decision-making

---

[1] Angang Hu, "The Distinctive Transition of China's Five-Year Plans," *Modern China* 39, no. 6 (2013): pp. 629–639.
[2] *Ibid.*

model, where diverse groups of stakeholders are consulted to create social indicators rather than top-down quantitative decrees in order to enhance the performance of the market (2001–2020).[3] The 14th FYP 2021–2025 is perhaps the most radical, where the public was asked to submit recommendations, views, and concerns to their local officials for nation-wide planning. This is not the democracy that the West wanted, but it can be seen as a "democratic" process in the Confucian sense of the word. It is a communitarian approach to decision-making where the final blueprint, by the time it has reached the National People's Congress, has seen dozens of configurations and been created through tens of thousands consultations and thousands of edits.[4]

Modern Chinese planning is informed by intensive investigation and analysis. Decrees are no longer handed down from the head of the party (although some of them will always make their way in). Stakeholders are not just consulted on the planning, they are hired as close and trusted advisers. A diverse swathe of industry representatives iron out what is possible, what is achievable, and what is a stretch (the stretch will always become the target). Finally, and most importantly, Modern Planning focuses on technology. Semiconductors, telecommunication, fintech, and the blockchain has become the oil of the 21st century that the planning programs are ready and willing to exploit. When the decrees are set by the bureaucrats, it enters the hands of private firms to innovatively implement the directives and compete among themselves. Table 1.1 demonstrates the leaders of the Made in China 2025 (MIC25) initiative. These will also be the companies that are leading the push to digitize property, which we discuss in Sections 2 and 3 of this book.

---

[3] *Ibid.*

[4] Patrizio Bianchi, Clemente Ruiz Duran, and Sandrine Labory, *Transforming Industrial Policy for the Digital Age: Production, Territories and Structural Change* (Cheltenham, UK: Edward Elgar, 2019).

Table 1.1.   State-owned and private enterprises divide the leadership in MIC25
core industries amongst themselves (selection).

Next-generation IT	Ownership	Business area
Huawei	private	network equipment, consumer electronics (-> smartphones)
ZTE	SOE	network equipment provider
Alibaba	private	AI research as well as all kinds of Internet related services
Tencent	private	AI research as well as all kinds of Internet related services
Baidu	private	AI research as well as all kinds of Internet related services
Beijing Bytedance	private	Internet media, smartphone applications, AI research
Sense Time	private	deep learning and AI research, face recognition technology
Cloudwalk	private	AI research, facial recognition technology
Yitu Technology	private	AI research in relation to health care, finance
iFlytek	private	AI, translation systems, voice recognition
Megvii Face++	private	AI, face and body recognition
Cambricon	private	IC, AI chips, semi-conductors
YMTC	SOE	IC/microchips
Horizon Robotics	private	IC/microchips
HiSilicon Technologies	private	IC
Jiangsu Changjiang Electronics Technology	private	IC packaging and testing
Automation and robotics		
Sense Time	private	deep learning and AI research, face recognition technology
DJI	private	intelligent aerial drones, AI research
Ubtech Robotics	private	humanoid robots
Siasun Robot & Automation	private	robots: industrial, mobile, service; intelligent logistics and assembly systems

Source: Max Zenglein Zenglein and Anna Holzmann, "Evolving Made in China
2025: China's Industrial Policy in the Quest for Global Tech Leadership," *Merics*,
July 2, 2019.

Cities have found an especially new prominence and importance
in the development model. Significantly, 2011 was the year when the
number of Chinese citizens living in major cities for the first time
exceeded those living in rural regions (Figure 1.2). Since Babylon,
Alexandria, and Chang'an, the world has known the fundamental
importance of the city. Socially, it is a point of amalgamation: where

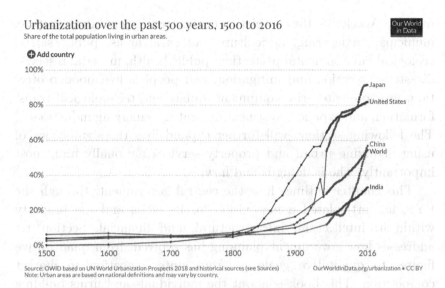

Figure 1.2.   Global urbanization rate (1500–2016).

Source: Ye Qi *et al.*, "China's New Urbanisation Opportunity: A Vision for the 14th Five-Year Plan," Coalition for Urban Transportation (The Hong Kong University of Science and Technology, Tsinghua University, 2020).

talent, knowledge, and dreams come together to produce the most extraordinary and unique human achievements. Materially, it is a source of accumulation: where money, worldly goods, and avarice come together to produce extraordinary wealth. Administratively, cities are a source of control: where taxation, laws, and security are easy to enforce. The amalgamation of human capital reaps the desire for financial capital, which necessitates administrative control. In 2011, China reached a point where, through a few cities and a few strategic technologies, it could easily touch the lives of most citizens of their country.

Most groundbreaking is the Central Committee's promotion of the proptech industry. For the first time in China's history, a significant conversation is taking place in the highest policy echelons about the need to digitize construction, urban planning, and property. In preparation for the newest FYP, the Party recommends a need to "Accelerate the completion of shortcomings in infrastructure, municipal engineering, agriculture and rural areas, public safety, ecological environmental protection, public health, material reserves, disaster prevention and mitigation, and people's livelihood protection, promote enterprise equipment update and technological transformation, and expand investment in strategic emerging industries."[5] The following sections will further expand into the significance of using digitizing urban and property services nationally and, most importantly, who is doing it and how.

This chapter outlines how the central government, through the FYP, has articulated a new vision for its cities and the property within it: intellectual, infrastructural, and financial. Section 1.1 addresses how government planning has evolved, from quantitative figures to qualitative goals — from state allocation to market competition. This book is about the individuals and firms building China, not the bureaucracies muddling in economic incentives. Outstanding and much more pointed investigations of the planning process have already been written by people like Jason Inch, Donghua Chen, and Angang Hu. Here, we offer an introductory overview of the planning process specifically as it relates to technology, urbanization, and property digitization. The 7th through the 11th FYPs ironed out some of the fundamental governance and financial inefficiencies. Starting from the 12th FYP (2011–2015), China reoriented itself toward publicly articulating social goals. Markets are now encouraged to innovate, integrate technology, and discover new markets.

Section 1.2 of this chapter outlines how the 13th FYP (2016–2020) begins to draw a new vision of China based on blockchain, artificial intelligence (AI), automation, and autonomous driving. This section will also address the MIC25 initiative that was discreetly folded into the 13th FYP. We emphasize the new policy tools that are used to reach policy targets (Box 1.1).

---

[5] "中共中央关于制定国民经济和社会发展第十四个五年规划和二〇三五年远景目标的建议", 新华网 November 3, 2020, http://www.xinhuanet.com/politics/zywj/20 20-11/03/c_1126693293.htm.

Box 1.1. Policy tools for MIC25.

1. Forced technology transfers in exchange for market access
2. Market access and government procurement restrictions for FIEs
3. Standards
4. Subsidies
5. Financial policy
6. Government-backed investment funds
7. Support from local government
8. Technology-seeking investments abroad
9. SOEs: mergers and politicization
10. Public-private partnerships

Source: "China Manufacturing 2025: Putting Industrial Policy Ahead of Market Forces (《中国制造 2025: 产业政策对弈市场力量》)," European Chamber of Commerce (European Union Chamber of Commerce in China, 2017).

Section 1.3 focuses on the 14th FYP (2021–2025), outlined in October 2020 and officially released in March 2021. Planned in the midst of a global pandemic, an escalating trade war, and on the heels of a chaotic US election, it is the most sweeping reassertion of China's bet on the 21st century: *dual circulation* (economic self-reliance), digitized property, blockchain, 5G, artificial intelligence (AI), and urban sustainability.

1.1. The Evolution of the FYP

In its earliest iteration, the first FYP in 1950 copied Soviet planning — in design, targets, and even name. While phenomenal history books have been written about the overwhelming ambition (and subsequent failure) of many of these mandates, these are outside the scope of this book. What is more central is that, in the 1990s, China woke up to a new world. Beijing bureaucrats watched the collapse of the Soviet Union and the dismantling of Saddam Hussein's command-and-control center in less than 24 hours during the Gulf War. Both signaled the changing world orders and the impossibility of the old. China's planning changed radically as a result, and it continues to change with every iteration. While we are not writing a history of China, it is important to briefly acknowledge the evolution of these mandates and how each FYP builds on the successes of the past. Above all, it shows how China, faced with occasional failures, pivots quickly and refocuses efforts toward new solutions. Our main point here is that FYP are no longer ideological — they focus on results. They have become brutally pragmatic — the mirror of pure ideology. The leaders want results from provincial and local leadership to improve lives, advance technology, reduce poverty, and improve the climate. In a word, it is valuable to understand the genealogy of Beijing's thinking. Readers may glean that the top-down "authoritarian" or "communist" planning of the 20th century has transformed into a "bottom-up" communitarian approach: government bureaucrats compete to implement effective policy, meet the bottom line, and satisfy their constituency.

The 7th FYP, published in 1986, was the first plan to come out on time and escape Mao Zedong's shadow. National growth targets were set at 6%, agricultural communities were scaled back, villages got access to credit, free trade and industrial development zones were roughly distributed throughout the country, and locations of infrastructure projects were delineated.[6] Early reforms are piecemeal, but they still take root.

While instituting certain market mechanisms, China's primary goal was to pacify the world that was on the brink of a rupture (fall of the Soviet Union) and to outsource domestic financing. As early as 1984, Deng Xiaoping noted "Foreign investment will doubtlessly serve as a major supplement in the building of socialism in our country."[7] The cracking of the economic window opened a conceptual door that was previously unimaginable. A new standard of effective bureaucratization was established, rewarding local government officials who could attract as much investment as possible,

---

[6]Hui Wang and Rebecca Karl, "The Year 1989 and the Historical Roots of Neoliberalism in China," *Positions: East Asia Cultures Critique* 12, no. 1 (January 2004): pp. 7–69.
[7]*Ibid.*

employ as many people as possible, and establish as many new industries as possible.[8] The goal was to meld old party rules with new marketization. Political promotions were tied to your county's growth, export penetration, and level of industrialization.[9] In two FYPs, Deng Xiaoping transformed local and provincial politicians into ambassadors for domestic and foreign business.

The FYP have never been perfect but remain a constantly evolving process of trial and error. Try! Stop! Observe! Get feedback! Start again. The 9th FYP (1996–2000) rearticulated China's commitment to a socialist market economy, but created robust financing models for the private sector.[10] It was under the 9th FYP that some of China's largest companies in existence today began to flourish — Alibaba was founded in 1999, SAIC Motor in 1995, China Mobile in 1997, Tencent in 1998, Evergrande Group in 1996, and JD 1998, to name a few (Figure 1.3).[11]

Though China was not significantly affected by the Asian Financial Crisis in 1998, it highlighted a need for more robust reforms. The 10th FYP (2001–2005) was still setting goals for yearly GDP growth and employment levels, but it began to articulate tangible and significant social measures. Soft metrics like improving the IT sector, reforestation, increasing urbanization, improving research & development standards, and accelerating educational attainment began to sit comfortably at the top of the priority list.[12] The 11th FYP (2006–2010), renamed to "program," focused on "sustainable development, growth model, innovation, and balancing urban-rural developments."[13] The 12th FYP (2011–2015) articulated a need to

---

[8] *Ibid.*

[9] *Ibid.*

[10] *Ibid.*

[11] William Goetzmann and Elisabeth Köll, "The History of Corporate Ownership in China: State Patronage, Company Legislation, and the Issue of Control," *Yale International Center for Finance*, June 2004.

[12] Han Huang, "China's Five-Year Plans," *South China Morning Post*, May 25, 2020, https://multimedia.scmp.com/infographics/news/china/article/3085903/china-five-year-plans/index.html.

[13] *Ibid.*

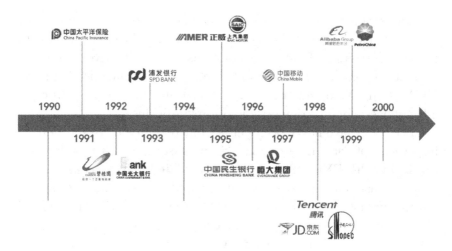

Figure 1.3.   China's Corporate Development after the 9th FYP.
Source: Schulte Research.

speed up urbanization, create more value-added industries, focus on research rather than manufacturing, and build sustainable growth (both environmentally and economically). In almost all regards, these goals were achieved. One of the more significant goals was the growth in education. In a matter of four years, the population of undergraduate and the postgraduate students more than doubled, producing millions of STEM experts yearly (Figure 1.4).[14]

Recent research on the fundamentals of the planning process has confirmed these bi-decennial developments. Over the past 30 years, "the Chinese government has introduced the market mechanism, which plays the fundamental role of resource allocation, while reforming the planning mechanism, thus facilitating the transition of planning itself from economic planning to public affairs governance planning."[15] Direct quantitative planning (economic and structural

---

[14] *Ibid.*

[15] Angang Hu, "The Distinctive Transition of China's Five-Year Plans," *Modern China* 39, no. 6 (2013): pp. 629–639.

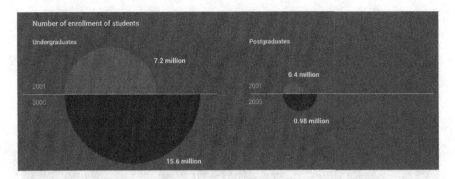

Figure 1.4. Number of enrolled students.
Source: Han Huang, "China's Five-Year Plans," *South China Morning Post*, May 25, 2020, https://multimedia.scmp.com/infographics/news/china/article/3085903/china-five-year-plans/index.html.

growth) have been almost nonexistent in the most recent plans. The Chinese government is now merely conducting Public Affairs management, working closely with private firms, and articulating social goals made in consultation with institutions, local governments, think tanks, and (regarding the most recent plan) the public. In the most halcyonic view, "the hand of the market aims to promote economic prosperity and the hand of the plan aims to promote a harmonious society; the hand of the market is engaged in providing private goods and the hand of the plan in providing public goods."[16]

In order to guarantee a future, steel production targets are out and Internet interconnection targets are in. These are intertwined with social goals: education, research and development, reforestation, CO_2 output, as well as urban/rural integration (Figure 1.5). What comes out is technology made for the individuals. It does not just exist in the abstract. Section 1.2 addresses the 12th and the 13th FYPs, which set the foundation for these technologies to flourish.

---

[16] *Ibid.*, p. 632.

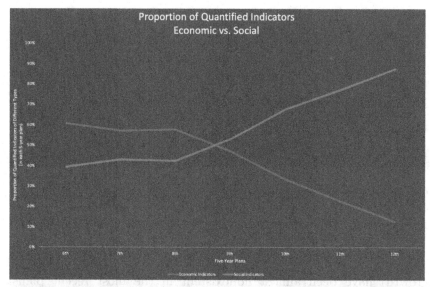

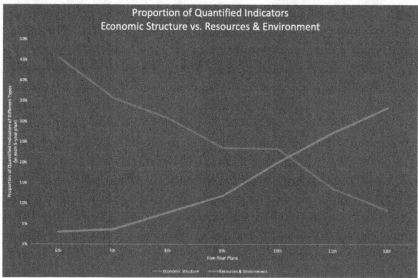

Figure 1.5.   Proportion of quantified indicators.

Source: State Council of the People's Republic of China, "The 13th Five-Year Science and Technology Innovation Plan," August 8, 2016; Angang Hu, "The Distinctive Transition of China's Five-Year Plans," *Modern China* 39, no. 6 (2013): pp. 629–639.

1.2. The 13th FYP (2016–2020): Technological Innovation as the Cornerstone of the 21st Century

The transition between the 12th and the 13th FYPs marked a major historic turning point in the path of global superpowers by creating the foundation of the digital world and proptech. China was addressing issues far different from the US. It was not bogged down by wars in the Middle East and Afghanistan. There was no opioid epidemic. There were no school shootings. Significantly, 2011 was the year when the number of Chinese citizens living in major cities for the first time exceeded those living in rural regions (Figure 1.6). China recovered from the Great Financial Crisis and it reasserted the role of major urban hubs as the foundation of Chinese development.

The planning of the mid-2010s is perhaps the most sweeping modernization of China's economy since the market reforms in the 1980s. In 2013, China launched the Belt and Road Initiative, intended to interconnect Europe, Central Asia, Africa, and China via land and sea routes. In 2015, the world saw the emergence of the MIC25 initiative, focusing on high-end manufacturing and import-substitution. All of these projects were integrated in the 13th FYP released in 2016. This section will focus on what the 13th FYP

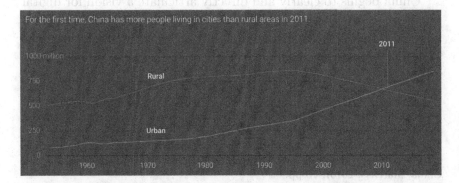

Figure 1.6. Population living in urban and rural areas in China (2011).

Source: Han Huang, "China's Five-Year Plans," *South China Morning Post*, May 25, 2020. Available at: https://multimedia.scmp.com/infographics/news/china/article/3085903/china-five-year-plans/index.html.

(2016–2020) articulated regarding self-reliance, technology, urban integration, and property. It will additionally highlight what industry leaders China has envisioned as the vanguard of its future.

Most importantly, clarity and transparency became the foundation of China's vision for the 21st century. China's leadership is not delusional; they have remained very aware and lucid about their limits, failures, and room for growth.[17] Long gone are the days when every report must be prefaced by 50 pages of praise. Now, central planners are setting out policies to address the "unbalanced, uncoordinated, and unsustainable growth" and working toward a "moderately prosperous society in all respects through innovative, coordinated, green, open, and inclusive growth."[18] This is the essence of modern urban development and digitization.[19]

Beyond a groundbreaking environmental policy that pushes for new standards of improved air, water, and soil quality, the plan directs heavy subsidies toward green industries. There is plenty of old in the new. The FYP seeks to once again speed up the rate of urbanization, reform data collection across the country, improve coordination between national and local urban planning, and more.[20] While this is an ambitious extension of previous FYP, the real innovation lies in the planners' awareness of a need for technological innovation.

China begins to clearly and directly articulate a vision for digital interconnection. Instead of building roads, the Internet took on a new importance: the undisputed digital highway for the future. The 13th FYP raised the goal of "fixed broadband household penetration

---

[17] Katherine Koleski, "The 13th Five-Year Plan," U.S.- China Economic and Security Review Commission, February 14, 2017, https://www.uscc.gov/research/13th-five-year-plan.

[18] Li Keqiang, "Report on the Work of the Government," Report on the Work of the Government (Fourth Session of the 12th National People's Congress, Beijing, China, March 5, 2016), 10 pp.

[19] Barbara Finamore, "China's Quest for Global Clean Energy Leadership," *Instituto Affari Internazionali*, January 2020.

[20] People's Republic of China, 13th Five-Year Plan on National Economic and Social Development, March 17, 2016. Translation. http://www.gov.cn/xinwen/2016-03/17/content_5054992.htm.

ratio from 40 percent in 2015 to 70 percent in 2020 and the mobile broadband subscriber penetration ratio from 57 percent in 2015 to 85 percent by 2020."[21] The plan hedged its bet on the fact that interconnectivity is the most important part of optimizing finance, education, healthcare, and manufacturing. Broadband penetration is a foundational necessity for everything from cloud computing, big data, to making an Internet of Things (IoT) world a reality.[22]

This is where China's new approach to market liberalization is clearer. The National Development and Reform Commission, and Ministry of Industry and Information Technology allocated US$179.1 billion (RMB 1.2 trillion) to build 56,000 miles of high speed fiber and 2 million 4G and 5G stations.[23] The Cyberspace Administration "launched the $14.9 billion (RMB 100 billion) China Internet Investment Fund in January to provide equity investment in Chinese Internet and IoT sector firms."[24] In the meantime, major State Banks have opened US$22.4 billion (RMB 150 billion) in credit lines for IoT firms that the fund already invests in.[25] We are seeing a state apparatus creating incentives for firms and research institutions to innovate, compete, and most importantly, interconnect every part of China. The only time this has happened before on such a national scale is when the US was building the world's Internet. Competition with the Soviet Union forced the US to activate every part of society around mutually empowering infrastructure. Competition with the US is forcing China to do the same.

Chinese planners couple concrete interconnection with softer targets to guarantee long-term externalities. The 13th FYP aimed to increase the R&D personnel (number of people with scientific

---

[21] *Ibid.*

[22] Katherine Koleski, "The 13th Five-Year Plan," U.S.- China Economic and Security Review Commission, February 14, 2017, https://www.uscc.gov/research/13th-five-year-plan.

[23] *Ibid.*

[24] "China Launches 14.6 Bln USD Internet Investment Fund," *Xinhua*, January 22, 2017, http://www.xinhuanet.com//english/2017-01/22/c_136004874.htm.

[25] In particular, The Agricultural Bank of China, China Development Bank, and the Industrial and Commercial Bank of China.

degrees per 10,000 people) from 48.5% to 60% by 2020.[26] It doubled the target of patents per 10,000 and raised the standards to align with the international citations and Patent Cooperation Treaty.[27] Finally, the FYP raised spending on R&D from 2.2% of GDP to 2.5% of GDP.[28] This brought China's total spending on research and development to US$1.2 trillion (RMB 8 trillion). As a great example of how the "two-hands" economic policy actually functions, the FYP also sets recommended targets for the private sector's spending on R&D (Table 1.2).

The 13th FYP additionally highlights China's points of weakness that the current initiatives will work on correcting.

First, there is an effort to move China away from being the factory of the world. In 2015, it produced 90% of the world's mobile phones, 60% of the world's TV sets, 50% of the world's refrigerators, 24% of the world's power, and 50% of the world's steel.[29] Much of this industry lies at the low-value-added, high-energy, and high-polluting end of the scale.

Second, there is a fear of the middle-income trap, where economic growth stagnates before a high level of GDP per capita is achieved. The 13th FYP explicitly mentions this concern, acknowledging that "in 2005, one RMB of credit produced one RMB of GDP, in 2008 the same RMB of credit produced less than 0.8 RMB of GDP, and decreased to less than 0.4 RMB of GDP in 2015."[30] This means that growth, going forward, can only be guaranteed through innovation.

Third, China has a quickly depleting eligible workforce (those between 15 and 59 years old): "China's National Bureau of Statistics

---

[26] Katherine Koleski, "The 13th Five-Year Plan," U.S.-China Economic and Security Review Commission, February 14, 2017, https://www.uscc.gov/research/13th-five-year-plan.
[27] *Ibid.*
[28] *Ibid.*
[29] "China Manufacturing 2025: Putting Industrial Policy Ahead of Market Forces (<中国制造 2025: 产业政策对弈市场力量》)," European Chamber of Commerce (European Union Chamber of Commerce in China, 2017).
[30] *Ibid.*

Table 1.2. The 13th Five-Year Science and Technology Innovation Plan's targets.

Target	2015	2020
Global innovation ranking	18	15
Contribution of science and technological advantages to economic growth	**55.3%**	**60%**
R&D as share of GDP	**2.1%**	**2.5%**
Number of R&D personnel per 10,000 people employed per year	48.5	60
Revenue of high-technology enterprises	22.2 trillion RMB	34 trillion RMB
Share of value-added knowledge-intensive services industries to GDP	15.6	20
R&D intensity	0.9	1.1
Global ranking for the number of citations in international science and technology papers	4	2
Patents filed under the Patent Cooperation Treaty per 10,000 patents	3.05	6.1
Patents filed per 10,000 people	**6.3**	**12**
National technical contract turnover	983.5 billion RMB	2 trillion RMB
Proportion of the total population possessing scientific degrees	6.2%	10%

Note: In this table, all targets in bold are key targets in the 13th FYP (see Appendix II).
Source: State Council of the People's Republic of China, 13th Five-Year Science and Technology Innovation Plan, August 8, 2016. Translation. http://www.gov .cn/gongbao/content_5103134.htm.

reported that from 2013 to 2014, the workforce will decline by 3.7 million, with a further decline of 4.9 million from 2014 to 2015."[31] The decline is mostly in rural areas, where the number of employed persons will halve. Simultaneously, the urban employment will increase by an estimated 22%.[32] In total, one in eight workers will leave today's workforce. Since the urban workforce is about

---

[31] *Ibid.*
[32] "China's Labour Force Is, and Is Not, Growing," *Global Demographics*, August 2018.

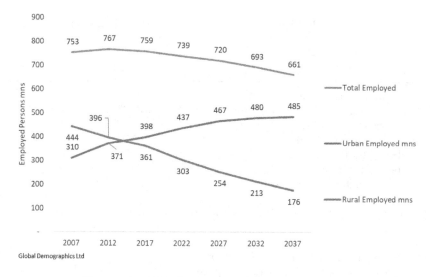

Figure 1.7.   The divide in rural/urban job growth.

four times more productive than the rural, this is a positive trend. Therefore, even though the employment decline mostly signals rising rates of urbanization and agricultural automation, an aging workforce is still a genuine concern (Figure 1.7). In order to get rich before they get old, China is doubling down on research and development.

Finally, China is late to the automation game. Xi Jinping said as early as 2014 that "China's foundation for science and technology innovation is still not firm. China's capacity for indigenous innovation, and especially original innovation, is still weak. Fundamentally, the fact that we are controlled by others in critical fields and key technologies has not changed."[33] None of these are deal breakers. The country's sober diagnoses of weakness and failures, and especially its public acknowledgment, is a sign of robust leadership. Figure 1.8 highlights China's divergence five years ago, in 2016. By the time this book comes out, that gap is quickly being closed: "China had

---

[33]Rainer Frietsch, Henning Kroll, and Koen Jonkers, "China's Development of an Innovation-Driven Economy," *Innovation and Development Policy* 2 (2019): pp. 85–103.

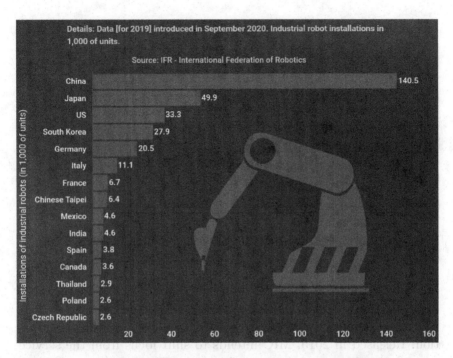

Figure 1.8.   Annual installations of industrial robots, 15 largest markets.
Source: "China's Global Leadership List — Charts and Facts, 2020." *World Affairs*, January 11, 2021. https://worldaffairs.blog/2019/09/23/chinas-global-leadership-list-2019/.

a density rate of 25 units in 2013 that grew to 97 in 2017. In 2019, that figure had grown once again to 187."[34] The difficulty is appreciating the speed of the growth considering China's population of 1.4 billion people. From 2016 to now South Korea, the most industrialized country in the world, went from 531 to 855 robots per 10,000 workers. During the same time, China went from 49 to 187, more than tripling. Despite the global trade war and international tensions on its manufacturing sector, China continues to digitize at the fastest rate worldwide.

---

[34]Niall McCarthy, "The Countries with the Highest Density of Robot Workers," *Statista Infographics*, September 24, 2020.

Box 1.2 Ten key priorities of MIC25 initiative.

(1) Next-generation IT
(2) High-end numerical control machinery and robotics
(3) Aerospace and aviation equipment
(4) Maritime engineering equipment and high-tech maritime vessel manufacturing
(5) Advanced rail equipment
(6) Energy-saving vehicles
(7) Electrical equipment
(8) Agricultural machinery and equipment
(9) New materials
(10) Biopharmaceuticals and high-performance medical devices

In response, Beijing is doubling down on high-value-added manufacturing. The MIC25 initiative isolates 10 strategic industries that will enhance productivity, quality, and most importantly, digitization. Released in 2015, MIC intends to shift focus from the service economy to the manufacturing value chain. The former central bank adviser Yu Yongding said "In the past, we emphasized an export orientation because [we believed] that export-oriented countries, especially small countries, were successful. In the future, we need to use more power to boost import substitution. MIC 2025 is a reflection of this aspiration, and support for this aspiration should be accorded."[35] The council focuses on 10 key priorities (Box 1.2).

As can be seen, the planning process is diverse, centralized, and cumulative. Thousands of bureaucrats pour the energies of their whole ministries over the course of a year into articulating the clearest vision. In the next four years, the energy goes into its actualization (Figure 1.9).

MIC 2025 accelerates the decoupling started in the aftermath of the Great Financial Crisis. Now, with an explicit focus on import

---

[35] Jude Blanchette and Andrew Polk, "Dual Circulation and China's New Hedged Integration Strategy," Center for Strategic and International Studies, August 24, 2020.

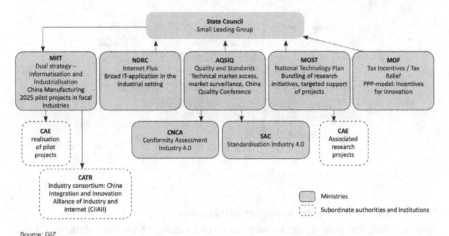

Figure 1.9. Political responsibilities and initiatives under China Manufacturing 2025.
Source: "China Manufacturing 2025: Putting Industrial Policy Ahead of Market Forces (《中国制造 2025 产业政策对弈市场力量》)" European Chamber of Commerce (European Union Chamber of Commerce in China, 2017).

substitution, the state council is pouring trillions of RMB into strategic industries, de-emphasizing imports/exports, and prioritizing self-reliance. As we will point out later in the chapter, in light of an exacerbating trade war and COVID-19, the 14th FYP set even more ambitious targets for the substitution industries (Figure 1.10).

Through the 13th FYP 2016–2020 and the MIC initiative, China is rearticulating a new class of industry that is not just strategic, but central to China's future. The firms that are prioritized in the process of decoupling receive favorable credit lines, are at the top of the list for government procurement, and are heading much of the local public–private partnerships.[36] However, it is not a

---

[36]Max Zenglein Zenglein and Anna Holzmann, "Evolving Made in China 2025: China's Industrial Policy in the Quest for Global Tech Leadership," *Merics*, July 2, 2019.

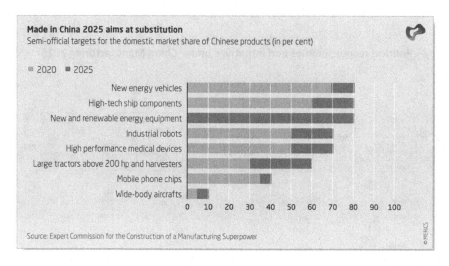

Figure 1.10.   MIC25 aims at import substitution.
Source: Max Zenglein Zenglein and Anna Holzmann, "Evolving Made in China 2025: China's Industrial Policy in the Quest for Global Tech Leadership," *Merics*, July 2, 2019.

one-way relationship. Leadership of major firms is often consulted on major decisions about technology, targets, and the state of the market. As just one example, the Internet Plus initiative to increase broadband penetration was created largely in consultation with the CEOs of Alibaba, Baidu, Huawei, and Tencent: "The internet plus strategy (互联网+) and a stronger emphasis on AI was largely driven by private tech companies" (Table 1.3).[37]

Industry leaders are spearheading the government's focus on AI. For example, the "recruitment of a national AI team by the Ministry of Industry and Information Technology in 2017 involved internet giants Baidu and Alibaba and the AI companies iFlyTek and SenseTime."[38] Chinese leadership is especially keen on consulting industry about emerging issues of technology, materializing a symbiotic relationship between private firms and

---

[37] *Ibid.*
[38] *Ibid.*

Table 1.3. State-owned and private enterprises divide the leadership in MIC25 core industries amongst themselves (selection).

Next-generation IT	Ownership	Business area
Huawei	private	network equipment, consumer electronics (-> smartphones)
ZTE	SOE	network equipment provider
Alibaba	private	AI research as well as all kinds of Internet related services
Tencent	private	AI research as well as all kinds of Internet related services
Baidu	private	AI research as well as all kinds of Internet related services
Beijing Bytedance	private	Internet media, smartphone applications, AI research
Sense Time	private	deep learning and AI research, face recognition technology
Cloudwalk	private	AI research, facial recognition technology
Yitu Technology	private	AI research in relation to health care, finance
iFlytek	private	AI, translation systems, voice recognition
Megvii Face++	private	AI, face and body recognition
Cambricon	private	IC, AI chips, semi-conductors
YMTC	SOE	IC/microchips
Horizon Robotics	private	IC/microchips
HiSilicon Technologies	private	IC
Jiangsu Changjiang Electronics Technology	private	IC packaging and testing
Automation and robotics		
Sense Time	private	deep learning and AI research, face recognition technology
DJI	private	intelligent aerial drones, AI research
Ubtech Robotics	private	humanoid robots
Siasun Robot & Automation	private	robots: industrial, mobile, service; intelligent logistics and assembly systems

Source: Max Zenglein Zenglein and Anna Holzmann, "Evolving Made in China 2025: China's Industrial Policy in the Quest for Global Tech Leadership," *Merics*, July 2, 2019.

bureaucratic demands. As one Chinese researcher put it, "replacing 'one hand' (the plan) with 'two hands' (both the plan and the market)."[39] On top of selecting the strategically important industries, the Chinese government also elevates their leadership.

---

[39] Angang Hu, "The Distinctive Transition of China's Five-Year Plans," *Modern China* 39, no. 6 (2013): pp. 629–639.

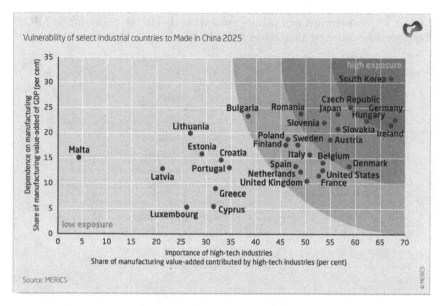

Figure 1.11.   Under pressure: Industrialized countries will face the heat of Made in China 2025.
Source: Max Zenglein Zenglein and Anna Holzmann, "Evolving Made in China 2025: China's Industrial Policy in the Quest for Global Tech Leadership," *Merics*, July 2, 2019.

China's development is not occurring in isolation, and there are plenty of nations vulnerable to its industrialization. Much of China's global diplomacy can be understood through Figure 1.11. Those nations closer to the top are more likely to make trade deals, investment treaties, and political conciliations. It is not the ultimate answer, but it serves as a helpful lens. For example, China and the EU's recent Comprehensive Agreement on Investment to open China up to European investment makes much more sense in light of the dangers that accelerating industrialization will pose to Germany.[40]

---

[40]Alexis Leggeri, "EU-China Investment Deal: Has China Revived Its European Diplomacy?" *The Diplomat*, December 31, 2020.

In conclusion, the Chinese government is articulating a new model and vision for how markets function by:

(1) Outlining social goals: The most important ones that we expand on in this book are accelerating urbanization, reducing the rural/urban disparity, creating technical self-reliance, increasing public/private partnerships, and national interconnection.

(2) Selecting the industries that are central to its strategic interests: IT, Robotics, high-value electrical equipment.

(3) Handing down to industry leaders the power to determine what is possible, what is necessary, and what will be important in the next decade: AI and IoT. In order to understand China, its technical innovations, and its future direction, the world must look to these companies, who have largely been allowed to steer the economic digitization. This book is particularly about them. We explain how *China's second hand* — Alibaba, Tencent, Ping An, Baidu, and dozens of start-ups — interprets the social goals, envision public–private partnerships, create new technology, and transform everyday life in China.

1.3. The 14th FYP 2021–2025: Renewed Focus on SMEs, Entrepreneurs, and Emerging Technology

While this book goes to print a few weeks before the 14th FYP is officially released, in October 2020, the central government met to outline and set priorities for it. The central documents to articulate the intention of the plan came from the party and Xi Jinping himself.[41]. While we do not know the exact targets that will be set, the words of the leadership serve as an important indicator of what

---

[41] "中共中央关于制定国民经济和社会发展第十四个五年规划和二〇三五年远景目标的建议", 新华网, November 3, 2020, http://www.xinhuanet.com/politics/zywj/2020-11/03/c_1126693293.htm. And "习近平: 关于《中共中央关于制定国民经济和社会发展第十四个五年规划和二〇三五年远景目标的建议》的说明," 新华网, November 3, 2020, http://www.xinhuanet.com/politics/leaders/2020-11/03/c_1126693341.htm.

China is doubling down on and where it is pivoting to in the next five years. On top of setting new priorities, it also signals China's cautious perception of the global order. The 14th FYP has shed significant new importance to three goals:

(1) Self-reliance through dual circulation.
(2) Scientific and technological reform.
(3) Support of entrepreneurs and homegrown talent.

Dual circulation entails strengthening and insulating the local market from international market fluctuations through import substitution. Expect more "Buy Chinese" campaigns in the next 10 years. Scientific and technological reforms will push the economy toward high-value-added industry and pull away from labor-intensive work. Investment in human capital is perhaps the more important infrastructure for national success. It will ensure that innovation and development can persist past any single political leader, FYP, or economic policy.

Chinese policymakers see this planning program as fundamentally different from its precedents precisely because of the method. While symposiums of experts have remained, meetings with entrepreneurs have taken on an important role in it of themselves. Xi Jinping has emphasized the democratic quality of this plan, saying "From August 16 to 29, the preparation of the '14th Five-Year Plan' began to solicit opinions online. The broad masses of people actively participated, leaving more than 1 million messages, and related parties sorted out more than 1,000 suggestions."[42] While it is unclear how the recommendations from the public were sorted and who was responsible for winnowing down public opinion into useful suggestions, the leadership is certain that: "This is a vivid practice of democracy within our party and socialist democracy."[43] Significantly, the most important goal of the FYP has remained the same: public

---

[42] "习近平: 关于《中共中央关于制定国民经济和社会发展第十四个五年规划和二〇三五年远景目标的建议》的说明," 新华网, November 3, 2020, http://www.xinhuanet.com/politics/leaders/2020-11/03/c_1126693341.htm.
[43] *Ibid.*

affairs. Now that it has abandoned its ancient task of setting quantitative targets, China's leadership has reaffirmed that "The recommendations of the Party Central Committee are mainly to manage the general direction and set the general strategy."[44] These recommendations are from some of the few public documents out of China that lets the outside world peak into its national strategy.

First, it is important to note what has been an extension of the 13th FYP. In a recent speech, Xi Jinping has continued emphasizing the importance of high-quality development, the need to address inequality, and doubled down on fostering social cohesion and stronger party rule. Despite predictions of China's economy surpassing the US, Xi Jinping acknowledges that:

(1) "Development is still our party's top priority in governing and rejuvenating the country...
(2) Development of the new era must be high-quality...
(3) The results must better benefit all people, and continue to realize people's yearning for a better life.
(4) We must enrich the guiding ideology and principles, strengthen the people-centered approach, expand the opening up to the world, and comprehensively govern the country according to law, and coordinate development and security."[45]

The goals of the 12th FYP (2011–2015) to improve the technological capability of the urban areas are maintained in the 14th FYP (2021–2025). Xi Jinping explicitly recommends "to improve the new urbanization strategy and enrich the content of urban planning and construction management."[46] Many threads have remained from the plan that the party drafted during the modernization push in the 12th FYP, and it has also embarked into unexplored territory (Figure 1.12).

The outside world has changed significantly since 2011, when China first started turning to technological innovation. If the 13th

---

[44] *Ibid.*
[45] *Ibid.*
[46] *Ibid.*

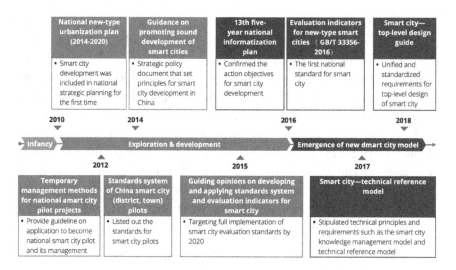

Figure 1.12.   Evolution of China's National Smart City Strategy.

Source: "5G Smart Cities Whitepaper: Deloitte China," Deloitte China, June 2020, https://www2.deloitte.com/cn/en/pages/technology-media-and-telecomm unications/articles/tmt-empowering-smart-cities-with-5g.html.

FYP intended to bring back the research and development, there is no way it could have predicted the trade war, COVID-19, or Donald Trump's loss in November. The past five years have opened a Pandora's Box of international anxiety that will not be closed anytime soon. The 14th FYP is being published on the heels of Western industries leaving China en masse, overwhelming sanctions on Chinese technology companies, and a propaganda campaign against China's responsibility over COVID-19. Regardless of how many doves sit on Joe Biden's National Security Council, the new American leadership will not be able to abate China's concerns: what if the next storming of the capital is successful, or what if in another four years a new president arrives and China once again ends up on the receiving end of a "tantrumatic" foreign policy? The comments of the party and Xi Jinping are hyper-lucid about the precariousness of the international order.

The 14th FYP emphasizes a significantly more inward-looking economic policy. Xi Jinping termed the policy "dual circulation" in

May 2020, and has re-emphasized its importance in his addresses: "In recent years, with the changes in the global political and economic environment, the trend of anti-globalization has intensified, some countries have practiced unilateralism and protectionism, and the traditional international cycle has been significantly weakened. Under such circumstances, we must put our development foothold in the country and rely more on the domestic market to achieve economic development."[47] While it does not explicitly entail a closing off to the outside world, there is an acknowledgment of the changing tides, "since the reform and opening up, we have encountered many external risk shocks, and ultimately we can alleviate the dangers. We must manage our own affairs."[48] Since the sector most impacted by the trade war has been technology, it is also the industry most heavily impacted by the new policy of dual circulation.

Emerging technology takes on outstanding importance in the 14th FYP's vision of a country insulated from outside tumult. The Proposal of the Central Committee for the 14th FYP outlines a vision for emerging industries, encouraging policymakers to "accelerate the growth of a new generation of information technology, bIoTechnology, new energy, new materials, high-end equipment, new energy vehicles, green environmental protection, aerospace, marine equipment and other industries."[49] The recommendations are not exclusively about abstract industry. Much of the recommendations focus on the development of specific technology like "artificial intelligence, quantum information, integrated circuits, life and health, brain science, biological breeding, aerospace science and technology, and deep sea," along with a push to further integrate "internet, big data, and advanced manufacturing."[50] Technology was a focus in both the 12th and the 13th FYPs, but in the most recent iteration it

---

[47] *Ibid.*

[48] *Ibid.*

[49] "中共中央关于制定国民经济和社会发展第十四个五年规划和二〇三五年远景目标的建议," 新华网, November 3, 2020, http://www.xinhuanet.com/politics/zywj/2020-11/03/c_1126693293.htm.

[50] *Ibid.*

has become the source of China's competitive advantage in the 21st century.

Not all the focus is on the emerging industries, and large enterprises continue to be well supported in the Party's priorities list. China's commitment to the private market focuses primarily on enhancing their "technological innovation capabilities." This is achieved by elevating enterprises to a "dominant position [within] innovation" and improving "the concentration of various innovative elements."[51] Expect the next five years to feature more economic incentives and political favors for the companies most committed to R&D. As another sliver of evidence that China in 2020 is not the China of the 1970s, the Central Committee highlights "the important role of entrepreneurs in technological innovation" striving to "encourage enterprises to increase R&D investment, and implement tax incentives for enterprises' investment in basic research."[52] Finally, and most importantly, is the emphasis on SMEs and common technology platforms to do business on. The Central Committee intends to "... give full play to the leading and supporting role of large enterprises, support the growth of innovative small, medium and micro enterprises as an important birthplace of innovation, strengthen the construction of common technology platforms, and promote the integration and innovation of the upper, middle and lower reaches of the industrial chain, and large and small enterprises."[53] It is in this statement that 5G, the Blockchain Service Network, and Central Bank Digital Coin can be detected: they are the foundational technological services that will bring tens of thousands of SMEs into the 21st century, offering both low price and ease of use.

The final development of the 14th FYP is its focus on local talent and entrepreneurship. This is what this book is about. It is about the individuals and firms in China working to kill the perception that

---

[51] *Ibid.*

[52] *Ibid.*

[53] Dorcas Wong, "What to Expect in China's 14th Five Year Plans After the Fifth Plenum?" *China Briefing News*, December 29, 2020.

they can only copy the West. The government has been long aware of this drive to facilitate risk-taking while ensuring contribution to society. The government is committed to:

(1) "Carry out the principles of respecting labor, knowledge, talents, and creativity;
(2) Deepen the reform of the talent development system and mechanism;
(3) Cultivate, introduce and make good use of talents in all aspects;
(4) Create more world-class technology leaders and innovative teams; and
(5) Cultivate international competitiveness."[54]

This is a policy that will encourage domestic innovation, but it is simultaneously a promise to the huge Chinese diaspora: if you return, your labor and talent will be used, respected, and well compensated.

---

[54] "中共中央关于制定国民经济和社会发展第+四个五年规划和二〇三五年远景目标的建议," 新华网, November 3, 2020, http://www.xinhuanet.com/politics/zywj/2020-11/03/c_1126693293.htm.

Chapter 2

5G and the Connection of Property

2.1. Introduction

When 1G came out in 1979, it paved the way for mobile communications, although telephones with 10-feet-long cords would remain in use until the 1990s. 2G (1991) and 3G (1998) allowed for messaging, internet access, and GPS. When 4G came out in 2006, it facilitated the creation of a multibillion-dollar mobile app-ecosystem and finally brought seamless streaming to the consumer. Each new generation of mobile technology gives birth to firms, markets, and products that could not have been imagined before. Every MBA program ridiculed Netflix, Facebook, and Google for misunderstanding the basics of business administration; however, it is now impossible to move through the world without using their services. Most importantly, because the US created 4G infrastructure quickly and in an early manner, the information giants could grow and dominate the world.

From the beginning of the Industrial Revolution — from the textile mills and the luddites to cryptocurrency and the bankers — every technology that threatens an industry is often rejected by the lizard brain of its most fervent supporters.[1] Unfortunately, when the amygdala speaks, the boardroom listens. This initial resistance has destroyed firms, put millions out of work, and elected demagogues

---

[1] Carl Frey, *Technology Trap: Capital, Labor, and Power in the Age of Automation* (Princeton University Press, Princeton, 2020).

into office. Western industries no longer send jobs abroad, rather they outsource innovation.

The existing urban infrastructure is lacking and not sophisticated enough to function beyond the basic exchange of information. Fixed-line broadband and 4G networks cannot meet the needs of any smart city scenario, primarily because the installation and replacement costs are too high, the infrastructure is not flexible, and coupled with long latency and low bandwidth, it means that a network cannot handle more than a few operations. However, when you combine every urban operation, with hundreds of terabytes of data flowing daily requiring ongoing input and output, the networks will inevitably get bottlenecked. For auxiliary technology (AI, big data analytics, and cloud computing) to transform city life, new communication pipelines must come into existence: i.e. 5G needs to be built now and it must be built fast.

While 4G might have capped the necessary speeds for inter-personal interactive communication, 5G is opening up new opportunities to interconnect the very infrastructure we use on a daily basis. Improved speeds, bandwidth, and reduced latency are already starting to upend transportation, healthcare, and real estate. Among all developed countries, China has been one of the few to declare 5G as one of its most strategically important infrastructures from the start of the decade. Considering that over 70% of current 5G users are in China, it is clear where the technological leadership lies.

The most jarring divergence between China and the world's development of new telecommunication is the impact of COVID-19. The pandemic catalyzed a gamut of new industrial applications of 5G and proved its potential. In March, Hunan Valin Xianggang (Iron & Steel Conglomerate) built the first multinational 5G+AR remote assembly to overcome the impact of the epidemic and conduct remote debugging and operation of equipment.[2] In April, Huawei helped develop the first 5G integrated coal mine in the Xinyuan

---

[2] "Hunan Mobile, Huawei and Valin Xianggang Jointly Promote the Integrated Development of 'Information Technology + Intelligent Manufacturing'," *Day News*, April 26, 2020.

Coal Mine in Shanxi.[3] In May, Cosco Shipping and Dongfeng Motor jointly released the country's first 5G full-scenario smart port at the Yuanhai Terminal in Xiamen, Fujian.[4] The Yunnan province used 5G drones to patrol and advise people to avoid gatherings. Near the Beijing National Stadium, 5G drones dispatched face masks and delivered hot meals to hospital patients from 1,800 km away. In Hubei, 5G drones circled the skies, spraying disinfectants.[5] Chinese firms continue to apply 5G technology to new fields. Every industry including supply chains,[6] drones,[7] healthcare,[8] public surveillance, shopping, mining, manufacturing, and driverless transportation[9] is being transformed. The extent of industrial innovation that will be widely accepted is still to be seen, but the seeds of a highly interconnected and responsive society have been planted.

This chapter will address why 5G will become the highway of the 21st century. Section 2.2 touches on its technical innovation and current global deployment. Section 2.3 addresses how private firms in China have adapted it for consumer use. Section 2.4 and Section 2.5 address the future potential for urban planning and real estate.

2.2. 5G and the Global Reach

Over the past 10 years, only one country in the world has been betting big on the evolution of mobile technology. When we evaluate the rates of global penetration of 5G towers, research, and complete urban integration, it becomes clear that China is at least three years

---

[3]Yuan Shenggao, "5G Helps Unearth More Efficiency in Coal Mines," *Chinadaily*, June 26, 2020. Available at: http://epaper.chinadaily.com.cn/a/202006/26/WS5 ef532c2a3107831ec75309a.html.

[4]Zoey Zhang, "COVID-19 Catalyzes Commercial Use of 5G in China," *China Briefing News*, May 26, 2020.

[5]"云南移动5G智慧无人机高空巡查创新疫情防控手段," Xinhua, February 13, 2020.

[6]"Chinese Shipbuilding Switches on to 5G," Royal Institute of Naval Architecture, May 2020, Available at: https://www.rina.org.uk/iqs/rp.5/rssnewsfeed.html.

[7]"Coronavirus Helps China Pull Ahead in the 5G Race," *Nikkei Asia*, May 6, 2020.

[8]*Ibid.*

[9]Charlie Wood, "A Chinese Firm That Makes Driverless Delivery Vans is Thriving Amid the Coronavirus Outbreak," *Business Insider*, March 9, 2020.

ahead of the rest of the world in telecommunications. However, if a consumer is asked how they feel about 5G, you might get a few blank stares. Why is this? Using the latest mobile technology to transfer photos, communicate with friends, and stream videos is equivalent to using the large hadron collider to staple your resume: it is a wasteful overkill. Add in the fact that it is more expensive than 4G that can accomplish all of the necessary consumer services perfectly fine and it becomes increasingly confusing why the second richest country in the world is so obsessed with 5G. The truth of the matter is that China does not just plan for two years out (a term of a US Congressional Representative) or four years out (the term of a US President). Chinese lawmakers have tangible policy goals for decades to come. 5G is not for consumers in 2020. It is for large-scale industrial use into 2024. Most importantly, it is for our property and cities in 2030.

Many of the modern tools are sufficient for speeding up the most basic task that we have been perfecting for millennia: exchanging information. Now, the modern world is run by individuals who are merely empowered by technology. The reaction time of a human is about 250 ms or 1/4th of a second. With proper training, the fastest an individual can get might be around 200 ms. If you have been to a baseball game recently (via zoom of course), then you know that the most interesting plays in the sport happen within the range of 200–250 ms. It is where human limits are tested, and success in this range is often what separates someone who has practiced a lot from someone for whom it is as instinctual as breathing. In telecommunications, this reaction speed is referred to as latency. Fourth-generation cellular communication functions at around 200–400 ms. If communication speeds are stopped now, all of the progress would happen in polishing around the edges of speeding up interpersonal exchange.

The technical capabilities of the next generation allow it to supersede merely interpersonal exchange. On balance, 5G cellular networks will be the harbinger of a fully automated world, bridging the communication gap between the individuals and the property they interact with (Figure 2.1). On the streets, fifth-generation technology has comfortable "air latency" speeds — communication

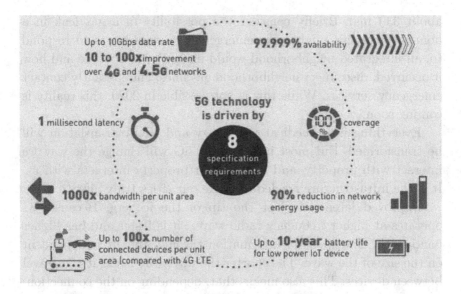

Figure 2.1.   5G capabilities and improvements.

Source: "Introducing 5G Technology and Networks (Speed, Use Cases and Rollout)," The Thales Group, December 2020. Available at: https://www.thal esgroup.com/en/markets/digital-identity-and-security/mobile/inspired/5G.

from a *cause* in equipment to *effect* at the server — between 10–20 ms.[10] In a lab, air latency has been registered between 1–4 ms. While this will not be possible for another few years on the streets of Shanghai, right now 5G is 10–300 times faster than 4G, and consequently, humans. Take a car accident for example. With property integrated 5G interconnection, your car would be able to analyze everything that has happened on the road, stop, send the information to a server, call emergency services, communicate with the transportation department for a public service announcement, and tell every other smart car in the city to divert traffic to a different location. All this before you can blink an eye (which takes

---

[10] "Introducing 5G Technology and Networks (Speed, Use Cases and Rollout)," The Thales Group, December 2020. Available at: https://www.thalesgroup.com/ en/markets/digital-identity-and-security/mobile/inspired/5G.

about 330 ms). Briefly consider the possibility of a gas leak in a home. While this might take emergency services hours to respond to, an integrated neighborhood would instantly note where and how it occurred, disconnect neighborhood gas lines, and instantly contact emergency services. While this is not possible in 2020, this reality is coming soon.

Everything from medical technology and VR to translation will be transformed. But most importantly, 5G will change the way we interact with property, and the way our property interacts with us. It is the infrastructure needed to make our cities truly alive.

Improved latency is just the tip of the iceberg. Because 5G operates at higher frequency radio waves, it is faster and has higher bandwidth. The speed of information through the air is dependent on the size of the wave. The shorter the wave, the faster it can travel between devices. This also means that, depending on the connection, it can have download speeds of 10 GB/s. Its network interconnection allows it to support thousands of devices at the same time, while putting minimal strain on battery life, naturally extending the life of whatever device is connected to it (Figure 2.2).

Admittedly, there are still issues with the rolling out, marketing, and applications of 5G. The 3rd Generation Partnership Project sets all the standards, and defines any system using 5G New Radio software as "5G".[11]

This presents two problems. First, "5G" can be anything from sub-6 GHz to 100 GHz (mmWave). This means there is a huge range in the actual speed, latency, and bandwidth of the network. Second, one does not have to build a standalone 5G network to call it "5G". The current standards allow a telecom provider to simply update the software on the existing 4G networks without changing anything but the price tag. There is an ongoing scandal with AT&T about its false advertising of "5G Evolution" for phones on its network that does not actually allow the phones to connect to 5G towers (and is

---

[11]Magnus Johansson, Matts Karreman, and Amalia Foukaki, "3rd Generation Partnership Project: Competition in the Developmental of Standardization Setting," *Academy of Management Proceedings*, 2017, no. 1 (2017).

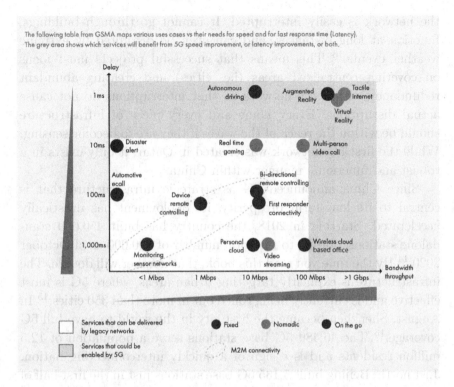

The following table from GSMA maps various uses cases vs their needs for speed and for fast response time (Latency). The grey area shows which services will benefit from 5G speed improvement, or latency improvements, or both.

Figure 2.2. Digital services and their internet speed requirements.

Source: "Introducing 5G Technology and Networks (Speed, Use Cases and Rollout)," The Thales Group, December 2020. Available at: https://www.thal esgroup.com/en/markets/digital-identity-and-security/mobile/inspired/5G.

hardly faster than 4G LTE).[12] American Telcos have become experts in putting lipstick on the pig, intent on maintaining their regional monopolies and squeezing their customers. As is the case with most emerging technologies, there will be the innovators, the emulators, and the grifters.

2.3.   International Rollout

For 5G to be successful, it requires a national project on the scale of the Federal Highway Act. Because of the high-frequency waves,

---

[12]Nick Statt, "AT&T Won't Remove Fake 5G Logo Even after Ad Board Says It's Misleading," *The Verge*, May 20, 2020.

the network is easily interrupted. It cannot go through buildings, function at long distances, and can even be disrupted by extreme weather events.[13] This means that successful projects must focus on covering centralized areas (i.e. cities) and creating abundant redundancy within the network so that interruptions do not cause actual disruptions. Every home and every piece of infrastructure should be within the reach of the waves if they are to become sensing. While the first 5G network was created in Qatar, it only exists in a robust and functional manner within China.

Since China announced 5G as strategic infrastructure that is central to its long-term prosperity, its deployment has drastically accelerated. Starting in 2018, the country has built 450,000 standalone stations, adding to the total number of 600,000 as of October 2020.[14] By the time you read this book, that number will double. The infrastructure is explicitly targeting urban areas, where 5G is most effective and is currently being rolled out in more than 350 cities.[15] In August, Shenzhen became the first city in the world to have full 5G coverage.[16] The 46,480 5G base stations serve a population of 12.5 million residents and is a sign of a quickly interconnecting nation. Just north, Beijing built 5,135 5G base stations just in the first half of 2020, expected to finish 13,000 stations by year's end (Figure 2.3).[17]

Chinese policymakers and producers are focusing specifically on working to make 5G applicable to consumers. China's national regulators are already creating incentives for companies to better articulate the importance of 5G to consumers and create useful applications. Under the guidance of the Ministry of Industry and Information Technology, the Broadband Development Alliance and

---

[13]Lina Xu, Anca Delia Jurcut, and Hamed Ahmadi, "Emerging Challenges and Requirements for Internet of Things in 5G." In *5G-Enabled Internet of Things*, CRC Press, 2019, pp. 29–48.

[14]Juan Tomás, "China to End 2020 with over 600,000 5G Base Stations: Report," *RCR Wireless News*, June 9, 2020.

[15]*Ibid.*

[16]*Ibid.*

[17]Juan Tomás, "Beijing Installs 5,135 5G Base Stations in H1," *RCR Wireless News*, July 30, 2020.

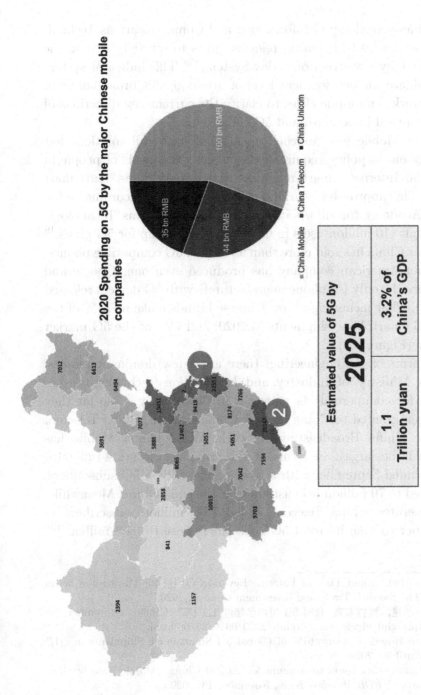

Figure 2.3. China's national 5G development.

Source: Joakim Abeleen and Thomas Larsen, "Beyond COVID-19: The Rise of 5G in China," The Swedish Trade and Investment Council, 2020.

the Chinese Academy of Information and Communications Technology took the lead in uniting relevant units to officially release the "Gigabit City Construction Index System."[18] This indicator system will evaluate the development level of urban gigabit broadband and 5G networks and guide cities to clarify the current key directions of gigabit optical bandwidth and 5G construction.

China Mobile has launched an all-gigabit overall solution that not only meets policy requirements but also the needs of people in industrial Internet, smart manufacturing, smart cities, and smart homes. This approach is working at least on paper. According to the China Academy for Information and Communications Technology, more than 110 million users in China have signed up for 5G plans.[19] This year China has sold more than 93 million 5G compatible phones, before an American company has produced even one (Google and Apple are the only US phone manufacturers with 5G devices released in 2020). That means right now Chinese brands make up 61% of the total 5G smartphone shipments in 2020, and 75% of the 5G market globally (Figure 2.4).[20]

In terms of the engineering, there are a few dominant players. China's Ministry of Industry and Information Technology issues licenses for commercial 5G networks in the country — so far they have been granted to China Mobile, China Unicom, China Telecom, and the China Broadcasting Network. While China Mobile has remained the largest in terms of subscribers, "the state-run telco said it ended September with a total of 114 million 5G subscribers, compared to 70 million 5G customers at the end of June. Meanwhile, rival operator China Telecom added 7.66 million subscribers in September to take its total 5G subscribers base to 64.8 million."[21]

---

[18] Joakim Abeleen and Thomas Larsen, "Beyond COVID-19: The Rise of 5G in China," The Swedish Trade and Investment Council, 2020.

[19] "**5G 新基建，智领未来' 我国 5G** 用户已超过 **1.1 亿**," Ctocio, September 16, 2020, http://club.ctocio.com.cn/club/2020/0916/38100.html.

[20] "Chinese Brands Capture 61% of Global 5G Smartphone Shipments in Q1," *CGTN*, April 30, 2020.

[21] Juan Tomás, "5G Users to Account for 20% of China's Mobile Base by June 2021: Huawei," *RCR Wireless News*, November 13, 2020.

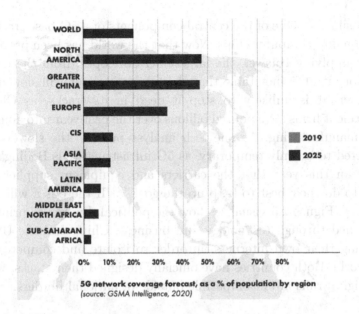

5G network coverage forecast, as a % of population by region
(source: GSMA Intelligence, 2020)

Figure 2.4.   Global 5G development.
Source: Kalvin Bahia and Anne Delaporte, "The State of Mobile Internet Connectivity," GSMA, September 2020, https://www.gsma.com/r/wp-content/uploads/2020/09/GSMA-State-of-Mobile-Internet-Connectivity-Report-2020.pdf.

While the telcos might operate the 5G, almost all of the construction is contracted out. In 2020, China Mobile gave out "37.1 billion yuan ($5.2 billion) in 5G contracts, with virtually all the work going to Huawei and smaller rival ZTE."[22] Huawei got a 57.3% chunk of the total tender, ZTE 28.7%, Ericsson 11.5%, and CICT 2.6%. Investment in 5G is expected to double in 2021.

However, there has been substantial slowdown as a result of the US–China trade war. As Washington's pressure and sanctions on Huawei escalates, so does China's de-Americanization. Nikkei reported in July 2020 that "both Huawei and ZTE told some suppliers to slow down shipments of certain 5G base station-related products in June, so the Chinese companies can redesign products and change some equipment to remove as much US content

---

[22] *Ibid.*

as possible."[23] One of the central components of a 5G base station is high-quality computer chips. Now that the world has been prevented from supplying Huawei, the largest 5G developer, from the central component, it is inevitable that the telecom rollout will slow down. However, it is unlikely to stop it dead in its tracks, as Chinese investment firms have poured billions over the past year into domestic chip manufacturing. As one tech analyst put it, "the slowdown is expected to be only temporary, as 5G infrastructure is Beijing's key ambition this year that the carriers and equipment suppliers will have to do their best to keep up the goal."[24] If there is a will there is a way. Figure 2.5 visualizes how the political divergence primarily happened through technology and business. China and the US are building their own internets, in order to isolate and compete from the world. Both countries have officially designed their stacks, where the digital rails are incompatible outside of national borders.[25]

2.4. Revolutionary Uses of 5G

Inside China, more 5G towers were built during the COVID-19 global pandemic than in the past three years combined. This stands in stark contrast to the experience of the rest of the world that has been forced to shut down. Even the US, the richest country in the world that invented pandemic prevention measures, fumbled its response to COVID-19. The US failure in controlling the pandemic has led to more than 555,000 deaths in the country. The Chinese government never tried to fix the symptoms by sending checks directly to its people. Instead it focused all of its energy on finding a cure for the source of the ailment. When the economic stimulus was introduced, it was largely in the form of policy loans to speed up the development of a few key industries collectively referred to as "New Infrastructure": 5G, Blockchain, and the Digital Coin (the latter two are addressed in

---

[23] Staff Writer, "Huawei and ZTE Slow down China 5G Rollout as US Curbs Start to Bite," *Nikkei Asia*, August 19, 2020.

[24] *Ibid.*

[25] Benjamin Bratton, *The Stack: On Software and Sovereignty* (Cambridge, MA: The MIT Press, 2016).

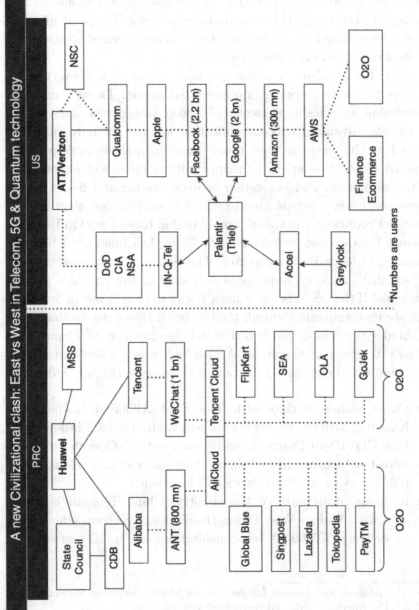

Figure 2.5. Comparing China and the US' military/civil fusion.

Chapter 3).[26] While an average of 1,500 Americans were dying a day, China was returning to normalcy. In the process, it was adding an average of 15,000 new 5G base stations every week. The pandemic, by virtue of requiring fast and reliant communication, tested commercial applications of 5G on a mass scale.

Once the pandemic started sweeping across China, every segment of the society sprang into concerted action. Those firms and government agencies implementing 5G were tasked with applying it in real life. Advanced telecommunication was not the only industry pushed to its extremes, as every experimental technology was directed toward the crisis. Fundamentally, a crisis will either lead to transformation and innovation or degeneration and destruction. There was never a debate about cashing in on the equivalent of the Defence Production Act (usually mobilized in time of war) in Beijing, because for the past 10 years, all of China has functioned like an extended Defence Production Act. The reality is that some degree of "socialist" national response is necessary in the face of a global pandemic. If the US feels like it must resort to laws of war in order to activate its communitarianism, then so be it. Hypocrisy be damned!

Across the board, much of the 5G development in China was initially targeted at hospitals. We list below just a few initiatives that were rolled out via 5G to combat the disease (Figure 2.6):

(1) China mobile worked with The First Affiliated Hospital of Kunming Medical University to launch an "Online Platform for Free COVID-19 Diagnosis and Treatment."[27] Operated on 5G infrastructure, it delivered timely diagnosis, contract tracing, and public service announcements within seconds.

(2) In more rural parts of the country, China Telecom cooperated with Wuhan West China Hospital and Sichuan University to deliver COVID-19 tele-consultations on a 5G network.[28]

---

[26] Joakim Abeleen and Thomas Larsen, "Beyond COVID-19: The Rise of 5G in China," The Swedish Trade and Investment Council, 2020.

[27] *Ibid.*

[28] *Ibid.*

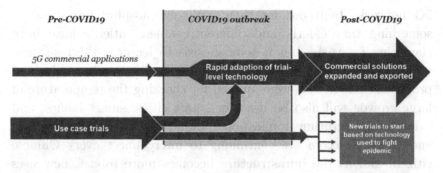

Figure 2.6. How the Chinese 5G ecosystem adapted to COVID-19 as an opportunity.

Source: Joakim Abeleen and Thomas Larsen, "Beyond COVID-19: The Rise of 5G in China," The Swedish Trade and Investment Council, 2020.

The hospital was able to move terabytes of data between 27 hospitals at high speeds and without interruption.

(3) China Unicom assisted in streaming the construction of "Xiaotangshan Hospital" through 5G.[29] Even Ericsson, the Swedish telecom firm, built 5G base stations in Wuhan at the peak of the crisis to ease the network load.[30] More than 100 hospitals used 5G systems for medical consultations.[31]

(4) Doctors from the People's Hospital of Zhejiang even used 5G to remotely control a robot to perform an ultrasound test on a COVID-19 patient at a hospital in Wuhan 700 km away. It is sometimes difficult to distinguish what is clever publicity and what is fundamental transformation of crisis management, but regardless, firms across China utilized 5G at a critical time both to save lives and demonstrate its applicability.

The transformation and development was delivered with endurance in mind. Telemedicine is slowly becoming a new normal across China, pioneered by the hospitals who have had robust

---

[29] *Ibid.*

[30] *Ibid.*

[31] Zoey Zhang, "COVID-19 Catalyzes Commercial Use of 5G in China," *China Briefing News*, May 26, 2020.

5G networks built out for them. "Virtual hospital visitation" is something that elderly and differently abled patients have been clamoring for years, but it took a crisis to leapfrog the resistance within hospital administration. Image recognition technologies and processing power that were applied for checking the temperature of large crowds will also be used for smart cities, smart homes, and smart manufacturing applications. China Mobile, China Unicorn, and China Telecom are continuing to interconnect every Chinese citizen, and as the infrastructure becomes more robust, new uses and applications will spring out of it.

One brief example of a company connecting office property is Kuban (Figure 2.7). Born out of the UrbanLab initiative, they are utilizing the existing infrastructure to connect Internet of Things (IoT) devices to manage retail space. Such integration requires IoT devices that are able to communicate seamlessly on an integrated telecommunication network that can handle hundreds of devices. It is one of the hundreds of companies rethinking how we interact with the space around us.

2.5.   Future Potential of 5G in Property and Smart Cities

While we have already seen diverse applications of 5G in a plethora of fields, large-scale and consumer-friendly applications will not be available for a few years. Before robust products can exist on a foundation of new communication infrastructure, the infrastructure must be widely available, reliable, and cheap. Only a few cities in China have reached full coverage or are nearing it, and there is a long road for it to become the status quo. In order to understand the true potential of 5G, this section will expand on the possibilities from its contemporary applications and start to imagine fields that are ripe for disruption and innovation within property.

As an infrastructure designed for cities and targeted at urban life, 5G's most fundamental transformation will be in the way we live in communities. A smart city fundamentally consists of four layers:

(1) The Terminal Layer
(2) Communication Layer

KUBAN

What do they do	Who is their boss	New Technology	How do they make money
Smart Workplace: • Kuban develops IoT software and hardware-based smart office solutions, including workstation, meeting, visitor and asset management systems. • Solution helps clients transform from fixed to flexible workplace.	• Jones Lang LaSalle (JLL) • One of twelve startup finalists chosen from UrbanLab Proptech Accelerator – joint programme by JLL, Swire Properties and Ping An Urban Tech	• Applied the concept of Urban Ecosystem by JLL to connect occupier, operator and employee via a platform of AI+IoT+SaaS • **Employee Access/Visitor management:** Combines AI and SaaS to optimise safety and well-being of occupancy levels • **Smart office space management:** Utilise highly precise IoT sensors to obtain real-time occupancy status of work spaces while using AI algorithm to maximise the efficiency of office equipment and facilities • **Integrated solution:** Connects with existing office systems via apps including WeChat, Dingtalk and Microsoft Office, reducing the cost of switching	• Partnering with prominent Smart Building and Workplace Solution businesses in China • E.g. Lenovo Commercial IoT Group to utilise Kuban's smart workplace software and hardware via Lenovo's edge devices and IoT products

Figure 2.7. Kuban — Smart Workplace.

(3) Service Layer and

(4) Application Layer.

From the infrastructure underground, to the apps that exist at the fingertips of every citizen, this is the foundation of every modern city.

The Terminal Layer is the gas, water, electricity, and roads that have made up urban infrastructure since cities started to exist. These are the foundations that make amalgamated living possible.

The Communication Layer is the fixed line broadband, the cellular networks, and auxiliary IoT technology that serve as pipelines for information. While in a modern city, the communication layer has become the terminal layer, for the sake of understanding the role of 5G, they will be separated for now.

The Service Layer is where data from the terminal and communication layer gets stored, analyzed, and processed. Most modern cities have not actually built out this layer. While they have all of the terminal and communication infrastructure, there is either no data being collected from it at all, or there is no centralized mechanism to analyze all of it in a cohesive form.

The Application Layer is the final step of a smart city. This is where the data from the Service Layer is used to create solutions. Ideally, self-functioning adjustment mechanisms are able to self-regulate, self-correct, and achieve largely decentralized objectives. Most of the world is very far from the Application Layer. What will take modern cities from the Communication Layer to the Application Layer is 5G (Figure 2.8).

Fundamentally, the modern Communication Layer is not sophisticated enough to function beyond basic exchange of information.

There are two fundamental characteristics of 5G that make smart cities possible. Technical characteristics will bring industrial and consumer innovations forward, i.e. low-latency, high-speed, high-bandwidth, massive digitized datasets and tokenized assets. However, there is much more required to bring innovation to property.

2.5.1. *Network slicing*

First, the 5G networks are equipped with network slicing. This is exclusively a benefit of the standalone core. This means that it

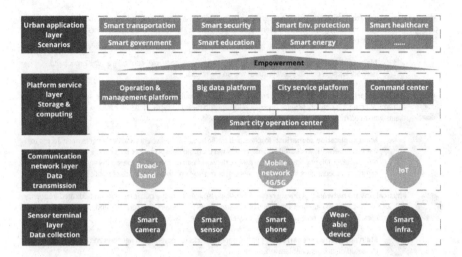

Figure 2.8. Smart City System Map.
Source: "5G Smart Cities Whitepaper: Deloitte China," Deloitte China, June 2020, https://www2.deloitte.com/cn/en/pages/technology-media-and-telecomm unications/articles/tmt-empowering-smart-cities-with-5g.html.

can categorize resources, edit functions, and create "on demand" virtual networks on the same infrastructure for radically different applications. The implication here is that traffic regulation, hospital administration, and crime prevention can be carried out without interruption on the same core network.[32] This makes battling over scarce spectrum resources unnecessary (Figure 2.9).

2.5.2. *Edge computing*

Second, a necessary function of 5G is edge computing. This allows standalone cores to process massive floods of data locally, instead of sending them to a centralized server. Edge computing will give birth to highly efficient cloud service systems, facilitating rapid development, efficient deployment, and quick response times. Being able to process high-definition video, AR/VR, and self-driving vehicles at the edge means access-delays are almost completely erased. This will

---

[32] "5G Smart Cities Whitepaper: Deloitte China," Deloitte China, June 2020, https://www2.deloitte.com/cn/en/pages/technology-media-and-telecomm unications/articles/tmt-empowering-smart-cities-with-5g.html.

Virtual private network: Wireless access to shared public network via end-to-end network slicing is a low-cost, quick-turnaround solution for industry clients who have temporary needs or have requirements that can usually be served by the public network.

 Main application scenarios: Network slicing can be used to quickly configure a large broadband network for high-definition event streaming on the media.

 Integrated private network: Wireless access to multiplex 5G public network on authorized spectrum, with customization on the network side for the right reliability and business separation, can fulfill the SLAs for industry clients who need more than what the public network can offer.

 Main application scenarios: Hospitals and traffic hubs, where patients and passengers need access to the public network, while staff and merchants need private networks. User data can be separated at the terminal level. Or, physical and virtual private networks can be merged to meet differentiated needs, by setting up independent internal core network or multiplexing the air interface of public network.

 Physical private network: A private network physically isolated from the public network on dedicated frequency with wireless equipment can meet the needs of industry clients that expect high reliability and privacy. This solution supports flexible customization, with high reliability and complete isolation.

 Main application scenarios: Physical private networks for government agencies and industrial parks via the setup of independent network facilities.

Figure 2.9.   5G + network slicing enables the private use of public network by different industries within the smart city.

Source: "5G Smart Cities Whitepaper: Deloitte China," Deloitte China, June 2020, https://www2.deloitte.com/cn/en/pages/technology-media-and-telecomm unications/articles/tmt-empowering-smart-cities-with-5g.html.

transform the way individuals move throughout the city. While the technology exists today to make the monitoring of smart vehicle and pedestrian traffic possible, it is neither fast enough nor widespread enough to be of practical use. When 5G is integrated with IoT and Cloud Data analytics, there might never be traffic again. Imagine this, a wide range of cameras, radiometers, signal lights, road signs, weather detectors, and laser monitors exist along every city road. At all times of the day, they are capturing the conditions of the road, car accidents, construction, movement of people, and everything in between. All of the information would be processed via the cloud core, learning from itself, and constantly improving navigation.

How will this be done? Some red lights are removed, some green lights are extended, some roads are temporarily shut down, some neighborhoods are rerouted, and violators instantly caught. This is far from futuristic though — this reality exists now, and all it needs is clever integration and public/private collaboration.

The real future unfolds once these same sensors can imagine what is not imaginable now. With proper understanding of neighborhood conditions, movement of people through the city, and the location of vital services (schools, hospitals, and grocery stores), the entire fabric of the city can be reimagined. In a world where we truly understand urban space, roads only facilitate obsolete, wasteful, and antisocial behavior: driving. If IoT, AI, and 5G is fully integrated with the citizen in mind, it leads to better public transportation, better locations of vital services, and can lead to critical solutions for urban ailments: poverty, substance abuse, and crime. All three are diseases of despair, often produced by a set of inflexible, outdated, and unequal urban conditions.

2.5.3. *5G and public safety*

We do not propose that technology will solve all urban problems. It is merely a tool. In the right hands, it has the potential to improve the way people occupy space. In the wrong hands, it could create considerable ethical problems. We believe that the infrastructure being built across China right now, and soon spread to the rest of the world, at least has the ability to shine a light and understand aspects of the city that have previously remained in the dark. There are plenty of auxiliary urban services that would greatly benefit from the speed, latency, and capacity of new-generation telecommunication. Hikvision is one of the many companies perfecting urban management through enhanced video monitoring services (Figure 2.10). While FTSE Russel recently removed HikVision from its index in light of US sanctions, demand for its services in light of COVID-19 is at an all-time high.[33] It currently creates one of the largest range of IoT products for surveillance, analysis, and response, facilitated by the foundation of 5G. The more widespread the infrastructure becomes, the more power Hikvision's products gain, from improved sensing and instantaneous analysis to seamless response. Property will be transformed only once it finds eyes and a capacity to act based

---

[33]Staff Writer, "US-Blacklisted Hikvision Zooms in on COVID Tracking Demand," *Nikkei Asia*, December 2, 2020.

What do they do	Ownership	New Technology
IoT and SaaS: • Provide IoT products (cameras, storage, accessories, etc.) • Offer software for monitoring purposes, crown control, traffic management, and urban administration	• Zhejiang HIK Information Technology Co., Ltd. has a 51% stake • Gong Hongjia has a 13% stake • Significant government links	• Artificial intelligence to process and auto identify visual input. • Cloud computing for large data analysis • Edge computing for on site processing • Facial Recognition

Figure 2.10.   Hikvision: Video surveillance.

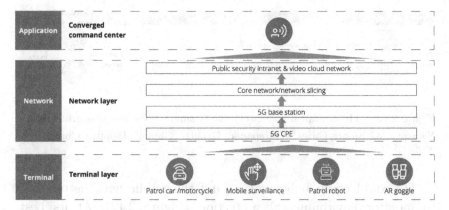

Figure 2.11.   5G network slicing empowers a secure and integrated wireless police system.

Source: "5G Smart Cities Whitepaper: Deloitte China," Deloitte China, June 2020.

on what it sees. Hikvision has recently been put on an entities list, which restricts its activities in the US for national security purposes.

5G can help us rethink public safety. In terms of policing, "wearable equipment that integrates innovative AR and AI technologies, such as mobile police terminals, body cameras, onboard mobile devices and wearable devices, connected with a back-end information management platform[34]" has the ability to keep police forces more accountable, reduce misinformation, better understand large-scale bias, and improve a community's security (Figure 2.11). Individuals and vehicles can be instantly cross-referenced with public databases, offering a transparent and publicly accountable end of profiling. Simultaneously, it can add technological authority to the bias that already exists. Technology that is fed very specific data sets for learning is just as capable of prejudice as a human. Most importantly, it almost never has the capacity for context that a complicated community security situation requires, unless it is consciously built with that in mind.

---

[34] "5G Smart Cities Whitepaper: Deloitte China," Deloitte China, June 2020, https://www2.deloitte.com/cn/en/pages/technology-media-and-telecommunications/articles/tmt-empowering-smart-cities-with-5g.html.

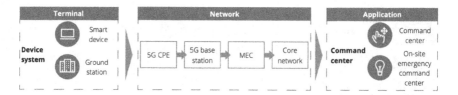

Figure 2.12.   The technical framework of 5G smart environmental protection.
Source: "5G Smart Cities Whitepaper: Deloitte China," Deloitte China, June 2020.

5G could equip policymakers and the public with better tools to monitor environmental protection (Figure 2.12). At its best, adequate industrial monitoring solves one of the most persistent economic dilemmas of free-riding. Pollution sensors (water, air, and earth) provide governments with a holistic tool to analyze regulation compliance as well as source and quality of pollution instantly. This guarantees that the poisoning of water and airways is not allowed to go on for decades before, as is usually the case, being first identified in hospital records of unsuspecting victims. Additionally, quick and proper monitoring of sensitive industry guarantees that industrial accidents are either not allowed to happen in the first place, or identified and responded to instantly. Simultaneously, we should not forget the type of waste that is produced via a massive 5G rollout. Couple that with billions of IoT devices, made from nonrecyclable material, and we could be looking at living on Trash Island.

Thoughtful application of 5G could create an urban framework for public health. Beyond remote consultations and telemedicine that we have talked about before, there are a plethora of preventative healthcare tools that better social data can facilitate. First, the research that would often take sociologists decades to carry out, involving extensive household surveys and long-term monitoring, could be done instantly. Take, for example, an excessive number of patients from the same neighborhood exhibiting similar symptoms. Today, since many of them would go to different hospitals and communicate with a diverse range of doctors that never talk to each other, it might take decades to understand that lead has been leaking into the water source of a community. In a world where

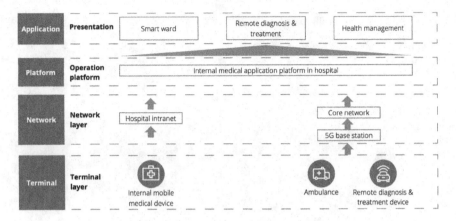

Figure 2.13.   The technical framework of 5G smart healthcare.
Source: "5G Smart Cities Whitepaper: Deloitte China," Deloitte China, June 2020.

5G data of all local hospitals is pooled, anonymized, and analyzed for patterns, regional problems can be discovered and addressed significantly sooner. The goal of 5G as a whole is to make the infrastructure communicate with itself, identify patterns that even experienced bureaucrats could not imagine, and find solutions that world-class urban planners might not think possible. Proper IoT and 5G integration would not just help curtail a disease outbreak, it would stop it before it ever had the chance to enter a hospital (Figure 2.13).

2.6.   Conclusion

The next generation of telecommunication will connect a whole new swathe of the intangible world, facilitate a massive influx of new data, and give our cities new sensing powers. 3G and 4G brought about the information revolution and the financial revolution by providing the means for institutions and individuals to communicate seamlessly. 5G, by virtue of its speed, small size, and increased processing capacity, will bring lightning speed telecommunication to every neighborhood. It is giving birth to the new Proptech industry, which is able to collect this data, analyze it, sell it, and solve endemic urban problems.

Chapter 3

Blockchain as the New Urban Trust Framework

In 2017, a tiny unknown company — Red Date — was creating smart city technology for municipal services. Their first large-scale application was called "Citizen Card." The service digitized civic identity to make paying bills, getting on the metro, and authentication available in one physical card. In 2020, Red Date is bringing their smart city tech to one of the largest infrastructure projects in China's history: the Blockchain Service Network (BSN). The goal of the new infrastructure is to integrate the digitization of logistics, banking, insurance, and property into a tradeable tokenized ecosystem. Where does BSN fit into China's larger technological ambitions, why now, and what does it have to do with property? This chapter addresses exactly the question at the center of China's 21st-century technology strategy. The Five-Year Plan (FYP) published in October 2020 lays the foundation of the BSN, which is now a vital part of Beijing's domestic tech drive and its global ambitions. The BSN, along with 5G, is the underlying digital infrastructure that supports the massive rollout of proptech. First, we briefly address the history of blockchain, its technical capabilities, and how it is the fundamental force in BSN and in digitizing property. Second, we outline how BSN came into existence, its technical foundations, and its expected impact on China and the world. Third, we analyze the Digital Currency/Electronic

Payments (DCEP), why China's nationwide blockchain network will bring ultimate financial integration, and how it will transform China's property sector.

3.1. The Foundation of Blockchain

3.1.1. *A brief history of trust*

Much of the technology that we now take as a vital part of the modern world was dismissed, disregarded, and bet against when they first appeared. Even the World Wide Web had their luddites: "why do I need email? I can just walk across the building to send this note." The Internet has only been around for two decades, and already much of the global stock market is made up of companies based on it. It no longer seems impossible to take a business from a US$0 to a US$1 billion dollar valuation in a matter of a few years, developing a purely digital product. For better or for worse, much of the global value has been summarily abstracted from the physical world. If one sees markets as a rational pool of individual interests, concerns, and expectations, then starting in the 1990s, it all promptly left the earthly surface and escaped to the cloud.

When universities and military research institutions were developing the Internet across the US, it was primarily to distribute the load of complex mathematical calculations. The real potential of constructing a secondary digital reality would not come until decades later. The Internet was revolutionary because it brought all human transactions to your fingertips. However, both because of libertarian dreams of its creators and the large infrastructure requirement to run a cross-country connection, the question of trust never entered the equation of packet switching (the algorithm that allowed different internet networks to function together, on one large platform). This means that interactions that might otherwise have to cross multiple time zones and take weeks, can now be performed at lightning speed — but it also means that they cross the globe mostly unsecured.

All the while, the function of individual interaction has remained the same: you want to conduct business, but you still lack the trust for the transaction to be guaranteed. Outside of the Internet, this trust function has been performed by banks, insurance companies, governments, the mob, your older relatives, or any other more powerful entity that can exert pressure so you uphold your side of the bargain (be it through artful persuasion, legal code, or a baseball bat). Much of the financial and bureaucratic safeguards created throughout human history have been erected to keep scammers at bay. (Question: What happens when scammers run the safeguards? Answer: Revolutions). Because lack of trust was the fundamental part of the Internet's design, it has made scamming faster, easier, and more profitable. The older institutions that were the beacons of trust are still trying to be the turnstile of Internet transactions, and they are failing miserably. Not only because they misunderstand the fundamentals of Internet trust, but also because they try to continue creating trust with hole-punchers and staplers. The fastest growing companies in the world have tried to upend these industries by abstracting trust faster, better, and making it stronger.[1] In less than a decade, these trust-infusing institutions have become household names: Visa, PayPal, Square, Stripe, Credit Karma, etc.

However, all of these companies simply try to abstract the power of hole-punchers and staplers to computer code. PayPal must still stand between you and your customer to guarantee the transaction will go smoothly and everyone upholds their side of the bargain. Yes, they are backed up by hundreds of engineers, but their fundamental job has remained hole-punching and stapling, even if it is now millions of transactions per second. Fundamentally, there is little difference between trust of the spoken word in the real world and trust given to you by a third party on the Internet. Authority is abstracted, but

---

[1]Paul Schulte, *The Next Revolution in Our Credit-Driven Economy: The Advent of Financial Technology* (Singapore: Wiley, 2015).

it nonetheless remains institutional. The hacks of Equifax should remain an admonition. No single institution of trust is safe from outside threats. The Code of Hammurabi and Moses' Stone Tablets both stand testament to the social need of permanent laws inscribed into an immutable source. Two thousand years later, we have finally gotten to a point where a permanent legal record can exist and it does not have to be guaranteed by an institution.

3.1.2. *A brief history of blockchain*

Blockchain is the immutable stone into which the laws of human transactions can be written into. It is backed by practically indestructible encryption (which is in turn backed by the fundamental laws of mathematics) and hundreds of computers trading their processing power for a reward. Both the way we understand blockchain and the way it technically functions has changed drastically. However, one fundamental foundation persists: the desire to create a decentralized authority out of the hivemind of computing authentication. Consider it the final iteration of Mandeville's *Fable of the Bees*: when each computer node pursues its individual interest, everyone benefits.

Before blockchain came Bitcoin. The original open-source protocol for this cryptocurrency was invented in 2008 by a group of researchers termed Satoshi Nakamoto. The first ever bitcoin mined to begin the distributed chain was tagged with the inscription "The Times 03/Jan/2009 Chancellor on brink of second bailout for banks." Cryptocurrency came into existence as a response to the inherent instability of fractional reserve banking. However, despite the lofty economic criticism, its early popularity with cyberpunks immediately landed the currency in online black markets. Between 2013 and 2015, other cryptographic assets began to emerge (ZCash, Monero, Ethereum, Ripple, Litecoin, Dogecoin, and everything in between). Some assets offered privacy and convenience, some did not, some grew and crashed within weeks, some continue to remain in circulation today. In the wild-west days of cryptocurrency, new digital assets were being created out of thin air.

The industry undulates from assets to infrastructure. The large leap for cryptocurrency was the realization that not all new digital assets are valuable, and the attention shifted to the underlying infrastructure. The infrastructure bitcoin was built on — blockchain — started to be used to manipulate old assets and create applications on top of it. "Companies like R3, Chain, Symbiont and Digital Asset 9 focused their efforts on re-platforming legacy financial products like 10 equities, bonds, derivatives and swaps."[2] The emergence of "smart contracts" allowed programmers to build computer programs into the existing blockchain system. Things like loans, bonds, and betting could now be represented on the blockchain, and hundreds of applications now found their technical foundation.[3] In 2020, innovations stem from using the infrastructure to create digital applications that can document and secure, not from creating new assets. Currently, our prognosis is that in the next 10 years, blockchain will return to creating assets. This time these assets will be born out of digitized property, the data upon which property sits, and the people who use it.

Before the return can be complete, two problems within blockchain must be addressed. First, every user in the chain must process every single transaction. This distribution makes for an extremely slow process that guarantees security, but sacrifices valuable computing power. The solution lies in Blockchain Scaling: "a scaled blockchain accelerates the process, without sacrificing security, by figuring out how many computers are necessary to validate each transaction and dividing up the work efficiently."[4] Second, different

---

[2] Jill Carlson, "How the Crypto Industry Seesaws Between Assets and Infrastructure," *Yahoo! Finance*, September 30, 2020.

[3] Vinay Gupta, "A Brief History of Blockchain," *Harvard Business Review*, August 21, 2019.

[4] *Ibid.*

blockchains are unable to talk to and between each other, let alone run different services for the same application instantaneously. Such disintegration was also the problem of the early Internet in the 1970s. While each university in the US ran their own Internet protocol, it was impossible to communicate between different networks until packet switching arose to centralize communication. We are now witnessing the creation of blockchain packet switching. China is building out the BSN across the country to solve both of these problems.

3.1.3.   *Blockchain's impact on property*

5G, Internet of Things (IoT), and AI are creating an explosion of data. Blockchain has come along just in time. Now, it needs new digital rails in order to prevent cities from collapsing into economic and social chaos. Why is this happening now? Currently, "more than 55% of the world population is living in urban areas...this rate is predicted to reach 70%, by 2050."[5] As our cities become smarter — and as commercial and residential property become more digitized — protection of data becomes vital for these systems to remain stable. This is because many of our cities will become digital villages, made up primarily of IoT devices, free flowing data, and instantaneous response neural networks. This creates potentially catastrophic insecurities. Blockchain is one of the best ways to secure this massive and continuous flow of information.

Figure 3.1 depicts the foundation of the digitization push. Smart Cities will create terabytes of data points regarding the movement of people, the consumption of electricity, the production of carbon, of traffic accidents, and so much more. The only way to make sure municipal services, research institutions, and private businesses can use this data securely is to guarantee it with a distributed ledger. The problem is that just one blockchain is not enough. BSN is China's infrastructure for digital cities of the 21st century.

---

[5]Khashayar Kotobi and Mina Sartipi, "Efficient and Secure Communications in Smart Cities Using Edge, Caching, and Blockchain," *2018 IEEE International Smart Cities Conference (ISC2)*, 2018.

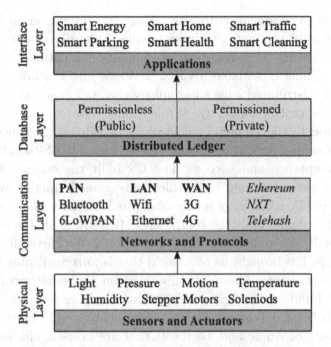

Figure 3.1.   How to secure smart cities using blockchain.

Source: Kamanashis Biswas and Vallipuram Muthukkumarasamy, "Securing Smart Cities Using Blockchain Technology," *14th IEEE International Conference on Smart City*, December 2016.

3.2.   BSN

The most transformative development in the integration of all blockchains is currently being undertaken in Beijing. The BSN was first announced by Xi Jinping in October 2019.[6] It was launched as a central tenet of China's National Blockchain Strategy. This both confused and surprised international experts, seeing as just a year earlier China banned any use of digital currency or blockchain association within the country. China's problem with global blockchains was not the services themselves, it was the lack of control. Decentralization is the founding principle of blockchain and it is the antithesis of

---

[6] Arjun Kharpal, "With Xi's Backing, China Looks to Become a World Leader in Blockchain as US Policy Is Absent," *CNBC*, December 16, 2019.

a central government authority. What Xi Jinping argued for in October 2019 was not a Chinese bitcoin; he outlined a strategy of commandeering its foundational technology for national needs. In essence, China articulated a vision of a new national infrastructure based on distributed ledger technology that will function under the aegis of a central authority. While China's stated goal stands in opposition to the foundational ideology of Bitcoin ("Chancellor on brink of second bailout for banks"), it is central to blockchain's long term acceptance and success. The US built the original Internet infrastructure (Internet 1.0), which only gained traction with the general public when large monopolies provided the tools to utilize it efficiently: Apple built the computers, Microsoft built the software, AOL built the online highways (Internet 2.0). Three decades of innovation has brought us to a world that is unrecognizable without this infrastructure. China is embarking on the same monumental task by building the BSN. This section analyzes how the BSN is currently being developed. The rest of the chapter will look at China's equivalents of Apple and Microsoft that are infusing efficiency and mass acceptance into Internet 3.0.

3.2.1. *The vision*

BSN was articulated as a way to bridge a diverse set of blockchain services. The architects envisioned the infrastructure to "represent an interoperability standard that allows different heterogeneous IT and datacenter ecosystems to interoperate," serving as a foundation for applications to function between different blockchain ecosystems: "cross-cloud, cross-portal, and cross-chain global public infrastructure."[7] Consider it the block for blockchains. The nodes allocating the computing power, storage, and bandwidth are distributed throughout China, interconnecting every major and minor city into a nationwide ecosystem. At its core, BSN is a commercial service built atop urban infrastructure.

---

[7]Ting Peng, "China's Blockchain Service Network: Integrates Three More Public Chains," *Cointelegraph*, September 15, 2020.

The project is initiated by four partners: China State Information Center, China Mobile, China UnionPay, and Red Date Technology.[8] Red Date is at the center of the project, responsible for deployment, R&D, and operations. The State Information Center is providing the authority and legal framework. China Mobile is offering the physical infrastructure. China UnionPay is responsible for the users and financial due diligence within the blockchains. The partnership of the project, the government support, and the existing rollout is important for its radical innovation. China is the first country in the world to nationalize blockchain services and to establish a platform for all blockchains, anywhere in the world, to function together seamlessly.

This will be integral for mass global adoption of blockchain technology. BSN has drastically lowered the cost of deploying a personal chain or building apps integrated within it. The minimal cost of BSN is US$300 per year.[9] The impact will be most disruptive in developing nations, where trust in financial services, taxation, and bureaucracy is the lowest. It should be noted that the countries that are considering Central Bank Coins are either some of the most financially integrated or the most desperate (Table 3.1).

BSN intends to integrate the majority of public chains in the world. At a rate of five chains a month, with hundreds of chains actively applying, the majority of the global blockchains will be integrated within the next two years. Red Date is thus operating Infrastructure-as-a-Service, acting like a toll operator collecting fees for traffic passing through. The problem of this metaphor is it does not fully credit Red Date's contribution. Because BSN is more than the tollbooth or a single road, it is the entirety of the highway system on which different chains (public transportation) is allowed to function on (Figure 3.2). As was the case with Federal Highways in the US, the fundamental goal is to connect all urban centers.

---

[8]Zheping Huang, "China-Backed Crypto Guru Wants to Unify World's Blockchains," *Bloomberg*, July 27, 2020.
[9]Wolfie Zhao and David Pan, "Inside China's Plan to Power Global Blockchain Adoption," CoinDesk, December 17, 2020.

Table 3.1.   Jurisdictions where retain CBDC is being explored (as of October 14, 2020).*

Bahamas (pilot underway; full launch in October)	Sweden (proof of concept started)
China (pilot launched)	Ukraine (pilot completed)
Eastern Caribbean (2020Q4 pilot launch)	Uruguay (pilot completed)
South Africa	
Where central banks have explored or are exploring issuing retail CBDC	
Australia	Japan
Brazil	Korea (proof of concept started)
Canada	Malaysia
Chile	Mauritius
Curaçao en Sint Maarten	Morocco
Denmark	New Zealand
Ecuador (completed pilot & project discontinued)	Norway
Euro Area	Russia
Finland	Switzerland
Ghana	Thailand
Hong Kong SAR	Trinidad and Tobago
Iceland	Tunisia
India	Turkey
Indonesia	United Kingdom
Israel	United States
Jamaica	
Where central banks have explored or are exploring issuing retail CBDC (according to reputable news sources)	
Bahrain	Lebanon
Egypt	Pakistan
Haiti	Palestine
Iran	Philippines
Kazakhstan	Rwanda

*Where central banks are in advanced stages of retail CBDC exploration.
Source: "Jurisdictions Where Retail CBDC Is Being Explored," *Kiffmeister Chronicles*, January 1, 2021.

BSN is built on city nodes that both create the backbone of the infrastructure and its final customer. Since BSN functions like a permissioned chain, the authenticating authority will be based on urban centers. As per Red Date's own expectations "Each city can build one or more public city nodes that are linked via the internet to form a nationwide (and in the future, worldwide) physical city node blockchain service network. Blockchain application publishers need only to deploy the application to multiple city nodes in the BSN

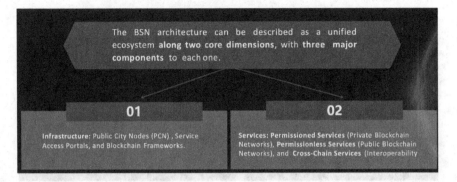

Figure 3.2. Infrastructure as a service.
Source: "An Introduction to the BSN," BSNBase.io (BSN Foundation, 2020).

(www.bsnbase.io), then participants may enter at practically no cost through the city node gateway."[10] This is the essence of proptech in China.

As a resource-sharing mechanism, it drastically lowers the cost of development of blockchain infrastructure. In the past, it cost approximately RMB 100,000–500,000 to build a consortium blockchain network area. With BSN, that cost is reduced to RMB 2,000–3,000 a year.[11] Instead of each household having to dig a well, the entire neighborhood can share a well. This is the basis of economies of scale (Figure 3.3).

3.2.2. The tech

There are four factors that make up the core foundation of BSN. The explanation and Figure 3.4 summarize the base.

(1) Public City Nodes described above, which are responsible for "access control, transaction processing, data storage, and

---

[10] "China's Blockchain Service Network on the Rise Despite Split," Nasdaq, July 27, 2020.
[11] "An Introduction to the BSN," BSNBase.io (BSN Foundation, 2020).

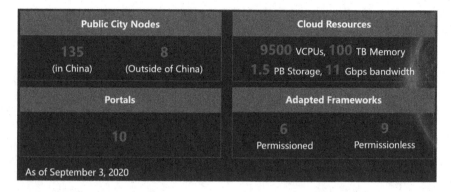

Figure 3.3.   BSN as urban infrastructure.
Source: "An Introduction to the BSN," BSNBase.io (BSN Foundation, 2020).

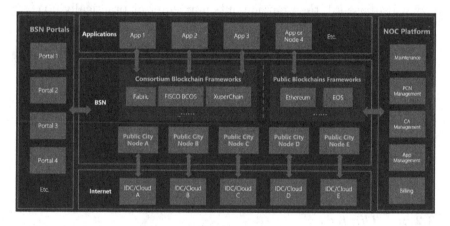

Figure 3.4.   The infrastructure of BSN.
Source: "An Introduction to the BSN," BSNBase.io (BSN Foundation, 2020).

computing abilities for blockchain applications."[12] Anyone with adequate computing resources can build a city node, download the appropriate software, and start operating a City Node.

---

[12] "Blockchain-Based Service Network Technical White Paper," BSNBase (BSN Development Association, April 25, 2020), https://bsnbase.io/static/tmpFile/B SNTechnicalWhitePaper.pdf.

(2) Consensus Order Cluster, run and operated by UnionPay, each node determines the transaction order and permanently writes it into the ledger. UnionPay will also be responsible for regulatory compliance for financial transactions.

(3) Permission Management Chain — this is a system level chain that manages the permission mechanism.[13] It is completely in the hands of the developer and utilizes application-role-based-control (ARBAC). The developer has two options of management: the consortium mode and the centralized authority mode. Under consortium mode, all participants are equal and jointly manage the application, and mechanism changes are subject to a vote of all members. Under the centralized management mode, the application publisher determines all internal application management. The developer has an ability to choose which form of management their application will abide by during the publishing phase.

(4) Smart Gateway. This is the business system of each participating organization on the applications, a personal server or website, which is linked to the blockchain services.

As an application creator, you have a choice over how much computing power you will require and how to manage your personal application. The publisher will choose the amount of city nodes necessary depending on the "the transactions per second, storage, and bandwidth" requirements.[14] The application creator has the freedom to do three things.

(1) Allocate rule;
(2) choose between private or consortium chains; and
(3) decide on the amount of user access that is allocated.

---

[13] *Ibid.*

[14] "Blockchain-Based Service Network Technical White Paper," BSNBase (BSN Development Association, April 25, 2020), https://bsnbase.io/static/tmpFile/B SNTechnicalWhitePaper.pdf.

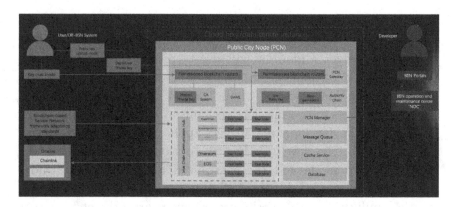

Figure 3.5. User and developer relationship on BSN.

Source: "Blockchain-Based Service Network Technical White Paper," BSNBase (BSN Development Association, April 25, 2020), https://bsnbase.io/static/tmpFile/BSNTechnicalWhitePaper.pdf.

In the process, participants and publishers can cooperate between applications and between chains without incurring any additional costs. The result is cost saving, ease of application development, convenience, and flexibility (Figure 3.5).

The regulation of the network is managed by the BSN Development Association. The Association consists of four units:

(1) The State Information Center
(2) China Mobile Group
(3) Unionpay Co., Ltd.
(4) Red Date Technology Co., Ltd.

These six organizations are responsible for determining "regulatory design, technical standards, development and operations management, running modes, price-setting for services, and external cooperation."[15] BSN has the backing of the highest industry and government apparatus in China. In essence, it will not be allowed to fail (Figure 3.6).

---

[15] *Ibid.*

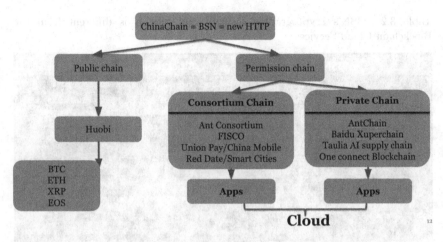

Figure 3.6.   The structure of BSN.

3.2.3.   *Privacy and security*

Privacy and Security have been emphasized within the BSN infrastructure. Partly for due diligence, partly to allay fears of the critics, BSN's White Paper emphasizes that "utmost priority is given to data security and user privacy protection."[16] There are many mechanisms in place for data security as these are critically important for the credibility of BSN — we lay them out in detail below. (Table 3.2 shows how the security of BSN is fundamentally different than that offered by Blockchain Cloud Services).

One, Data Encryption, which is required prior to launch of service. Two, developers have a choice of how public and private keys are developed (created locally or auto-generated by the system). Three, developers have an option to provide each user with their own encrypted private key. Decentralized Applications (DApps) distribute trust via different roles, and the developer has the choice of how data is read and written and by whom. Four, developers have the option to allow private users to query and implement different

---

[16] "Blockchain-Based Service Network Technical White Paper," BSNBase (BSN Development Association, April 25, 2020), https://bsnbase.io/static/tmpFile/B SNTechnicalWhitePaper.pdf.

Table 3.2. BSN's cryptographic security and how it is different from the Blockchain Cloud Services.

BSN	Blockchain Cloud Services
Cross-cloud, cross-framework, cross-portal	The same cloud, a few frameworks, and a single portal
All applications on the BSN can interchange data easily through different clouds and different frameworks	Every application is totally isolated, deployed individually with a different framework and a different encryption algorithm
Blockchain developers on the BSN do not require prior blockchain knowledge. One-day learning curve	Developers require blockchain knowledge and programming ability
A blockchain system administrator is not required	A system administrator is required to maintain the production environment
All applications on a PCN share system sources based on TPS and Requests. Costs are less than 10% of the cost of cloud services	One peer node uses one VCPU. Ten times more expensive than BSN
One user can use one private key to access all permissioned applications deployed on any given PCN with one gateway and one set of APIs	One user needs to have one private key, one gateway, and one set of APIs for each permissioned application they want to access

Source: "An Introduction to the BSN," BSNBase.io (BSN Foundation, 2020).

data transaction operations privately. On balance, it is completely in the hands of the DApp developers to decide how much control and privacy they are able to allocate to their users. This could mean either that applications compete on who provides the most privacy or users forego certain protections for auxiliary services. Five, individual users are not stored on BSN itself as "it is only possible to track which portals have distributed any given DApp and how many users are using this DApp. There is absolutely no detailed information about the DApp's developer and no detailed information about the DApp users."[17] Whether this is enough to allay concerns of certain users remains to be seen.

This entire technical infrastructure guarantees one thing: ease of adoption. Much of the world is already aware of the benefits of blockchain technology. The ongoing problem is creating the ease of use that will take it from a niche technical fetish to a broadly used service provider. As Xi Jinping mentioned in

---

[17] *Ibid.*

2020, "Blockchain applications have already extended to fintech, e-commerce, robotic factories, supply chain management and other various digital assets... expediting blockchain technology with socio-economic elements will lead to unparalleled developments."[18]

BSN is a central component of the proptech movement for two reasons. First, it is a distributed trust network. No longer are banks, government offices, or insurance companies necessary to validate contracts, prove ownership, or transfer deeds. In fact, blockchain and BSN will bring ownership of property online, where it will be tokenized and tradeable. Second, it will help bring the physical world to life. Based in every major city, and backed up by the resources of urban infrastructure across China, BSN will become the infrastructure to secure massive inflow of data from IoT and 5G solutions. BSN will ensure that important diagnostics from smart cities cannot be corrupted and it will allow the whole city to sense its surroundings.

The profile of the first benefit of BSN is Liquefy: a company working on tokenizing assets on the blockchain (Figure 3.7). Their vision is to make it easy for investors to buy into a small part of illiquid assets and to make it easier to raise capital. The process still requires large institutions to structure the security and issue the coins for investment, meaning that for now, it is little more than a blockchain-backed kickstarter. Nevertheless, Liquefy has opened a conceptual door for breaking down property, tokenizing it, and making it tradable. BSN will greatly expand its reach.

The profile of the second benefit of BSN is Bitmark: a company working to make massive urban data collection straightforward, anonymous, and actionable (Figure 3.8). Sean Moss-Pultz is one of the leading innovators in the provenance movement, and Bitmark is an early example of how blockchain can be used to animate our cities and secure property online: "digital property rights are the missing link that will allow the Internet to enable a far

---

[18] "Xi Stresses Development, Application of Blockchain Technology," *Xinhua*, October 25, 2019.

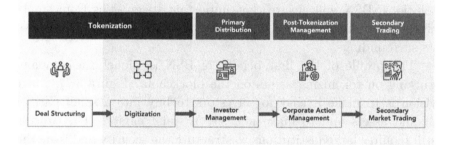

Figure 3.7.   Case Study: Liquefy.
Source: Hannah Jeong and Rita Lau, "Real Estate Tokenization," Colliers International, 2020.

more inclusive economy."[19] BSN will be the rails upon which data provenance is brought to SMEs across the Greater China area.

Tencent is the company that is bringing blockchain, data provenance, and automation to urban planning and property (Figure 3.9). Much of their work is carried out through intimate government partnerships. We go into significant detail about Tencent's ongoing work in Chapter 6.

---

[19] "Alibaba, HTC Invest in Blockchain Property Rights Startup (Bitmark)." *Ledger Insights*, September 4, 2019.

Bitmark - Property Rights and Urban Data

What do they do	Leadership	New Technology & Projects
Data Provenance: • Secures data provenance through registration and transfer on a blockchain • Offer privacy and anonymity for large scale data collection through blockchain	• Startup backed by Alibaba, HTC, WI Harper, and DCG • Sean Moss-Pultz, and Casey Alt,	UC Berkeley, KKBOX, and Pfizer use the Bitmark Protocol to increase trust in valuable data. In total, the Protocol is securing more than one million data records in healthcare, music, art, finance, and more. - Pfizer and Health2Sync crowdsource data directly from patients while protecting their privacy. - Allows for widespread urban data collection while ensuring anonymity.

Figure 3.8. Case Study: Bitmark.

Tencent - Smart City

Tencent 腾讯

What do they do	New Technology
Urban Digitization: • "We City 2.0" builds up a comprehensive smart solution for digital government affairs, urban management, urban decision-making and industrial interconnection.	- Automation: of tax services, data collection on the local economy, tourism management, and public security. - Blockchain: infrastructure as a service for voting, community fund management, ownership and dispute management. - Net City: an entire urban center built in Shenzhen focused on sustainability

Figure 3.9. Tencent — Smart City.

3.3.   Central Bank Digital Coin

The majority of Central Bank Digital Coins (CBDCs) are not based on blockchain, but it is nonetheless central to their success. The digitization of currency and the digitization of trust must be understood in tandem, because their success is tied to each other. China has been leading the charge of currency digitization, launching a virtual version of the Yuan in 2020, officially titled the Digital Currency Electronic Payment (DCEP). Beijing saw the writing on the wall years ago, and has launched DCEP as the last ditch effort to challenge the US dollar and Facebook Libra. Although, DCEP is not built like Bitcoin atop a blockchain — it is issued directly by the Central Bank — blockchain will be central to its success and complete integration of urban life throughout Greater China. The following section will address why CBDCs are central to the digitization of the 21st century, how they are being implemented (including the early challenges), and how they, in combination with blockchain, will transform regulation of property across China.

DC/EP is vital to the proptech movement for two reasons. First, because a fully convertible tokenizable foundation to trade physical assets with is vital. You cannot abstract property and continue to use paper and metal to exchange it. Crypto enterprises that allow exchange of property — like Bithome — are already popping up. DC/EP is a government-backed version of it. Second, a fully digital currency becomes a gold mine of vital data. It is still to be seen how DC/EP is fully implemented but a digital currency offers insight into where people shop, how they move, what they value in the city, and so much more. Admittedly, the idea of tracking spending is much less popular in the West. However, a digital coin, fully integrated with the urban fabric, could easily point out food deserts, underdevelopment, gentrification, and other concerns that usually remain invisible until it is far too late.

3.3.1.   *DC/EP*

There are quite a few straightforward benefits of a Digital National Currency. It enhances payment competition amid the banking cartels, reduces costs of coinage, expands financial inclusion, smoothens out monetary policy responsiveness, improves economic data collection, and reduces the power of privately issued currencies (kneecaps Bitcoins of the world and brings the power back to the Central Bank). In addition, it improves local FX attraction. There are the outward goals that any central bank leadership will stand by when rolling out a digital currency.

Moreover, there are plenty of hidden benefits that come with getting rid of paper and metal. DCEP brings about improved surveillance. The digital currency will catch money launderers, tax evaders, terrorists, and capital flight suspects. DCEP is not your local anarchist's money supply anymore. While cryptocurrency was originally premised on separating money from the state, DCEP retains all of the improved operations of digitization while reeling in all of the control.

Figure 3.10 explains how the PBOC understands the theory, practice, and implementation of DCEP. How is this happening? The digital currency is actively tested. The Central Bank has been carrying out testing since August 2020, so far facilitating 3 million transactions worth 1.1 billion yuan (US$162 million). To attract publicity, the digital currency has been given out as bonuses, used in lotteries, and interconnected with public transportation. More than 100,000 personal digital wallets have been downloaded during the testing phase as of this writing. Much of the charge has been led by the government of Shenzhen, which rewarded 5,000 medical and healthcare workers dealing with COVID-19 with financial rewards in DCEP. It also launched a lottery that gave out 10 million yuan in October.[20] The winners are supposed to download a renminbi app to receive the e-yuan and are able to spend it at 3,000 local shops. Approximately 50,000 people won and can now test out DCEP at merchants as small as your local mom-and-pop shops or as large as

---

[20]Kevin Helms, "China's Digital Currency Has Been Used in 3 Million Transactions Worth Over a Billion Yuan So Far," *Bitcoin News*, October 8, 2020.

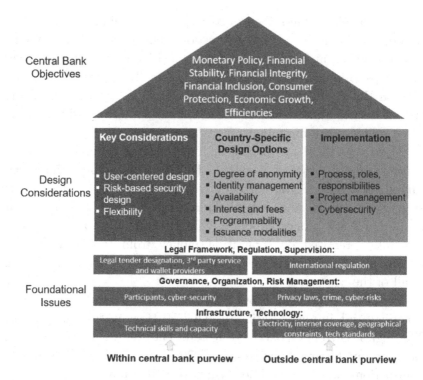

Figure 3.10.   Key topics for development of digital currency.
Source: John Kiff, "Central Bank Digital Currency Landscape," International Monetary Fund Landscape, June 13, 2019.

Walmart.[21] As the Chinese government explained during the launch, citizens "can use the digital wallet to top up accounts, withdraw money, make payments, and transfer money after registering with their mobile phone number."[22] All of the major banks are testing out the currency and the wallets, and it has been expanded to Beijing, Hong Kong, and Macau.

Figure 3.11 shows the Financial Industry Regulatory Authority (FINRA) mental blockage regarding digital currency. Money is

---

[21] Arjun Kharpal, "China Hands out $1.5 Million of Its Digital Currency in One of the Country's Biggest Public Tests," *CNBC*, October 12, 2020.

[22] Kevin Helms, "China Testing Digital Currency in Major Cities, Including Beijing and Hong Kong," *Bitcoin News*, August 17, 2020.

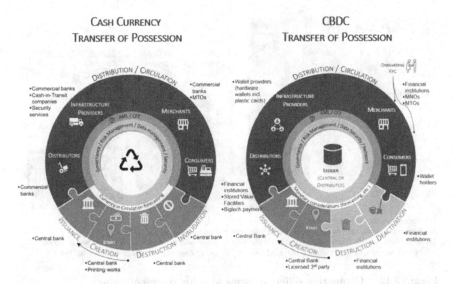

Figure 3.11.   Difference between partial reserve money distributed by banks (left) and full reserve central bank coin (right).

Source: John Kiff, "Central Bank Digital Currency Landscape," International Monetary Fund Landscape, June 13, 2019.

currently distributed to people and corporations through the banking system. Initially, the money enters the banking system through bank deposits. These banks use these deposits on a leveraged platform to create credit. With a reverse ratio of 10%, US$1 in bank deposits makes US$10 for the economy in credit. A digitized currency (fundamentally different from a crypto coin) is directly usable by persons without the bank and is usable for ALL debts public and private. It is much more than a coin and has the capability to digitize any and all assets. If this DC/EP is moved on the BSN rails, it can conceivably bypass the domestic and international banking system and attach itself to all digitized physical assets. Hence the power of digitized physical assets of the property sector (Figure 3.12).

What is the connecting argument here? The largest portion of bank assets (funded by deposit liabilities on the other side of the balance sheet) is PROPERTY. This new digital rail system can allow the banks to recede from the picture and heal from massive losses due to COVID-19. Moreover, digitized property assets can then be

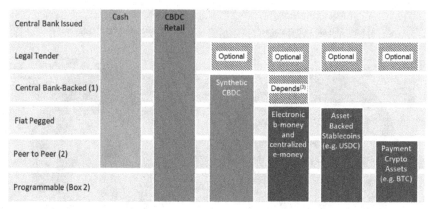

(1) Backed by deposits at the central bank
(2) Person to person, bank to bank, merchant to merchant, person to merchant etc.
(3) B-money is typically fractionally backed by central bank reserves, whereas centralized e-money may or may not
be. For example, Kenya's M-Pesa is not, but China's AliPay and WeChat Pay are fully central bank-backed.

Figure 3.12.   Comparing different forms of value representation.
Source: John Kiff, "Central Bank Digital Currency Landscape," International Monetary Fund Landscape, June 13, 2019.

traded outside the broken leveraged system of a fractional reserve system.

The rapid acceptance of proptech is predicated on the marriage of Super Apps, BSN, and Tokenized assets

The existing payment providers in China are central to DC/EP's internationalizations, and we have shown they are also central to the rollout of proptech (Figure 3.13). Chinese users are happy and able to download the Central Bank digital wallet and use it to transact outside of Alipay and WeChat. More importantly, SMEs (who operate buildings, housing complexes, logistics networks, etc.) are now mostly connected to super apps like DingTalk, Lark, and WeChatPay, which are a fertile ground for trading tokenized physical assets.

This cannot be said for the Chinese diaspora across the world, let alone foreigners. Alipay and WeChat are some of the most dominant online wallets in the developing world, making their participation in DCEP vital for the Yuan to have a truly global impact (Figure 3.14). However, the rapid acceptance of the new rails of BSN (managed

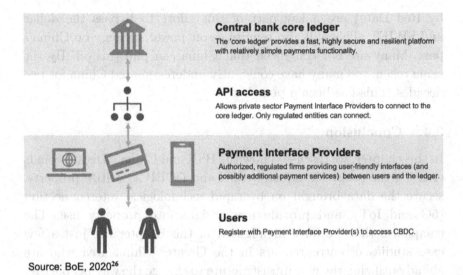

Source: BoE, 2020[26]

Figure 3.13.   Digital Coin M0 Distribution Map.

Source: John Kiff, "Central Bank Digital Currency Landscape," International Monetary Fund Landscape, June 13, 2019.

Figure 3.14.   Where you can pay with China's mobile payment systems?

Source: Julianna Wu, "A Surprising Number of Countries Now Accept WeChat Pay or Alipay," *South China Morning Post*, September 20, 2019.

by Red Date) are a key part of this effort to bypass the dollar and SWIFT. This will also require a soft power strategy on China's part. Many are not convinced that China can pull this off. By the same token, too many have constantly underestimated China for two decades. This has been a poor bet.

3.4. Conclusion

In this chapter, we discussed how the BSN and China's Digital coin is creating the proptech industry. BSN and DCEP securitize property, secure the data brought on by rapid technological interconnection (5G and IoT), and provide new insight into property use. The companies that we have highlighted in this chapter are just a few case studies of entrepreneurs in the Greater China area who are already utilizing the new infrastructure to change the way people live. Digitizing urban planning and property requires massive government build out, without which private firms would be unable to exist, let alone compete. The Chinese government is creating a new market before our eyes.

Section 2

The Giants

China's long-term planning offers the private sector reliable signals from which they can build innovative businesses. Public infrastructure projects are aligned with and sit next to private entrepreneurs. In this case, China has rolled the dice on digitization of the entire economy in record time, and it intends to tie these digitized assets to a new set of tokenized digital rails where the Central Bank Coin (and cryptocurrency) can run — both internally and internationally. In addition, China has made 5G a top priority to manage and interpret the billions of digitized data points from which new industries will arise and which can employ millions of people. The purpose is to create appropriate infrastructure for the future, solve societal problems, and discover new unrealized applications.

Like the "two-handed" model previously explained in Chapter 1, one hand points and the other executes. Across China, a few entrepreneurs with great insight — and who were early on the scene in Hangzhou and Shenzhen — have been able to capture the largest market share, attract the best talent, and be successful in capturing most of the profit. The big three — Alibaba, Ping An, and Tencent — started as heavy hitters in e-commerce, insurance, and gaming. Since then, they have expanded into fields as diverse as healthcare, urban planning, property development, and finance. They are both the executors of national policy for urbanization, rural equity, and sustainability as well as its designers (often advising the national entities that are drafting policies). They function independently, empowered by China's unique digital environment: super apps that become an small- and medium-sized enterprises' (SMEs) remote control for every function in the city. We argue in this section that the largest tech firms in China have placed a large bet on technology to reimagine the ways citizens exchange property and the government manages it.

We can say that proptech encapsulates what China is doing in the Belt and Road Initiative (BRI). The central tenet of the BRI was and will be infrastructure — both analog and digital. It is about building out both the physical AND the digital network of smart cities among and between China, Africa, and Europe. In addition, it is about educating the local population to a new digital age. The project touches 68 countries, 65% of the world's population, and 40% of the global economy.

At a basic level, the BRI is about bringing political stability to a region that has been wracked by religious and civil wars for two centuries. China's neighbors include Afghanistan, Pakistan, Kashmir, Vietnam, North Korea, Russia, and the entirety of Central Asia. It is not a great neighborhood. Many of the nations on the New Silk Road do not have strongly defined property rights. There are two ways to solve this problem. Either you strong-arm weaker states into changing their political system in your image (US tried this for 30 years in Central and South America in the 1950s–1970s, to little avail) or you provide them with the infrastructure that creates property rights outside of traditional legal channels on their terms (i.e. blockchain). In the implementation of a digital or blockchain-based system, Beijing is not rewriting the Washington Consensus. It will be offering nations along the Silk Road a four-fold package that will be delivered by China's leaders in digitization:

(1) Secure currency (DC/EP).
(2) A system to secure their property (Blockchain Service Network [BSN] or AntChain).
(3) Infrastructure (5G, Roads, Ports, Cloud Computing, etc.) and
(4) All of this is on a person's cell phone in a super app which offers a huge array of goods and services.

Chapter 4 begins with Alibaba, China's poster child for modernization. Founded in 1998, it has grown to become the largest e-commerce business in the world, running most of China's transactions, developing smart city projects, and modernizing Chinese bureaucracy. Starting in 2020, pitfalls have emerged in the government's relationships with Jack Ma's empire. After the halting of the Ant Group IPO and opening of an antitrust probe, the future of the company has been shaken, but it certainly has not been derailed. Its global expansion, municipal partnerships, and research & development continues unabated, and is unlikely to disappear anytime soon. Most important to property, Alibaba's City Brain project has successfully digitized much of Hangzhou municipal operation, signaling interesting potential for all urban management. Alibaba is chastened and has had a humbling lesson in trying to create an alternative universe from the one that tens of thousands of people have created through the Five-Year Programs (FYPs). Tencent and Ping An have chosen a wiser path.

Chapter 5 focuses on Ping An, an insurance titan that has expanded into artificial intelligence (AI), healthcare, fintech, and smart city development. Ping An offers an intriguing case study of how traditional industries must adapt in the age of cloud computing and AI. After spinning off a plethora of their affiliates and entering into practically every possible financial industry, their most recent focus on property is indicative of the technology trend in the Greater Bay Area. In the past decade, their innovation in big data and AI has transformed insurance, wealth management, and healthcare provision. Now the same technology is being applied to smart cities, government services, and real estate management.

Chapter 6 looks at Tencent and the creation of the urban remote control. Through its control of WeChat, the most popular messaging app in the world, Tencent has been able to learn about billions of people, everything from how they shop and move to where they live and what they watch. This data bank of information has allowed them to venture into smart city development, integrating government services, commercial activity, personal verification, data collection, and industrial management. It has already been implemented in cities across China and has the potential to become the management service for firms managing smart communities, government offices managing small cities, or governments managing nations. We conclude that Tencent is, by far, the most innovative company in proptech globally!

The following chapters give a glimpse into how the invisible hand of the market actualizes the directives of a government obsessed with catapulting all parts of China into the digital age. These three companies study the plans — and occasionally pivot away from them — and use their comparative advantage in talent and tech to innovate in new and previously unexplored areas. There are potentials as well as dangers in this. We see that their super apps can be easily inserted into existing proptech infrastructure for new projects. However, they can fall into prideful monopolies, which then crash to earth. They can abuse data, and they can become involved in national security issues, which might further the state, but hurt the consumer. These are identical issues also confronting the US and Europe each in their own way.

Chapter 4

Alibaba

China has two hands working together to create a digital economy. The intentions of the "state hand" are manifested by the National Development and Reform Commission (NDRC) after years of bottom-up consultation and consensus. The "market hand" of execution is manifested by aggressive entrepreneurs who not only seek out opportunities as these plans are enacted but also help to formulate these same plans. In the process, however, China is very keen on maintaining competition at all levels, both private and public. This establishes a foundation of innovative and competitive firms.

It is not just the government sending down decrees to the economic frontlines. Rather, it is a uniquely Chinese communitarian plan for development, where guidance is sought from the ground up and then formulated at a multi-cabinet level. This uniqueness is best understood through the industry of Property Technology (proptech), one of the fields that Chinese firms have created and are continuing to lead. Proptech touches what belongs to me and who I am: from physical buildings to my body, my identity and my intellectual property. No firm has been better at defining these than Alibaba. It played a key role in helping Xi Jinping learn about the digital world when he was a senior official in Hangzhou more than 15 years ago. It plays a (much chastened) role in adhering to regulatory rails but also in helping to formulate policies.

Incidentally, many wonder why the Chinese are willing to offer over their data to large digital firms like Alibaba while people in Western countries do not. There may be one simple answer to this. The West had a Great Financial Crisis (GFC) in 2008 and 2009, which caused a massive property crash, impoverished millions, and shattered confidence in institutions for many Westerners. China did not have a crisis. On the contrary, the West looked to China to offer a massive fiscal spending package to help bail out the world while the former was on its knees. Therefore, the Chinese people have maintained confidence in the institutions that represent the digitization of physical assets. So far, they see very clear benefits to handing over data to the likes of Alibaba and Tencent.

Since its founding in April 1998, Alibaba Group has transformed the way China shops, produces, pays, moves, and lives. From a struggling e-commerce firm to a multinational conglomerate, the story of Alibaba is often told alongside that of China itself: partly because it has been on the leading edge of every digitizing industry and partly because the careers of both Jack Ma and Xi Jinping started to ascend in tandem in Hangzhou. Alibaba was founded with the mission of creating a platform for millions of SMEs to excel in the modern world. Today, Alibaba has 742 million active buyers and 1.3 billion active sellers. It went from 18 employees to 82,000 in two decades, beating out international competitors on price, technology, and ease of use. At its founding, Alibaba's main technological product was trust: it created a platform that both sellers and buyers could use, with the confidence that their product would arrive on time and in the quality that it was described. Jack Ma's second largest creation, Ant Financial, also specializes in trust. However, in the process of being spun out into a separate company and almost becoming the largest IPO in history, it is completely reimagining trust toward property. We discuss later why Ant has hit hard times.

In recent years, the Ant Group's attention has shifted to public urban projects. In late 2019, the leadership of the Hangzhou Housing Authority reached a strategic cooperation with Alibaba and Ant Financial. The city's rental housing will introduce Zhima Credit. Zhima Credit is a live credit score for each user of Ant, which incorporates hundreds of criteria. It employs real-person authentication, comprehensive credit profiles, and other capabilities to build "integrity archives," cut off the dissemination of fake listings, as well as remove fake information from the mechanism.

Hangzhou is additionally using Alibaba's City Brain to aggregate much of the city's data into a smart response system. According to city officials who gave a briefing, "Alibaba's traffic control pilot programme showed that by controlling signals and predicting traffic trends there has been an 11% increase in speed on road sections."[1] There are hundreds of additional ongoing partnerships with universities, nonprofits, and hospitals. Alibaba is — quite literally — creating the proptech industry out of thin air.

Ant is working alongside municipal entities by designing the remote control for the city, a super app that aggregates the most important aspects of one's life. Alipay, while starting off as purely an online payments platform, has expanded into wealth management, insurance, municipal services, and so much more. It has now become the one stop shop for Chinese citizens to control their life. The integration of physical activity in life with the financial and civic offers the greatest capability for proptech. That is why super apps are vital to get to the next step. These traits — physical, financial, and civic — are then digitized and placed on tradable platforms based on blockchain. This provides authentication, fraud reduction, anonymity, cheap smart contracts, and the ability to trade any tokenized physical asset as it relates to finance (Figure 4.1).

The super app platform that Ant offers is optimal for proptech for one simple reason. Proptech is about creating a three-dimensional digitized world of ownership, physicality, and tradability via a new set of blockchain-based rails. We saw in Chapter 3 that the creation of the Blockchain Service Network (BSN) is an ideal way for these digitized assets to run and revolutionize marketing, advertising, merchandising, working capital management, and lending.

---

[1] "Hangzhou and Alibaba; Making Public Private Partnerships Work," *Smart City Hub*, March 22, 2017, http://smartcityhub.com/technology-innnovation/hangzhou-alibaba/.

Figure 4.1.   The Alipay ecosystem.
Source: "The World's Largest Fintech Is Going Public. What's Next?" *CB Insights Research*, December 18, 2020, https://www.cbinsights.com/research/ant-group-success-obstacles/.

The one area where this phenomenon of connecting the physical with the financial lies with SMEs, a sector that has been traditionally deprived of credit by banks. Why? It is in the "too hard" box for banks and has never been given attention. In other words, banks have never found a way to achieve economies of scale for companies with 10–100 employees.

Enter the SME super apps. There are three mainstream apps that occupy Chinese business apps market: Ding Talk, WeCom, and Lark, which are developed independently by three companies: Alibaba, Tencent, and Bytedance, respectively. We list their common points for comparison in Table 4.1.

These business and communication apps just may be a vital linchpin to the evolution of proptech as well as the more widely used public apps for personal use. We summarize functions that are vital to the real estate sector:

(1) Cloud address book

Real estate is a highly targeted and planned industry. The project master control plan guides the daily work and behavior of various

Table 4.1. Comparison of Ding Talk, WeCom, and Lark.

Ding Talk, WeCom and Lark		

	Ding Talk	WeCom	Lark
Customers	More than 15 million companies registered, over 300 million customers	More than 4.3 million companies registered, over 130 million customers	Increase sharply during covid period
Ranking(Most downloaded Business Apps)	1	3	56
Company	Alibaba	Tencent	Bytedance

Ding Talk, WeCom and Lark		

	Ding Talk	WeCom	Lark
Fundamental Function	Message read(unread), safety watermark, calendar, red envelope, nail plate, emoticon reply, audio and video conference	Message read(unread), Security watermark, schedule, red envelope, audio and video call	Message read(unread), security watermark, multi-device login management,
Unique Function	"Ding", message through train, message grouping, secret chat, group live broadcast, circle, smart hardware	Add WeChat users, join WeChat groups, customer circle of friends, take a break	"Pin", voice + text, group member calendar, shared calendar, offline document editing
Applications	Check-in, log, work summary, approval, customer management, reimbursement, procurement, operation and maintenance, security	Customer contact, schedule meeting, corporate email, We Cloud storage, Micro Document, live broadcast, approval, colleague bar, emergency notificatio., smart hardware	Check-in, questionnaire, approval task management, Google Analytics, Gitlab assistant, Jenkins CI assistant, Salesforce

departments. The master control plan is deconstructed into construction, planning, and is then broken down into weekly plans at all levels.

(2) Cloud goal setting and log

The real estate industry is a highly mobile industry, and once employees are hired, they aim to get started quickly. Address book Cloud storage can not only be retrieved quickly anytime and anywhere but can also be queried across groups. It can provide organizational structure, department settings, personnel ownership, and subordinate relationship.

(3) Instant communication

They provides free Internet calls, which saves phone bills for employees to a significant extent. You can also hold N to N video or Internet phone conferences to facilitate real-time team communication. They also provide a group-building function, which can form various virtual teams according to different needs. You can post notices or send messages. The best thing is that you can see who has read and who has not.

(4) Human resource applications

New employees can put all their knowledge and requirements on a cloud disk for employees to learn after they are hired; they can also establish a private group for new employees to conduct onboarding guides, and human resources colleagues to communicate in real time to grasp the employees' adaptation to the working environment. Real-time attendance can be presented anytime and anywhere, allowing employees to more freely control working hours and greatly reducing the workload of attendance.

Ding Talk is really the foundation of proptech and finance. It connects the physical movement of people and goods through and between the physical infrastructure. It does this by linking procurement and inventory to working capital. Imagine if the working capital is connected through the supply chain via apps such as these. Imagine if revenues and costs (including payroll) are delivered through the app. Imagine if payroll is delivered directly through PBOC distributed coin onto people's phones. Banks are bypassed. No need for payroll checks, waiting in line at the bank, and hidden fees. What if the ongoing cash flow can be constantly checked against existing orders and inventories? This means working capital loans can be released in line with the supply chain evolution. This can be marked against logistical activity at the warehouse. This is where the physicality of proptech merges with the digital rails that have been laid between the Central Bank Coin and the super app. No country is close to this. It is truly revolutionary.

4.1. The Vision

This section addresses the Vision of Alibaba and Ant, the services they provide, the partnerships they foster, and the impact they have on Chinese property and citizens.

The year 2020 was transformative both for Alibaba's operations and also for its imaginations. At the Smart City Expo in Chongqing, Jack Ma gave a speech ruminating on both the trend of digitization in the age of COVID-19 and also the emerging sectors that are prime for disruption.[2] He stated that the great breakthrough in the past was e-commerce. Today, however,

> "all industries such as agriculture, logistics, and service industries are facing an unprecedented huge opportunity to use digital technology to increase research and development to reduce the [cost of] advertising, supply chain, labor and management."[3]

Over the past five years, Alibaba has become increasingly aware that its business of being a platform has brought thousands of mom-and-pop shops to the market, yet it is only beginning the process of digitization. Acknowledging the diminishing importance of his own online-mall empire, Ma continued:

> "In fact, there will not be another industry called the Internet industry in the future, because all industries will use Internet technology. The only difference between traditional industries and future industries is whether they have used new ideas and new technologies to change themselves."[4]

---

[2]Yu Xiaoming, "Smart China Expo Opens in Chongqing," *Chinadaily.com.cn*, September 15, 2020, https://www.chinadaily.com.cn/a/202009/15/WS5f60743d a31024ad0ba79a9b.html.

[3]Jack Ma, "Jack Ma Speaking at Smart City Expo in Chongqing in September 2020," YouTube (Venturous Group, October 9, 2020), https://www.youtube.co m/watch?v=h4ZMymGM1yQ.

[4]*Ibid.*

His understanding of the changing nature of cities is most important to the future of industry in China. Their old foundations are waning and a new source of development is being established. Ma concluded:

> "In the past Chongqing was built because of water, and developed thanks to water. I believe that in the future Chongqing will prosper because of data, because the future development of cities depends on who has more data, computes faster, understands data better, protects data security and privacy better, and uses data to improve economics and social development."[5]

The problem remains that even while there might exist platforms for physical property to be exchanged (Alibaba, Alipay, Taobao), there is little digitization of the actual property itself. In Jack Ma's two simple sentences lie the vision of both China and Alibaba for the 21st century. Now, the most innovative companies are those that are creating the platforms for "traditional industries to use new technologies to change themselves."[6]

Jack Ma and Alibaba have been quickly pivoting the operations of Ant from pure e-commerce. For much of the past two decades, Alibaba has fulfilled its mission "to make it easy to do business anywhere," by bringing buyers and sellers together online.[7] Outside of the pure platform, Alibaba has expanded its commerce business to offering marketing, research, and data analysis. The company continues to lead in core commerce through its network of firms. In gross merchandise revenue, it is the largest retail commerce business in the world. Within China, Taobao and TMall generate 65% of its revenue.[8] Outside of China, Lazada, AliExpress, Kaola, Trendyol, and Daraz dominate global transactions.

However, Alibaba might be considered the most innovative outside of pure e-commerce. Much of its public reports have explicitly

---

[5] *Ibid.*

[6] *Ibid.*

[7] "Alibaba Group Fiscal Year 2020 Annual Report," SEC Disclosures, December 2020, https://www.sec.gov/Archives/edgar/data/1577552/000110465920082881 /0001104659-20-082881-index.htm.

[8] *Ibid.*

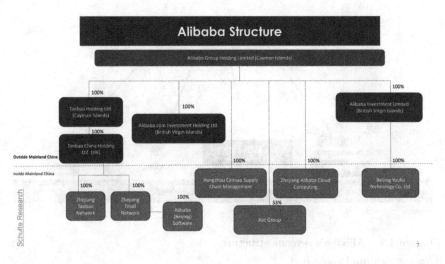

Figure 4.2.　Alibaba structure.
Source: Schulte Research.

de-emphasized it: "Our businesses are comprised of core commerce, cloud computing, digital media and entertainment, and innovation initiatives. In addition, Ant Group, an unconsolidated related party, provides payment services and offers financial services for consumers and merchants on our platforms."[9] What Alibaba has worked towards is becoming an economy in itself (Figure 4.2). According to their own estimations, the Alibaba economy generated RMB 7,053 billion (US$1 trillion) in 2020.[10]

> "... a digital economy has developed around our platforms and businesses that consists of consumers, merchants, brands, retailers, third-party service providers, strategic alliance partners and other businesses"[11]

Its firms outside of commerce give a glimpse into what Alibaba understands as emerging priorities. Alibaba is the world's third

---

[9] *Ibid.*
[10] *Ibid.*
[11] Louise Lucas, "Alibaba Bets on Do-It-Yourself Globalisation," *Financial Times*, May 22, 2017, https://www.ft.com/content/8f5e79ba-30ab-11e7-9555-23ef563ec f9a.

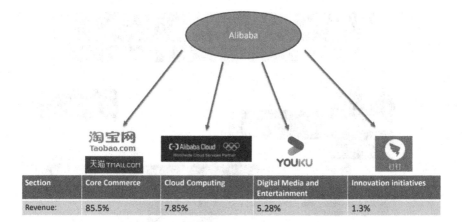

Figure 4.3.   Alibaba's revenue structure.
Source: Schulte Research.

largest and Asia-Pacific's largest infrastructure as a service (IaaS) provider.[12] However, for now, it is still a tiny portion of Alibaba's revenue stream (Figure 4.3). If e-commerce was the company's bread and butter, Alibaba-Cloud will become the ciabatta and caviar. One just has to look at the services it provides to understand its digitizing impact:

> "Alibaba Cloud, our cloud computing business, offers a complete suite of cloud services, including elastic computing, database, storage, network virtualization services, large-scale computing, security, management and application services, big data analytics, a machine learning platform and IoT services, serving our digital economy and beyond."[13]

The data Alibaba collects from their core business is used to power their digital media and entertainment arms, bringing the right content to the right user, through Youku, the third largest online long-form video platform in China, while Alibaba Pictures "covers

---

[12] "Alibaba Named by Gartner as Third Biggest Global Provider for IaaS and First in Asia Pacific," *Business Wire*, April 28, 2020.

[13] "Alibaba Group Fiscal Year 2020 Annual Report," SEC Disclosures, December 2020, https://www.sec.gov/Archives/edgar/data/1577552/000110465920082881/0001104659-20-082881-index.htm.

content production, promotion and distribution, intellectual property licensing and integrated management, cinema ticketing management and data services for the entertainment industry."[14]

Alibaba's innovation initiative is the company's betting arm, where it focuses on emerging trends and technologies for the future. It includes two important companies. The first is Amap, the largest provider of digital maps and navigation in China. The second is Ding Talk, which focuses on workflow management and facilitates network collaboration among team members and enterprises. In all of its official documentation, Alibaba continuously emphasizes that they "feel a strong responsibility for the continued development of the digital economy and (we) take ownership in this development."[15] At the center of Alibaba's digital economy infrastructure is the Ant Group, the financial infrastructure for every other interaction in China to go smoothly (Figure 4.4).

This vision of a purely digital economy with wholly digitized property is carried more explicitly in the Ant Group. As the darling of the world's fintech, Ant operates almost 60% of China's digital payments, but it has never wanted to be defined as a financial company. It brands itself as a tech company, for good reason.

Ant had come so close to creating an ecosystem that could have been a solid foundation for digitizing the physical world and then allow these digitized units to be traded through the new set of rails being rolled out via the BSN. There is one problem. The post mortem on the cancellation of the ANT IPO revolves around the question of Ant's commitment to the underlying success of the BSN. As we have laid out extensively, the BSN has been given a great deal of thought and is a vital link to China's digitized central bank coin as well as an international escape from the US-dominated SWIFT system. Everyone else signed up for BSN — Tencent, Huawei, JD, and Ping An. Everyone except for Ant, that is. Chinese Kremlinology is a difficult task at any time, but the Ant's slow acceptance of

---

[14] *Ibid.*
[15] *Ibid.*

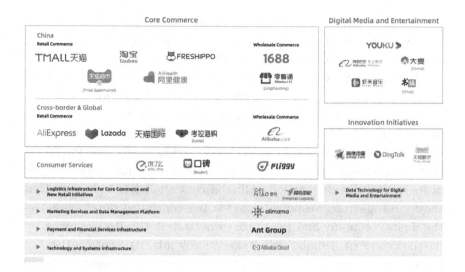

Figure 4.4.   Infrastructure elements of Alibaba digital economy.

Source: "Alibaba Group Fiscal Year 2020 Annual Report," SEC Disclosures, December 2020, https://www.sec.gov/Archives/edgar/data/1577552/000110465 920082881/0001104659-20-082881-index.htm.

and participation in BSN very likely angered people in the Central Bank and at the very top of the government. Ant is a chastened organization now, but its supremely clever structure — designed to digitize the physical world and put it on a cloud-based and blockchain-run machine — has been truly dashed.

Ant is still alive and kicking, but the regulators are very likely to force it to break up. This is unfortunate as the ecosystem it created would have been ideal for the world that is proptech. For the purposes of this book, we will point out where the property digitization of each division overlaps. This section will mostly outline the major financial services that the Ant Group offers and how it is working to digitize property: Alipay, AliCloud, Zhima Credit, AntFortune, MYBank, and AntChain (Figure 4.5). A different creature will certainly emerge after the regulators are finished with it, but the raw material is certainly there to do amazing things. And these things must be done in line with the agenda as set forth in the Five Year Program (FYP).

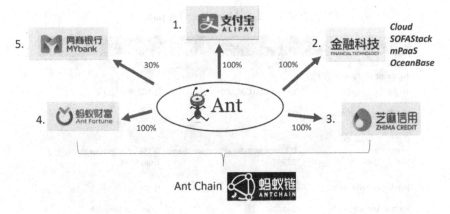

Figure 4.5. Ant is a technology-driven company.
Source: Schulte Research.

That is the way it works. Even Xi Jinping cannot change the FYPs once they have been created by tens of thousands of people and approved by the State Council and the National People's Congress. Did Jack Ma see himself and Ant as above the State Council's power to promulgate these programs? Some say yes. We cannot confirm this.

(1) Alipay has come a long way from its primitive uses 15 years ago. It now has one billion active users and has become much more than just a payment service. A Chinese resident can hail a taxi, make a doctor's appointment, and purchase wealth management products all in one app. In-store payment service covers over 50 markets across the world, and Alipay tax reimbursements are supported in 35 countries. Compared domestically to TenPay, Ant Group continues to dominate on price, support, and reach. Compared internationally to a company like PayPal — one of the leading digital payment platforms in the US, whose original founders have gone on to completely dominate the US tech space — Alipay is in a league of its own. It is available in 1 million restaurants, 40,000 supermarkets, 1 million taxis, and 300 hospitals. However, payment services are not an end in

Table 4.2.   Alipay vs. Tenpay.

Aspect	Alipay	Tenpay
Market Share (Amount of Payment)	48.44%	33.59%
Users	Over 1,000,000,000	1,100,000,000
Number of currencies supported	18	9
Fees	0.1% for withdrawals more than $2897	0.1% for withdrawals more than $153
Fee for merchants	0.55%	0.6%
Escrow Service	Support	Does Not Support

Source: Schulte Research.

themselves — they are a gateway to a vast digital ecosystem of products and services (Table 4.2).

(2) Ant Cloud is the financial technology arm of the Ant Group. It focuses purely on financial intelligence, security, distributed architecture, mobile development, blockchain, and distributed databases. It is completely independent from the public cloud and works with institutions to facilitate simple and streamlined digitization. Ant Cloud is actively updating outdated banking infrastructure, integrating internal and external data, and providing comprehensive risk management and offers a flexible marketing platform to engage with customers. It basically does everything that modern banking is supposed to be: easy, secure, flexible, and personalized. Similar services are provided to integrate insurance.

(3) Zhima Credit is a third-party credit agency under Ant Group. It uses cloud computing, machine learning, and big data processing to create a more objective credit profile. Through its smarter analytic algorithms, Zhima Credit operates a loyalty program, where a higher credit score and better payment history will bring with it social perks. It currently has more than 260 million users.

(4) Ant Fortune is a comprehensive wealth management app to manage all finances in one app. The group already holds

A loyalty scheme for an entire country, sponsored by certain companies:

- 600+ points – take out a Just Spend loan of up to 5,000 yuan (around £565) to use to shop on an Alibaba site

- 650+ points – rent a car without leaving a deposit. Faster check-in at hotels, use of VIP check-in at Beijing Capital International Airport

- 666+ points – get a cash loan of up to 50,000 yuan (£5,700 from Ant Financial Services)

- 700+ points – apply for Singapore travel without supporting documents such as an employee letter

- 750+ points – get a fast-tracked application to a coveted pan-European Schengen visa

Figure 4.6.   Zhima credit rewards scheme.
Source: Schulte Research.

more than 100 patents in blockchain technology, it has fully configured Interactive Voice Response (IVR), interactive robots, voice recognition, etc. Many have called it the Amazon moment for asset managers in China, allowing both institutions and individuals to manage all of their property through one simple user interface. With 180 million users, it is one of the largest wealth management services in the world. Ant Fortune allows users to purchase other Ant Financial services like insurance, take out a line of credit, or check your credit score.

(5) MYBank. The institutional financial arm of the Ant Group is MYbank. As one of the earliest private banks in China, it is focused on SMEs. Since its founding, it has lent US$290 billion to 16 million SME. A single loan takes less than three minutes to complete. The bank approves four times more loans than traditional lenders. The default rate is 1%.

While China has some of the highest saving rates in the world, the ease of credit facilitated by places like MYbank could become a tension point for China's economy (Figure 4.6). In the past five years, China's "household debt has surged to 128% of household income, and 56% of Chinese GDP."[16] This is partly due to mortgage

---

[16]Logan Wright and Allen Feng, "COVID-19 and China's Household Debt Dilemma," Rhodium Group, May 11, 2020, https://www.rhg.com/research/china-household-debt/.

and consumer credit cards. Consumers have been slow to catch up to the credit train until recently, "from the end of 2014 to 2019, China's corporates added an astonishing 37.9 trillion yuan in new formal borrowing ($5.5 trillion). But China's households joined in the party for the first time, adding 32.2 trillion yuan in debt from banks alone ($4.6 trillion)."[17] Some reports have emphasized that what has happened in the past five years is awfully similar to 2008: "the surge in China's household borrowing is comparable in size to the run up in US household debt in advance of the global financial crisis (although household debt was not the only factor involved in that crisis, of course). US household debt rose by US$5.1 trillion from Q3 2003 to Q3 2008."[18] Removing access to credit is definitely not the solution, and as China increases the size of its middle class, consumption and consumer credit become an inevitable part of the national economy anyway.

AntChain is the final and perhaps most promising Ant Group venture. In Chapter 3, we expanded on the intention, the architecture, and the potential impact of BSN that was rolled out in China in 2020. However, while BSN functions as the integration of disparate chains, it is the chains themselves that do the heavy lifting, provide the services, and attract users. AntChain currently has the ability to process one billion user accounts and transactions every day.[19] It holds 212 blockchain patents, making it the world's leading innovator in the space. Over 100 million digital assets are secured with AntChain on an average day. The Ant Group themselves claim that AntChain has been used in more than 50 cases so far in IT leasing, shipping, insurance claim processing, cross-border remittances, and

---

[17] Amanda Lee, "How Big is China's Debt, Who Owns it and What is Next?" *South China Morning Post*, December 15, 2020.

[18] Logan Wright and Allen Feng, "COVID-19 and China's Household Debt Dilemma," Rhodium Group, May 11, 2020, https://www.rhg.com/research/china-household-debt/.

[19] "Ant Financial Opens Blockchain Platform to Developer and SME Community," Finextra Research, April 17, 2020.

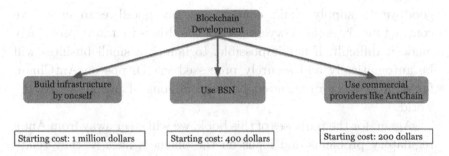

Figure 4.7.   Cost comparisons for Blockchain buildout.
Source: Schulte Research.

charitable donations, according to a company statement.[20] To truly understand the scope of BSN and AntChain integration, one has to look no further than the launch date: On July 22, 2020, PBOC released technical standards on security and performance for all blockchain operators in China; on July 23, Ant Group announced the launch of AntChain, already preconfigured to all of the technical qualifications (Figure 4.7).

AntChain will be transformative for China, and will perhaps become Ant Group's cash cow. Jack Ma captures the potential impact of such a reliable, authorized third-party trust network as AntChain: "There are still 1.7 billion people in the world who have no bank accounts, but most of them have mobile phones. The impact of blockchain on the future of humans may be far beyond our imagination."[21] AntChain will almost operate as a telco, providing the resources for SMEs to exchange contracts, verify transactions, automatically file taxes, integrate supply chains, and so much more. Say goodbye to the Big 4 accounting firms, say

---

[20] "Ant Group Creates New Blockchain-Based Technology Unit," Finextra Research, July 23, 2020, https://www.finextra.com/newsarticle/36269/ant-group-creates-new-blockchain-based-technology-unit.

[21] Luke Thompson, "Alibaba Launches Two Blockchain Subsidiaries," *Asia Times*, February 18, 2020, https://asiatimes.com/2019/03/alibaba-launches-two-blockchain-subsidiaries/.

goodbye to supply chain consultants, say goodbye to expensive contract monkeys (i.e. lawyers). All of the things that have previously made it difficult, if not impossible, to launch a small business will be automatically and securely processed via DApps on AntChain, for a small price distributed between billions of people across the world.

Again, for the purposes of this book, we will steer away from Ant's regulatory problems and focus on the business lines as they relate to proptech. AntChain will likely go through the most aggressive changes from regulators since BSN is really designed as the main rails for all the "train companies" to ride on, i.e. JD, Tencent, and Ping An. Ant did not agree on this format and presumably thought it could be a parallel set of tracks. The State Council disagreed.

AntChain offered two major types of services to businesses. First is Blockchain as a Service (BaaS) — the developers can build their own applications on an already existing and integrated chain, with minimal upfront fixed costs. Second is the Open Consortium Chain — it is a blockchain service network that uses a quick-build platform or dozens of contract development templates to achieve "low cost and low threshold on-chain" pricing by users on demand.

So do it yourself or plug-and-play. Depending on the type of business and the services provided, both offer all the necessary capabilities and support. The chain is also integrated with a variety of privacy measures. Ant Blockchain platform introduces Ring Signature technology to realize the concealment of transaction accounts. It introduces a variety of homomorphic encryption and zero-knowledge proof technologies to protect privacy. Its Native Data Authorization Access Scheme can support data isolation under the same network characteristic. These services are already being applied to logistics, contracts, and risk control. The final product is convenience and a low price. If this sounds awfully close to the services of BSN, it is because it is.

Figure 4.8 offers great clarity on what is an open system and what is a closed system. We hope it helps. The top left in the traditional purist version of bitcoin — proof of work. It is slow and clunky but public and permissionless. Anyone can use it — no questions

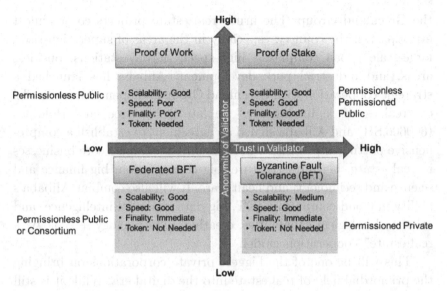

Figure 4.8. Anonymity vs. Trust Matrix.
Source: Schulte Research.

asked. Various chains like AntChain, Ping An, or JD are, we think, permissioned public — this is the top right. Central Bank Coins (and all the acronyms thereof) are, we think, permissioned private. This is the bottom right. In this way, they are the polar opposite of the hallowed bitcoin White Paper and so have earned the enmity of the cypherpunks. However, the PBOC coin, which will run along the BSN, will also allow several cryptocurrencies to operate with total cryptological anonymity. Therefore, it will very much be a hybrid. Lastly, the system bring rolled out by Facebook (Libra now called Diem) can be seen as the bottom left. Although this is subject to discussion. The new and improved Diem is morphing quickly and could end up resembling BSN, but who knows.

4.2. Partnerships

4.2.1. *Domestic partnerships: Greenland Group*

Perhaps the best example of an Ant partnership directly related to proptech is with Greenland. A partnership was recently formed with the Greenland Group. The firm's real estate projects cover almost every part of the country, especially in the areas of super high-rises, large-scale urban complexes, high-speed railway stations, business areas, and industrial park development. Alibaba has launched a strategic cooperation with Greenland Group and opened a new model of "real estate + intelligence." In late 2020, Greenland Holdings (600606.SH) and Alibaba signed an agreement to establish a comprehensive partnership, which will focus on Greenland's core businesses in real estate, big infrastructure, big consumption, big finance and science and technology, and healthcare. It will also combine Alibaba's ability in cloud computing, IOT, big data, artificial intelligence, and other technological capabilities, creating a "technology + ecology + real estate" cooperation model.

This will be one of the biggest private corporations on bringing the primordial field of real estate into the digital era. While it is still too early to project how daily life will change, it marks a major shift in two of China's biggest company's priorities: tech is moving toward property and property is moving toward tech.

4.2.2.   *International reach*

In summary, we lay out below how property will be a logical next step in the Internet of everything — digitize finance, tokenize physical assets, and trading these assets both through Central Bank and crypto coins. In practical terms, the first step is to create a secure digital payments system. The second step is to build out the infrastructure (blockchain, roads, Central Bank Digital Coin). The third step is to build out the cities. This is where local talent will congregate, learn from each other, and innovate. China is doing this on a regional basis — this is the digital Silk Road.

The central part of the BRI was and will be infrastructure — both analog and digital. It is about building out the core infrastructure between China, Africa, and Europe, educating the local population, and making them rich. The development of the region is vital for China. It touches 68 countries and 65% of the world's population, but only 40% of the global economy. The goal is to turn almost 5 billion people, who have not reached full economic development, into consumers of Chinese goods and their producers.

The BRI is a strategic move to reorient the economic gravity of the world back East. At its foundation, however, it is mostly about bringing political stability to a region that has been wracked by religious and civil wars for a century. China's neighbors include Afghanistan, Pakistan, Kashmir, Vietnam, North Korea, Russia, and the entirety of Central Asia. China has not fired a single shot in the past 30 years and wants to deepen economic ties.

Digital property will be central to the development of the BRI. First, many of the nations on the New Silk Road do not have strongly defined property rights. There are two ways to solve this problem. Either you strong-arm weaker states into changing their political system in your image (the US tried this for 30 years in Central and South America in the 1950s–1970s, to little avail) or you provide them with the infrastructure that creates property rights outside of traditional legal channels on their terms (i.e. blockchain). In the implementation of a digital or blockchain-based system, Beijing is not rewriting the Washington Consensus. It will be offering nations along the Silk Road a three-fold package:

(1) Secure currency (DC/EP)
(2) A system to secure their property (BSN or AntChain) and
(3) Infrastructure (5G, Roads, Ports, etc.).

China's national and regional agenda includes diverse climate change mandates. This includes rebuilding existing cities to make them adaptable to climate change, urbanization, and big data. The BRI lies along much of Central Asia and Africa, filled with abundant land and large rural populations. This will be the area where the new future metropolises could be built. It also includes some of the largest cities located along coastlines vulnerable to rising water levels. These countries need help or risk much of their population ending up underwater within 20 years. The first step is to create a secure digital

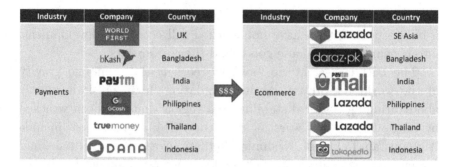

Figure 4.9.   Alibaba payments and e-commerce stakes across Asia.
Source: Schulte Research.

payments system. The second step is to build out the infrastructure (blockchain, roads, Central Bank Digital Coin). The third step is to build out the cities. This is where local talent will congregate, learn from each other, and innovate.

Digitization has occurred through both strategic partnerships and investments. The Ant Group invests in the majority of the dominant digital payment services within Asia: Paytm in India, TrueMoney in Thailand, BankWare in South Korea, and GCash in the Philippines (Figure 4.9). Additionally, it has collaboration agreements with the leading payment services in much of the Western world. Ant Financial has been unofficially spearheading China's BRI and helping the developing world leapfrog into digital payments.

One of the best concrete examples of overseas cooperation in the area of proptech is with CapitaLand. The firm manages about US$144 billion yearly, and is one of the largest real estate firms in the world. The Group has mostly focused on Singapore and China. In the past five years, it is trying to expand into India, Vietnam, Australia, Europe, and the US (Figure 4.10). On September 2017, CapitaLand (China) and Alibaba signed a strategic cooperation framework agreement in Hangzhou. The cooperation will use CapitaLand's operations and ecological capabilities in the real estate field, coupled with Ali's technology and ecological capabilities, to help urban innovation and jointly build a "future urban ecology." While the rhetoric on the surface looks pie-in-the-sky, the most important

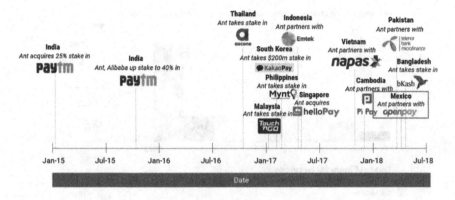

Figure 4.10.   Ant's globalization strategy: Local partnerships.
Source: "What the Largest Global Fintech Can Teach Us About What's Next in Financial Services," CB Insights Research, July 6, 2020, https://www.cbinsights .com/research/ant-financial-alipay-fintech/.

aspect here is priorities, and where each industry is pouring their attention, resources, and innovation.

4.2.3.   *Southeast Asia: A real battle ground with regional giants*

Southeast Asia is ripe for financial disruption, and the Ant Group is tapping into a regional need for credit. Three in four adults in Southeast Asia have subpar financial access (Figure 4.11). Almost 200 million are completely unbanked, 100 million are underbanked. This is an incredible amount of human capital and entrepreneurship that is locked out of the banking system. Perhaps the most expected and unfortunate reality is that the underbanked populations are in the poorest countries, with the worst financial infrastructure, and with the highest need for young and bright people to take risk for the benefit of their local community. Much of the public policy community forecast that lending will increase fourfold in the region in the next five years. It is primarily due to services like Ant, which can utilize existing mobile infrastructure to facilitate lending seamlessly.

The Ant Group has been riding this wave for the past five years, and they are ready to bring the convenience of digitization and data provenance to Southeast Asia. Since 2015, Ant has been investing

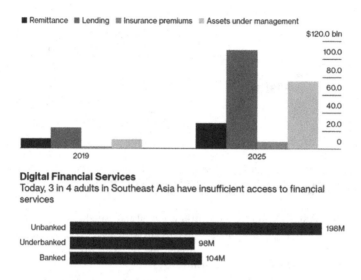

Figure 4.11.   Digital financial services are taking off in Southeast Asia.
Source: Yoolim Lee and Lulu Yilun Chen, "Indonesia's Ovo is Close to Merger with Dana to Fight Gojek," *Bloomberg*, June 12, 2020.

aggressively abroad, by taking revenue stakes and collaborating on key technologies.

4.3.   Conclusion

Some claim that Alibaba and Ant Financial have recently attempted globalization on their own. Instead of partnering with BSN, they have invested heavily in AntChain. Instead of following the FYP, some say that they tried to write their own. Alibaba continues to dominate the global e-commerce market and the property digitization push. Their brain trust continues to develop products for nations across the Silk Road. It continues to bring SMEs into a future with digitized property. It is moving offices, taxes, and government documents online.

However, in the short term, some claim it has been undermined by the curse of Icarus. Icarus ignored the advice of his father and flew too close to the Sun with wings made of wax. They melted and he fell to earth. It is still uncertain how the Jack Ma Empire will emerge. We feel confident that it will be a far more carefully regulated entity from all angles. In the mean time, Tencent and Ping An have both kept a low profile. They study FYPs very carefully to see how they can benefit rather than challenge it. They are stepping in to fill the vacuum left over. In the next chapter, we will see how Tencent and Ping An are taking bold and imaginative steps in proptech. The companies are turning Shenzhen into a showcase for the new smart city model.

Chapter 5

Ping An

Since its founding in 1988, Ping An has grown to become the biggest insurance company in the world and one of the leading technological innovators. The two are not as incongruent as is initially apparent. The insurance industry was one of the first to realize the interconnection between personal property and securitization. The conception of property, as early as the mid-19th century, extended from real estate and assets to your body and life. Most recently, intellectual property is being insured en masse. Perhaps it should not be surprising that the most successful and technologically integrated insurance companies in the world are leading the charge to digitize its core product: securing every form of property. Ping An's technology unit has been developing the core technology for the swathe of its subsidiaries.

One of the newest — and most central to Ping An's mission — is the expansion into physical space and proptech. Peter Ma, the CEO and Chairman of the company, spoke at the 19th National Congress of the Communist Party of China and echoed the common sentiment at the meeting: in order for China to develop, its cities must transform first. The Chinese government has been promoting and pouring money into modernizing urbanization, and private firms have been actualizing that vision. Ma doubled down, expressing that urban development requires "new technologies and the means to

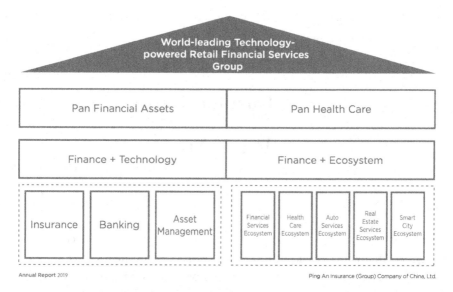

Figure 5.1.   Overview of Ping An group.

Source: "Ping An Insurance of China: Annual Report 2019," *MarketScreener*, March 18, 2020, https://www.marketscreener.com/quote/stock/PING-AN-INS URANCE-GROUP-1412620/news/Ping-An-Insurance-of-China-Annual-Report -2019-30182330/.

improve the operational management efficiency of a city, and build a modern community with immense soft power capabilities."[1] To actualize this vision, the company launched the "1 + N" smart city integrated platform for cities to do everything from data collection, municipal services, traffic reduction, environmental protection, and security to healthcare, education, etc. (the services are customizable by the city).[2] The platform is redefining urban governance through four key technologies that Ping An had developed and perfected for its financial and insurance units: smart recognition, artificial intelligence, blockchain, and cloud computing. This chapter explores how Ping An understands its technology, how it is digitizing property, and how — from health to wealth — it is rethinking every aspect of an individual's life (Figure 5.1).

---

[1] "Ping An Unveils First Smart City Integrated Platform and Solutions in China to Empower Development with Technology," PingAn, August 21, 2018.
[2] *Ibid.*

5.1. Vision

Despite being in an old and fundamentally conservative industry, much of the company's vision has a laser focus on innovation. Ping An's mission in 2020 has extended far beyond just customers and shareholders: "We influence our society with finance and technology, use our expertise to create value for the shareholders, customers, employees, communities, environment and partners, and pursue sustainable development together with the stakeholders."[3] The company has embraced the stakeholder capitalism model of governance, expressing, at least rhetorically, a commitment to the community, employees, and their environment. While remaining an insurance company at the core, it has expanded both its vision and method of impact. Ping An's self-professed vision is to "become a world-leading technology-powered personal financial services group."[4] It has been on track to do exactly that. So far, Ping An has invested more than CNY50 billion into emerging technology and holds the most patent applications in China's financial industry. Yu Ning, head of Ping An's technology entrepreneur division, has expressed on multiple occasions that the "ultimate goal is to develop core technologies that can be copied and expanded in various cities," while continuing to invest at least 1% of their annual revenue (about 10 billion yuan) to continue expanding the technology business.[5]

So far, this investment has paid off generously. In the first half of 2020, Ping An's operating profit increased by 1.2% to RMB 74,310 million, bringing the annualized operating Return-on-Investment to 21.6%.[6] Technology was a large chunk of that pie. In the first half of 2020, the technology business "increased by 11.2% year on year to RMB 42,732 million."[7] Since the middle of 2020, the valuation of its tech companies — focusing on financial

---

[3] "Building a Tech-Enabled Ecosystem," McKinsey & Company, May 11, 2019.
[4] *Ibid.*
[5] Daniel Ren, "China's Biggest Insurer Turns its Big Data toward Building Smart Cities," *South China Morning Post*, September 3, 2019.
[6] "Ping An Reports Steady Growth of 1.2% in Operating Profit Attributable to Shareholders of the Parent Company," *Cision PR Newswire*, August 27, 2020.
[7] *Ibid.*

Figure 5.2. The public/private impact matrix.

Source: "Smarter Life, Better Future: Ping An Sustainability Report," Ping An, December 2018, http://www.pingan.com/app_upload/images/info/upload/ba7a d86a-64e5-40d1-a1c2-1b090e2cd8af.pdf.

services, healthcare, auto services, real estate services, and smart city services — "reached USD70 billion, and the market values of Ping An Good Doctor and OneConnect increased by 108% and 84%."[8] Ping An Technology is the leading fintech developer in China, followed by Hundsun Technologies founded by Ant Financial.

From this wellspring came startups including peer-to-peer lender Lufax,[9] set up in 2012, fetching a valuation of US$18.5 billion in a fundraising two years ago; Ping An Good Doctor,[10] a healthcare portal with 30 million-plus monthly active users whose recent IPO raised US$1.1 billion in Hong Kong; and Ping An Healthcare And Technology,[11] a mobile app for booking hospital visits used by 800 million customers across 70% of cities in China. To consumers, the offer is often free mobile apps. However, there is a

---

[8] "Ping An Unveils First Smart City Integrated Platform and Solutions in China to Empower Development with Technology," PingAn, August 21, 2018.
[9] https://www.lu.com/.
[10] https://www.jk.cn/.
[11] http://www.pagd.net/.

Artificial intelligence: summers and winters

The current artificial intelligence boom began around seven years ago, following decades of "summers" and "winters" as faith in the promise of AI rose and waned. More recently, leaps in computing power have enabled vast amounts of data to be compiled and shared, opening up new uses for AI technologies; AI patent families swelled by an annual average of 28% between 2012 and 2017.

Other developments | AI patents filed with the World Intellectual Property Organization (number of patents)

1956 (9): The term "artificial intelligence" coined at a Dartmouth College conference; AI founded as an academic discipline in the U.S.

1956-74: The golden years of AI; generous government funding goes to promising developments in logic-based problem-solving technology

1970 Computer vision — Quality inspection; surveillance; vehicle navigation

1974-80: Overly high investor expectations collide with limited capacities of early AI programs, leading to first "AI winter," with reduced funding and interest in research

1974 (169)

1982-86 Robotics; planning and scheduling; knowledge representation and reasoning

1980-87: A new branch of AI, knowledge-based expert systems, brings successes. Fresh research and funding pivots toward this form of AI

1980 (207)

1992 Natural language processing — Chatbots; customer service

1987-93: Second "AI winter" triggered by sudden collapse of the specialized hardware industry in 1987. AI hype is countered with negativity from governments and investors, as expert systems hit limitations and prove expensive to update and maintain

1987 (693)

1996 Distributed AI — Trading strategies; modeling flows of vehicles, people

1993 (3,049): **1993-2011:** Increased computing power fuels new optimism about AI; industry becomes data-driven. In 1997, IBM's Deep Blue beats world champion Garry Kasparov at chess. In 2002, Amazon uses automated systems to provide product recommendations. In 2011, Apple releases AI-powered digital assisant Siri

2003 Predictive analytics and control methods — Risk assessment; sales forecasting; managing medical conditions

2012-17: Increased availability of data, connectedness and computing power allow for breakthroughs in machine learning, mainly in neural networks and deep learning. In 2012, Google driverless cars navigate autonomously; in 2016, DeepMind's AlphaGo beats world champion Lee Se-dol in complex Japanese board game Go. In 2017, China announces its New Generation Artificial Intelligence Development Plan, which lays a path to a full-fledged domestic AI industry by 2030

2011 (12,473)

2017 (55,660)

Source: World Intellectual Property Organization

Figure 5.3. History of artificial intelligence development.

Source: Yifan Yu, "Why China's AI Players Are Struggling to Evolve beyond Surveillance," *Nikkei Asia*, December 18, 2019.

business-to-business app: OneConnect,[12] linking 2,400 banks and non-financial institutions and valued at US$7.4 billion in its last funding round.[13]

Proptech is about capturing a massive influx of data and a built world that is able to respond to it. Ping An's wide array of businesses creates a treasure trove of data to make proptech a reality. The company is able to study a community's movements, health patterns, saving tendencies, insurance trends, and small- and medium-size enterprises (SME) penetration. If applied well, Ping An can understand the invisible trends of a house, neighborhood, or whole city. The future of cities is not just about people more adaptive and responsive to the "built" world around them. The future is also about making property responsive to the people. In order to actualize this reality, infrastructure needs to be able to sense and respond. The centralization of teams means centralization of data. Ping An will bring diverse data sets from disparate industries together, allow intelligent algorithms to find previously unseen patterns, and apply them to create solutions at the source: where people live, buy, and learn (the home).

One of the main reasons for the success of the technology business lies in its ability to use the entirety of the Ping An ecosystem for testing its products within its service network (Figure 5.4). Hu Wei, a member of Ping An Group Executive Committee and Ping An Smart City co-president and CTO has mentioned that if it was not for the network of its business, partnerships, and initiatives, it would be harder to quickly determine a failing from a successful product: "Before we apply the technologies... we tested and incubated the technologies within the system of Ping An's own businesses."[14] The whole company functions under a sink or swim mentality. Jessica Tan, the Co-CEO of Ping An and its technology czar said "we no

---

[12]https://tech.pingan.com/en/sass_h_account.shtml.

[13]Shu-Ching Jean Chen, "Chinese Giant Ping An Looks Beyond Insurance to a Fintech Future," *Forbes*, June 8, 2018.

[14]Mei Yang, "Ping An 'Has Advantages for Supporting Smart City Projects'," *Shenzhen Daily*, November 15, 2019, http://www.szdaily.com/content/2019-11/15/content_22629809.htm.

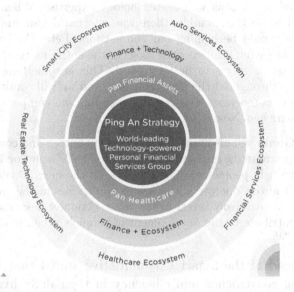

Figure 5.4. Ping An strategy.

Source: "Smarter Life, Better Future: Ping An Sustainability Report," Ping An, December 2018, http://www.pingan.com/app_upload/images/info/upload/ba7a d86a-64e5-40d1-a1c2-1b090e2cd8af.pdf.

longer have an incubation center. We have top-down and bottom-up approaches. The top-down is at the beginning to identify where we want to be. Then we set up a company. The bottom-up is the management team tasked to get the business off the ground. We close down underperforming companies."[15] Across the industry, these advances are powered by qualified personnel. The 1% of revenue toward R&D goes to 30,000 research professionals and more than 500 big data scientists.[16] Tan outlined the company's future vision:

> "Over the next ten years our strategy is very clear: to have our core financial services businesses continue to grow. We want to provide

---

[15] Shu-Ching Jean Chen, "Chinese Giant Ping An Looks Beyond Insurance To A Fintech Future," *Forbes*, June 8, 2018.

[16] Alice Ekman, "Towards Urban Decoupling? China's Smart City Ambitions at the Time of COVID-19 European Union Institute for Security Studies," European Union Institute for Security Studies, May 14, 2020.

financial services as well as technology expertise. When we first started to do this, frankly, there was internal debate and worries that we would be helping our competitors. Peter [Ma] was very strong in saying that we want to serve the entire market, we don't want just ourselves to be very good. This is something that we stuck to throughout the past ten years, and we will continue to do for the next ten years. Our consumer lending was completely offline four years ago. Now it's completely online."[17]

"The Group will also take advantage of its fintech and comprehensively promote the implementation of the "1+N" solution for smart cities to help people enjoy better lives. In the next 30 years, Ping An will also cooperate with various enterprises in the smart city industry, to actively invest in the construction of new smart cities and contribute to the development of people's urban livelihood in China."[18]

The head of the Smart City initiative stated that "only when people feel convenience and efficiency in their daily lives will they gain a sense of happiness."[19]

5.2.   Services

Ping An's leadership is aware that technology is not an end in itself. Its Technology unit supports the functioning of services that are intended to transform the entire life of an average citizen: from how they go to the doctor, shop, save, and buy property. While the technology originated with insurance and finance, it has expanded dramatically, and now supports every subsidiary with valuable expertise.

"The group has a 110,000-strong technology development team — larger than the commercial-banking divisions of all but the biggest banks — including 3,000 scientists. It submitted 4,625 technology

---

[17]Shu-Ching Jean Chen, "Chinese Giant Ping An Looks Beyond Insurance to A Fintech Future," *Forbes*, June 8, 2018.

[18]"Ping An Unveils First Smart City Integrated Platform and Solutions in China to Empower Development with Technology," *Ping An*, August 21, 2018.

[19]Mei Yang, "Ping An 'Has Advantages for Supporting Smart City Projects'," *Shenzhen Daily*, November 15, 2019, http://www.szdaily.com/content/2019-11/15/content_22629809.htm.

patents in the first half of the year alone. The tools developed within the group's technology unit are often used across the company."[20]

This has allowed Ping An to continue innovating in every field it partakes in, creating an ecosystem that makes interaction with every form of property substantially easier. From healthcare, to auto, to smart cities, Ping An has practically erased paper and staples that used to dominate these industries. Now they are being expanded into property and the built environment (Figure 5.5).

The technical platform is made up of three key services: (1) Artificial Intelligence (AI), (2) Blockchain, and (3) Cloud Computing.

First, Ping An's AI is being trained on more than 100 million data sets, leading to more than 18 cutting-edge technologies used in "intelligent cognition, intelligent prediction, intelligent risk control, and intelligent services."

Figure 5.5.   Ping An ecosystems.
Source: "Smarter Life, Better Future: Ping An Sustainability Report," Ping An, December 2018, http://www.pingan.com/app_upload/images/info/upload/ba7a d86a-64e5-40d1-a1c2-1b090e2cd8af.pdf.

---

[20] "How Ping An, an Insurer, Became a Fintech Super-App," *The Economist*, December 3, 2020.

Second, the Blockchain Hyperledger has been in development since 2014 and is currently being used in asset transactions, real estate transactions, financing loans, as well as medical and healthcare services.

Finally, Ping An's cloud computing has been in operation since 2012, when Ping An "put all [of the] systems on the cloud — this is unthinkable. No organization in the world was doing this."[21]

Ping An Group is a good example of the "multiple organization" or "matrix" governance model, with subsidiaries and centralized teams. It has established five subsidiaries, which focus on finance, healthcare, the automotive industry, real estate, and smart cities (Figure 5.6). Ping An guarantees flexibility and freedom regarding

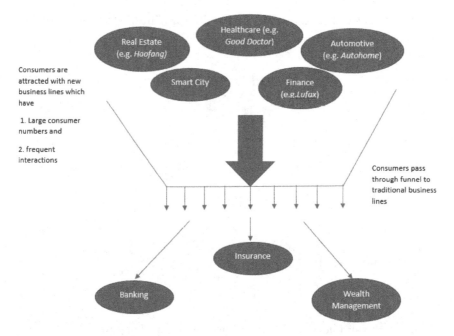

Figure 5.6.   From consumer business lines, to profit business lines.

Source: Arun Prakash, "The Ping An Ecosystem — How an Insurance Company Reached the Forbes Top 10 Ranking," *Medium*, May 3, 2020.

---

[21]Shu-Ching Jean Chen, "Chinese Giant Ping An Looks Beyond Insurance To A Fintech Future," *Forbes*, June 8, 2018.

funds, talent recruitment, and management for each subsidiary. It also provides coordination and support for the subsidiaries through a series of centralized teams.[22] The centralization of teams means centralization of data. Ping An will bring diverse data sets from disparate industries together, allow intelligent algorithms to find previously unseen patterns, and apply them to create solutions at the source: where people live, buy, and learn (the home).

5.2.1. *Smart city*

One of the most striking and global applications of this technology has been in urban management. Ping An's "1 + N" smart city platform is a customizable and responsive AI and Internet of Things (IoT) software for city managers to use for everything urban: finance, administration, transportation, healthcare, customs, education, agriculture, judiciary, environmental protection, and community management. It currently exists in more than 100 cities, including Beijing, Shanghai, Shenzhen, Guangzhou, Chongqing, Nanning, Tianjin, Xiamen, and a swathe of regions along the Belt and Road. Ping An does not offer a single urban management product — it provides and operates the technology that will address a specific problem of a municipality.

Although it has only been in operation for two years, 1 + N has already created tangible solutions. At the end of 2018, Ping An was contracted to ease traffic congestion in Shenzhen. Notorious for road problems, during the Golden Week, traffic could last up to 21.7 hours. After a year of operation by the Shenzhen traffic police, 1 + N completely eliminated traffic congestion.[23] A year later, Shenzhen partnered with Ping An to create an e-government app "i-深圳" (I-Shenzhen). Built with blockchain to facilitate better privacy controls, the app "offers more than 4,000 services that make it

---

[22]Joydeep Sengupta, "Winning in a World of Ecosystems," McKinsey & Company, April 9, 2019, https://www.mckinsey.com/industries/financial-services/our-insights/winning-in-a-world-of-ecosystems.

[23]Shu-Ching Jean Chen, "Chinese Giant Ping An Looks Beyond Insurance To A Fintech Future," *Forbes*, June 8, 2018.

much easier and efficient for residents to handle government-required procedures."[24] Additionally, Ping An has been able to forecast Shenzhen's economic growth and industry changes for six to nine months ahead.

> "Ping An Smart City, which is committed to promoting sustainable city development with services to government, business, and citizens in China, served 118 cities, nearly 600,000 enterprises, and over 87 million citizens. In government services, Ping An helped local governments increase their efficiency in fiscal, performance and environmental management through its integrated smart government service platform. The smart government system has been deployed in 25 cities and 52 commissions, offices and bureaus throughout China. In business development, Ping An's smart market supervision platform covers more than 600 supervisory scenarios and more than 8,000 risk points. The accuracy rate of early warning recorded was more than 90% and the accuracy rate of risk identification was as high as 85%."[25]

Ping An's Smart City division has remained in high demand. Hong Kong contracted Ping An to develop an electronic ID to use for a range of government services. Ericson Chan, CEO of Ping An Technology, said: "Face recognition was key for Ping An Technology to win this project. The e-ID project is the framework for building a smart city network in Hong Kong. Participation in the project is conducive to helping Ping An Technology further develop overseas practices for smart cities."[26] The Shenzhen Government reported that this year they will work with Ping An to launch a blockchain-backed tax system.[27] In addition, Ping An is currently building a blockchain-based e-license platform to secure electronic medical

---

[24]Mei Yang, "Ping An 'Has Advantages for Supporting Smart City Projects'," *Shenzhen Daily*, November 15, 2019, http://www.szdaily.com/content/2019-11/15/content_22629809.htm.

[25] "Ping An Unveils First Smart City Integrated Platform and Solutions in China to Empower Development with Technology," PingAn, August 21, 2018.

[26]Yiran Zheng, "HK Partners with Ping An Technology for e-ID System," *Chinadaily*, April 2, 2019.

[27] "China's Shenzhen to Launch Blockchain Tax System with Ping An," Ledger Insights, January 9, 2020.

records, marriage certificates, and government service payments.[28] These all stand as a testament that the demand in China for digitizing urban planning and service is at an all-time high. Hu Wei, Ping An's Smart City co-president, has signaled a global turn, saying "Ping An has [already] secured 200 or so smart city projects in more than 100 cities and in the future Ping An will seek cooperation in the South East Asian countries including Singapore, Indonesia, Vietnam and Malaysia."[29]

5.2.2. *Healthcare*

Ping An's technology has extended to the healthcare space. Through their insurance division, experience dealing with hospitals and facilitating communication between patients and medical practitioners, a glaring problem presented itself: "Chinese doctors spend on average, per patient, three to four minutes, especially in top-tier hospitals. Informal statistics show 30-odd% of misdiagnosis or missed early detection."[30] As a result, Ping An began working separately with both patients and hospitals to address their individual concerns, be it technological or logistical.

In the past five years, Ping An has led medical innovation with AI, cloud computing, and personalized medicine. As of 2020, Ping An has become "number one in AI medical imaging, for instance, with more than 95% accuracy in the authoritative LUNA rankings for imaging in two categories for lung diseases, ahead of Alibaba Health."[31] Ping An's Good Doctor has become the dominant online-to-offline healthcare platform for both the care and the insurance needs of patients. As of last year, "Ping An Good Doctor's revenues were RMB 1.4 billion, generated by a family doctor service (~15%), consumer health care (~45%), a health mall (~35%), and health

---

[28]Mei Yang, "Ping An 'Has Advantages for Supporting Smart City Projects'," *Shenzhen Daily*, November 15, 2019.
[29]*Ibid.*
[30]Shu-Ching Jean Chen, "Chinese Giant Ping An Looks Beyond Insurance To A Fintech Future," *Forbes*, June 8, 2018.
[31]*Ibid.*

management and wellness services (∼5%)."[32] In five years, it has become the largest online portal for healthcare services with an average of 53,500 daily consultations.

COVID-19 has only accelerated the expansion of telemedicine. Currently Ping An Healthcare and Technology has a 70% share of China's telehealth market.[33] Over the past decade, it has spent more than 20 billion yuan on healthcare technology, and it has pledged to spend another 30 billion yuan in the next five years in light of the

Figure 5.7.   Diverse uses of health risk.

Source: "Smarter Life, Better Future: Ping An Sustainability Report," Ping An, December 2018, http://www.pingan.com/app_upload/images/info/upload/ba7a d86a-64e5-40d1-a1c2-1b090e2cd8af.pdf.

---

[32] Joydeep Sengupta, "Winning in a World of Ecosystems," McKinsey & Company, April 9, 2019, https://www.mckinsey.com/industries/financial-services/ou r-insights/winning-in-a-world-of-ecosystems.

[33] "Ping An Healthcare & Technology: The Undiscovered Gem In Telehealth," *SeekingAlpha*, November 25, 2020.

global pandemic.[34] Jessica Tan said, "COVID has really accelerated digitization even for us, and we have always been on the forefront of digitization."[35] In the first half of 2020, "Ping An Good Doctor saw an average of 831,000 medical consultations daily, up 26.7% year-on-year."[36] The need for telemedicine is expected to further increase as more people move into large cities, as rural areas continue to lack vital medical personal, and as the pressure on existing medical infrastructure continues to exacerbate.

5.2.3. *Real estate*

Founded in 2014, Ping An Real Estate covers development and investment, commercial real estate, financial products, industrial development, and other fields. While it fundamentally functions as a real estate management company, it heavily cooperates with the Ping An Smart City and Technology divisions to develop new proptech applications. It has developed industrial parks in Zengcheng, Hangzhou's multilevel urban complex, and is currently developing the Guangdong–Hong Kong–Macao Greater Bay Area combined port project service platform.[37] As the real estate division builds, the attached subsidiaries apply blockchain, big data, artificial intelligence, and cloud computing create solutions (Figure 5.8). Chen Xinying, Co-CEO of Ping An Group, said:

> "The Guangdong-Hong Kong-Macao Greater Bay Area has a container throughput of more than 70 million containers and a cross-border trade volume of more than 15 trillion yuan, ranking first among the four bay areas in the world. Trends in global trade in the context of constant changes, how can the Guangdong-Hong Kong-Macao Greater Bay Area maintain its competitiveness? The first problem is how to integrate the 37 ports in the entire Greater

---

[34]Eric Ng, "Insurer Ping An Aims to Fill Gaps in China's 'Underresourced' Health System, to Spend up to US\$4 Billion on Health Care Tech Development," *South China Morning Post*, September 22, 2020.

[35]*Ibid.*

[36]*Ibid.*

[37]"OneConnect and China Merchants Group Launch 'Linked Port' Blockchain Project," Port Technology International, November 25, 2020.

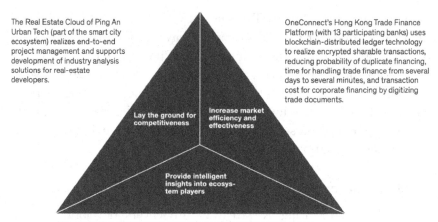

The Real Estate Cloud of Ping An Urban Tech (part of the smart city ecosystem) realizes end-to-end project management and supports development of industry analysis solutions for real-estate developers.

OneConnect's Hong Kong Trade Finance Platform (with 13 participating banks) uses blockchain-distributed ledger technology to realize encrypted sharable transactions, reducing probability of duplicate financing, time for handling trade finance from several days to several minutes, and transaction cost for corporate financing by digitizing trade documents.

Lay the ground for competitiveness

Increase market efficiency and effectiveness

Provide intelligent insights into ecosystem players

Ping An Healthcare Insurance Technology expands the healthcare ecosystem using a medical database and a knowledge map to build an end-to-end smart platform with a goal to satisfy the needs of patients, service providers, and payors so as to deepen government cooperation, enable corporate development, and improve patient experience.

Figure 5.8. Combining Healthcare, Blockchain, and Proptech.

Source: Joydeep Sengupta, "Winning in a World of Ecosystems," McKinsey & Company, April 9, 2019, https://www.mckinsey.com/industries/financial-servic es/our-insights/winning-in-a-world-of-ecosystems.

Bay Area? General Secretary Xi Jinping mentioned the "new infrastructure" many times. To implement this concept, with the support of the Shenzhen Municipal Government and the promotion of Shenzhen and Guangzhou customs, our two companies upholding the "Shekou Spirit" jointly build this platform."[38]

5.2.4. *Automotive*

Ping An's concept of property security does not stop at healthcare or urban space. In April 2020, the Ping An Auto Owner app surpassed 100 million registered users. The app functions as a one stop shop for any auto-related concerns using "leading artificial intelligence (AI), cloud computing and big data technology in a platform to connect car owners to car dealers and other automotive service providers."[39]

---

[38] *Ibid.*

[39] "China's Insurance Giant Is Morphing Into a Tech Company," *Bloomberg*, December 3, 2019.

A user can do everything from find a place to fix their car, get insurance, sell or buy a vehicle, move titles, and more. It actively serves 100 original equipment manufacturers (OEMs), 26,000 auto dealers, and 30,000 used car dealers.

5.2.5. *Finance*

The final piece of Ping An's ecosystem puzzle is its finance group. Insurance has been the core product and the company's cash cow since its founding. The goal of the automotive and healthcare divisions has always been to make day-to-day operations easier and, more importantly, to bring new customers under its insurance arm. Lufax, the company's financial arm founded in 2011, matches borrowers and lenders, and takes a slice of the pie along the way. However, beyond its sophisticated algorithms, it primarily functions as a middleman. Ping An's overflowing abundance of customer data and technological R&D make all of these services convenient and efficient. It was only a matter of time before the company extended its expertise into financial technology. If Lufax is mostly for consumer convenience, then OneConnect is to make the institutional gears turn smoother and quicker. As of June 2020, it has served all of China's major banks and 53% of its insurance companies through "end-to-end solutions of intelligent marketing, products, risk control and operation to financial institutions."[40]

OneConnect is based on the same core technologies that ensures the success of Ping An's other subsidiaries: AI, blockchain, and big data analytics. This year that company has become one of the largest commercial blockchains in the world, operating 44,000 blockchain nodes for more than 3,000 financial institutions, running almost 50,000 transactions per second.[41] It is this blockchain tech that is currently being used to "establish core port logistics data standards and platforms" in the Guangdong–Hong Kong–Macao Greater Bay Area.

---

[40]Michael Hytha, "Ping An's OneConnect Flat in Debut After $312 Million IPO," *Bloomberg*, December 14, 2019.
[41]Wolfie Zhao, "Ping An's New Pitch for Blockchain: Shared Ledger, But Banks Keep Clients," *CoinDesk*, December 3, 2018.

In this project, Ping An is also using its AI backbone to model the flow of goods, predict the port's turnaround, and reduce the reliance on port officials for clearance: "the overall duration of import and export logistics is reduced from 5–7 days to 2 days, efficiency is increased by 60%, and corporate transportation and customs declaration costs are reduced by 30%."[42] The port construction has become another example of the two-hand model — the government speaks while private companies innovate. Ye Wangchun, Chairman and CEO of OneConnect, said:

> "The Guangdong-Hong Kong-Macao Greater Bay Area Combination Port project has responded to the country's call for "new infrastructure" and helped regulators achieve precise risk control through customs supervision model innovation and technological innovation. At the same time, the project also reduces the cost of customs clearance and logistics for trading companies, improves the efficiency of capital turnover, and contributes to the high-quality development of the comprehensive construction of port logistics in the Greater Bay Area."[43]

COVID-19 has only accelerated the need for OneConnect's technology. There is new urgency for contact-free banking. OneConnect has made lending to SMEs considerably easier, creating a platform in a time when many would have gone out of business.

> "By September 2020, [Ping An's] platform had access to a total of 250 government data from 34 government units, and collected comprehensive information for more than 13 million SMEs in the province. More than 350 financial institutions have launched more than 1,000 financing products on the platform, more than 500,000 enterprises registered, and the total amount of financing has exceeded RMB30 billion."[44]

The pandemic has accelerated Ping An's expansion as well (Figure 5.9). In 2020 alone, the company secured 50 clients in more 10 Southeast Asian countries. Michael Fei, the board secretary of

---

[42] *Ibid.*

[43] *Ibid.*

[44] Daniel Ren, "Ping An's OneConnect Expects COVID-19 to Drive Growth in Southeast Asia," *South China Morning Post*, August 24, 2020.

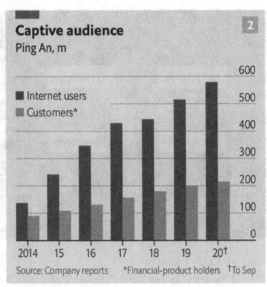

Figure 5.9. Captive audience for Ping An (in millions).

Source: "How Ping An, an Insurer, Became a Fintech Super-App," *The Economist*, December 3, 2020.

OneConnect, has pointed out: "COVID-19 is ushering in increasing orders for our products, such as AI-based call centre technologies and operations support service."[45] While China has considerable advantage in digital banking to the rest of the world, Southeast Asia is still prime for technological integration of finance. With an outsized unbanked population, Indonesia is adding 10 million new smartphone users every year.

5.3. Partnerships in Proptech

One of Ping An's largest sources of innovation and global reach comes from their international partnerships and relationships. Although many of the partnerships' utility should be taken with a grain of salt (it has become increasingly difficult to distinguish marketing from

---

[45] *Ibid.*

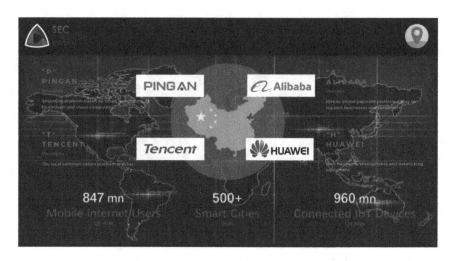

Figure 5.10.   China "PATH" initiative.

Source: "China PATH Smart City Initiative," Smart Eco City, October 27, 2020.

innovation), there is at least some grain of long-term vision within each project. We can begin to map Ping An's sister institutions, source of talent, and desire for new markets.

In 2018, Ping An brought together the largest tech firms in China to collaborate on a national smart city project called PATH, titled after the four companies leading it (Ping An, Alibaba, Tencent, Huawei) (Figure 5.10). Alibaba brings fintech with AliPay while its Cloud and its City Brain projects focus on urban mobility. Tencent facilitates digital communication through China's largest social media platform, WeChat. Huawei manufactures the smartphones, telecom hardware, and lays the maritime Internet cables. While official only in press releases, the quad has mostly carried out individual SmartCity projects. Each firm develops their individual urban and real estate technology solutions. However, cumulatively, each serves as an technological pillar for the national push to digitize its urban spaces.

Take the delineation of proptech as an industry. In October 2020, Ping An partnered with Sino Group (leading property developers in Hong Kong) to establish PropXTech, a corporate innovation program. It intends to highlight the work of promising tech companies in the Greater Bay Area for the real estate market. "During the five-month programme, participants will attend intensive training sessions and workshops, gain access to Sino Group's innovation ecosystem to develop pilots and proofs-of-concept, as well as test and fine-tune their solutions in a real-world environment."[46] They then will be connected with investors, potentially producing products that either Ping An or the Sino Group can adapt into their operations. This will be the first proptech-specific development program, potentially serving as a harbinger for a global conversation on urban and property technology. The CTO of Ping An Smart City, Hu Wei has remarked:

> "The "PropXTech" programme symbolises our efforts to assist the real estate and smart city industries in the Greater Bay Area to innovate and digitalise through the application of the latest technologies. With partners like Sino Group, we believe we could contribute to building the next generation of modern cities together."[47,48]

The firms will provide technical solutions in "geospatial technologies, drones, business process, robotics, smart city, smart home, smart buildings, modelling, data analytics, AR/VR, IoT, big data, machine learning, and sensors."

This is not the first venture Ping An has embarked upon to support entrepreneurs. In 2019, Ping An led a partnership with Swire Properties and Jones Lang LaSalle to establish UrbanLab, China's first corporate accelerator program that focuses on property technology. The partnership was formed after Ping An began to imagine innovation outside of its company walls, "We felt that we have reached the goal when our senior leaders concluded that, 'we need to engage in more technology collaboration in the future.'"[49]

---

[46] "Sino Group and Ping An Smart City Launch 'PropXTech' Innovation Programme to Foster and Drive PropTech Innovation in the Greater Bay Area," *Yahoo! Finance*, October 29, 2020.

[47] "Sino Group and Ping An Launch New PropTech Programme," *FutureIoT*, November 16, 2020.

[48] *Ibid.*

[49] Yingying Zhu, "Featured Femmes Interview with Alice Guo From Ping An Urban Tech," Women in PropTech, April 6, 2020.

The goal was to create a platform for rapid sourcing, testing, and adoption of new technology across the real estate market.

> "Screening more than 100+ digital solutions, each of us selected 4 startups to partner with in this accelerator program. Swire as an owner-developer focuses on startup ideas on smart building, retail innovation, energy management, e.g. Giga IoT (giga.build). JLL as a service provider focuses on building operations and data analytics. Ping An Technology has an important pillar focusing on smart city and construction tech and has therefore partnered with a few technology companies in these fields such as XKool Map (xkool.ai), who uses AI to automate zoning analysis and assist master planning and concept design, and Palmap (palmap.cn), who provides indoor mapping and orientation services to buildings including hospitals and parking lots."[50]

Ping An gives considerable acknowledgment to the motivation they receive from the government.

> "In China, the government is the invisible hand. There are a few policies acting as the key drivers for the tech scene in China. *Smart City* — China's urbanization rate has edged up to 60% in just over a few decades... Because of the rapid transformation in urban life, the cities are motivated to promote innovation to combat its negative side effects such as air pollution and traffic congestion. *Made in China 2025* — China has been making great strides in transforming its economy away from just being the hub of low-level manufacturers. *Internet+* — This policy means to integrate the internet with the traditional industries such as "Internet+ Finance" or "Internet+ Agriculture". The governments support startups working on these initiatives from the perspectives of funding, government purchase and tax policies."[51]

Wei Baisong, Chief Technology Officer at Ping An Urban Tech said:

> "We are providing an opportunity to urban innovators to test their solutions in Chinese Mainland, specifically technology solutions that can change the urban planning, real estate and infrastructure industries. With the spirit of a financial services firm, Ping An

---

[50] *Ibid.*
[51] *Ibid.*

Urban Tech also hopes to find a model that can seamlessly integrate these technology solutions with its finance and technology ecosystems. We hope to form an urban ecosystem that can benefit our customers and partners in the long run. I think *'UrbanLab'* is a good starting point."[52]

While cultivating domestic talent, Ping An also sought out collaboration with Western firms. In 2020, Intel and Ping An were planning to "cooperate on products and technology, and form a joint project team in areas of high-performance computing, including storage, network, cloud, artificial intelligence (AI) and security."[53] It is still unclear what the partnership will entail, and neither have disclosed financial terms. However, Ping An Technology CEO Ericson Chan said the partnership will "give Ping An an edge" to boost its cloud technologies and to "supercharge" its AI-based products and services.[54] Rose Schooler, Intel's Corporate Vice President, mentioned that "the two parties will explore joint development in technology areas including AI, high performance computing, visual computing and FPGAs using the full range of Intel's data-centric portfolio. We plan to innovate and support an open ecosystem Ping An Technology's Ping An Cloud."[55] The partnerships in the US come as Ping An is also looking for investments. In October 2020, the company announced the closing of the Global Equity Selection Fund and the Global Equity Fund for investments abroad. Cumulatively, the funds raised US$875 million.

5.4.   Conclusion

Ping An's greatest potential in proptech lies in its access to a diverse set of data on a range of human activity in its physical locations. The company has accumulated knowledge on savings, healthcare,

---

[52] "JLL, Swire Properties and Ping An Urban Tech Launch Chinese Mainland's First Corporate PropTech Accelerator — 'UrbanLab' Swire Pacific Limited, July 19, 2019.

[53] "Ping An Technology and Intel to Establish Joint Innovation Laboratory," *Business Insider*, January 10, 2020.

[54] *Ibid.*

[55] *Ibid.*

investments, risk, and movement. It is now able to bring it all together into a cohesive digital solution for the physical world.

Digitization of offices, homes, hospitals, and eventually whole cities begins and ends with data. What if Ping An was to simplify every aspect of one's life? Imagine a young woman in her thirties who owns a small business. She wakes up and is able to instantly receive a report on how well she slept, what her heart rate was, and how her diet has been impacting her sleep. Her body monitor notifies her that she got a cold, so the air in the room becomes more oxidized, her doctor is notified, and she is written a prescription all before she gets out of bed. After she dresses herself, her breakfast is automatically made in the kitchen. The prescription is already delivered to her door.

Her spacious living room transforms into an office. Before she opens her computer, she is updated on the payment that automatically went through to all of her employees via her SME app. She also gets a blockchain report about her real estate investments, which are blockchain-based fractionalized investments. Three of the investors have exited the position and seven more have bought in, all exchanged instantly via a digital currency. Her orders for goods shipped through Blockchain Service Network and smart contracts are done. This triggered working capital to be released from the bank to pay for the goods. She needs to get to the city so she orders an autonomous driving taxi, which picks her up and drops her off at the edge of her neighborhood (cars are not allowed into most of the city because public transportation has been automated and moved underground and all roads have been turned into parks). This is just a glimpse into a future that is mostly unimaginable to us. Proptech will make sure that body, building, and business are digitized and offer an array of connected benefits, which we barely begun to understand.

Chapter 6

Tencent

Tencent plays a vital part in Chinese people's lives, both inside China and overseas. About 1.2 billion people use WeChat worldwide, 1 billion of which are Chinese. According to a survey of more than 1 million Chinese people, 98% of the Internet users have a WeChat account. Even among those who do not have a WeChat account, (many who are born after 2005), most of them have a QQ account, which is another communication app developed by Tencent.

This is the impact of Tencent. It is like Facebook in the US, but with more popularity in one single country. Alibaba commands the heights in shopping and payments. Baidu dominates as a search engine. However, Tencent rules the waves as "unintentional" data, i.e. data that is chat and does not involve merchandise receipts.

Among these three, Tencent has the most ambitious plan for proptech and smart cities. It has established a complete and thorough proptech development structure based on the customers it has on WeChat. This is an example of a super app offering an entrée into vast new industries through unintentional data.

From Figure 6.1, we get a glimpse at what Tencent's plan are. Its services mainly focus on government, companies, and public.[1] For the government, it provides digital government and administrative

---

[1]See Tencent's solutions about future city at https://cloud.tencent.com/solution/ wisdom-city-details.

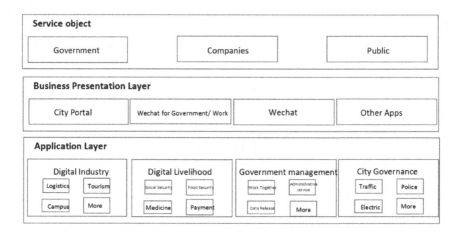

Figure 6.1.   Tencent's smart city structure.

service to improve the efficiency of governance. For companies, it offers a large menu of services — smart campus, intelligent logistics, automated factories. It also provides traffic monitoring to the public. These applications rely on several methods to implement, such as city portal, WeChat, and WeChat for Work/Government.

6.1.   Technologies[2]

Tencent's White Paper for proptech development brings out several key technologies that are essential to the technology. We note that most of these technologies are based on 5G.

6.1.1.   *Artificial intelligence*

As an important productivity supplement, algorithms related to artificial intelligence (AI) can greatly improve the supply efficiency of urban medical care, education, and other related resources. Take medicine as an example. From assisted virus analysis and drug development to intelligent identification of medical images and public signs, AI technology has significantly speeded up medical work.

---

[2]Tencent's WeCity 2.0 White Paper brings out several key technologies. https://cloud.tencent.com/developer/article/1701770.

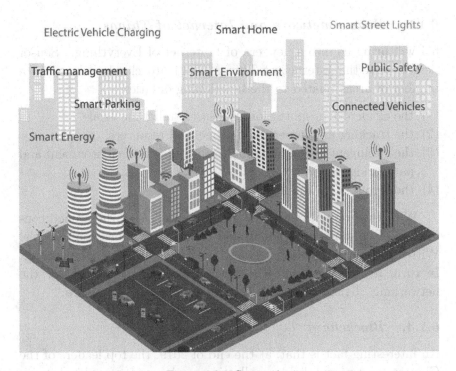

Figure 6.2. Smart city.

Besides medical treatment, educational resources are also one of the most concerned and scarce resources in cities. AI is helpful to promote the popularization and individuation of education.

6.1.2. *Cloud computing*

Cloud connectivity can help us build a more resilient city. With computing power in the cloud and greater flexibility, a large number of daily activities can break through the limitations of urban physical space and run online. For example, during the epidemic period, typical applications such as home office, online education, and online entertainment greatly enhanced the public's ability to enjoy urban public services in a special period. The virtually untapped capacity provided by cloud computing will provide the ground floor support for the implementation of various applications in the future city as well as providing security at home and abroad.

6.1.3. *Sensor network and Internet of Things*

5G will bring us into a new era of "Internet of Everything." Sensor devices and the Internet of Things (IoT) are closely related to a number of areas related to the functioning of cities:

(1) the efficient transportation of disaster relief materials,
(2) the tracking and supervision of medical resources,
(3) the intelligent perception monitoring of medical environment and patient signs, and
(4) the layout of an intelligent home.

With the gradual reduction of application costs, the unified connection of all kinds of differentiated terminals will become possible. With this comes a sensor network (provided by edge compacting). In turn, IoT may become the core supporting technology for the networking, digitization, and AI of smart cities in the future.

6.1.4. *Blockchain*

An interesting fact is that, at the end of 2019, the top leaders of the Chinese government held a collective study session on blockchain. The resulting working paper clearly pointed out that blockchain should be regarded as a breakthrough point for independent innovation of core technology. The non-tampering and multiparty participation feature of blockchain technology is an important tool to improve social governance. Blockchain has natural advantages in the field of people's livelihood and public services. In the future, it will gradually reveal its application value in a number of areas, which are part of life in the city:

(1) Education: Transparency and the non-tampering of data are fully applicable to student credit management, academic employment, qualification certification, industry–university cooperation, etc.[3]
(2) Employment: Blockchain can help establish a distributed platform to support management services such as registration, task

---

[3]http://www.woshipm.com/blockchain/1672640.html.

distribution and collection, task submission, and settlement of social laborers.[4]

(3) Identification: Blockchain functions can simplify the operation of security authentication of different subject identities. This is the foundational idea of provenance.

(4) Elderly care: The blockchain can store individual high-continuity and complete health data, which contains the medical data of each person. In addition to basic data, it can also efficiently and accurately record all information about medication records, doctor's diagnosis, health testing and maintenance services. The comprehensive historical data related to healthcare personnel, locations, and events is valuable for precise physical therapy and nursing aid.[5]

(5) Targeted poverty alleviation: The insurance mechanism is used to link the social poverty alleviation forces. The donations of donors, public welfare organizations, and poor families are linked together on the chain, thus forming a transparent and efficient blockchain poverty alleviation model.[6]

(6) Medical and healthcare: Medical and health data can be shared across the network in a safer and faster way, which will better facilitate the development of smart medical care.[7]

(7) Commodity anti-counterfeiting: With the help of blockchain technology, information on the farm to market process can be integrated and written into the blockchain to trace the following processes: [8]

   (i) raw material inventory process,
  (ii) production process,
 (iii) finished commodity distribution process, and
 (iv) marketing.

---

[4]https://www.sohu.com/a/350423369_112531.
[5]http://www.360doc.com/content/19/1027/14/497185_869350092.shtml.
[6]http://bgimg.ce.cn/xwzx/gnsz/gdxw/202004/08/t20200408_34639684.shtml.
[7]https://www.cn-healthcare.com/article/20191122/content-526568.html.
[8]https://zhuanlan.zhihu.com/p/91539846.

(8) Food and drug safety: Blockchain technology has created a new era of traceability in the food supply chain, which is conducive not only in ensuring and improving food safety conditions but also improving the efficiency of traceability and reducing corporate costs.

(9) Public welfare: Blockchain can distribute information about charitable projects on various nodes on the Internet. It is extremely difficult to tamper with the data of all nodes on the entire network. This prevents a certain organization or individual from manipulating a charity project for their own benefit.

According to predictions by IDC, Statista, and other domestic and foreign authorities, the investment in 5G, sensors, IDC data center, and other ICT infrastructure directly related to smart cities will have a compound growth rate of 20%–35% in the next three years. Middle and downstream industries, such as cloud computing, Augmented Reality (AR) and Virtual Reality (VR) and IoT, will grow at a compound rate of more than 35% over the next three years. Based on this, the entire market space will grow about 30% in the next two years. Each smart city pilot project will invest about 600 million yuan on average.

6.2. Tencent's WeCity Solutions

In 2019, Tencent announced WeCity 1.0 Project,[9] which is a concept of smart city construction in the future. By promoting this project, the company hopes to build up a comprehensive smart solution for digital government affairs, urban management, urban decision-making, and industrial interconnection. In December 2020, WeCity 2.0 was announced by Tencent as the next most significant step of its proptech development. WeCity 1.0 mainly expresses Tencent's concepts and plans about the future of cities. Figures 6.3 and 6.4 explain Tencent's plans.

---

[9]http://www.geekpark.net/tags/%E8%85%BE%E8%AE%AFWeCity.

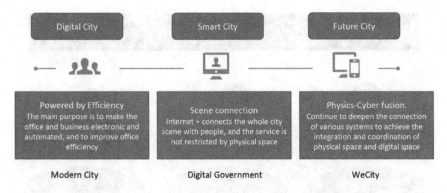

Figure 6.3. Tencent's concept of Three Phases of City.

Tencent has three phases for city development. The first is "digital city," which concentrates on local efficiency, such as smart factories, smart logistics, and robotics. However, it still lacks the ability to connect everything together. Let us remember we are in the very early stages.

The second step is "smart city." It connects the whole city scene with people using IoT. Examples of this are the massive traffic control system in cities and the smart citizen card system.

As to the third step, which is what Tencent is now focusing on, is WeCity. It aims to deepen the connection between people and cities, constructing an integral system using physical space and digital space. Figure 6.4 provides an illustration of the characteristics of WeCity. It has three major characteristics: Neural Network Intelligence, Central Nervous System, and Truly Inclusive. We explain all of these below.

From Figure 6.4, we can clearly see the structure of WeCity. The row on top, which includes the basic services, has four aspects: Digital Government, City Management, City Decision, and Industry Connection.

The middle platform has specific apps, data collection and management, as well as algorithm development.

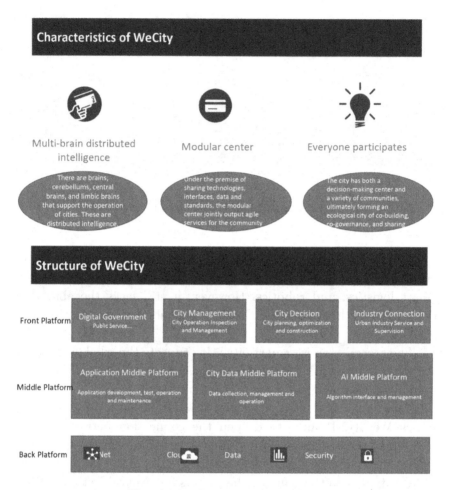

Figure 6.4.   Structure of smart city.

The bottom layer includes cloud, data storage, and security. The middle layer connects the storage and cloud services to the smart city services.

WeCity 2.0 is now under construction.[10] Its aim is to offer specific solutions. It is these solutions which gets us closer to the real essence

---

[10]Tencent's WeCity 2.0 White Paper. https://cloud.tencent.com/developer/article/1701770.

of proptech. For example,

(1) Improving service
(2) Supervision
(3) Decision
(4) Management ability, and
(5) Industrial ability.

We discuss these five proptech issues below. As Tencent has taken tremendous care and thought into this, the closer startups are to this configuration, the higher are the chances of success.

(1) **Improving service**

"City code" promotes the integration of government services and commercial operations.

Through "city code," Tencent's block chain system achieves the following:

(i) One Person, One Code: Improves the convenience of identity verification, access control, epidemic prevention, commercial consumption, and other application fields by combining entry and identification information.
(ii) One Enterprise, One Code: Promotes the implementation of national supervision and creditworthiness in urban economic development and governance.
(iii) One Thing, One Code greatly improves the efficiency of urban management, IoT rollout, as well as community governance.
(iv) Service on code: Through one code, Tencent can implement management and service integration.

On the one hand, based on entity identification, it can effectively solve ordered authentication and random authentication. On the other hand, it provides online and offline connection means for:

(a) Urban public emergency linkage and safety scheduling. Through "One Person, One Code," the government can have a clear view of the emergency gathering places for people, so that it can dispatch emergency services accordingly.

(b) Behavioral track tracing. Through city codes, the government can trace one person's path everyday, e.g. which bus and train he or she took. This would help epidemic prevention, ease congestion, and reduce crime.

(c) Market supervision. Through "One Thing, One Code," information commodity raw material circulation, production, and marketing processes are integrated.

In the field of city management and decision-making, "city code" can efficiently combine governance together into a unified platform. In the field of urban commercial operation, "city code" covers public transport, aggregation pay, hotel, medical services, education, and training business scenarios. It can boost the sustainable development of the urban economy.

(2) Supervision[11]

Supervision is an important element to guarantee the sustainable development of a city's economy. WeCity2.0's ability to upgrade supervision is mainly based on Tencent's big data and AI technology.

The whole regulatory system of WeCity2.0 is built on a nationwide supervision of big data and the governance of that data. This is derived from Tencent's experience from battling hackers in the past 20 years. It integrates social and government data and has real-time information flows. On top of it is the supervision AI system, which provides a flexible combination of various advanced tools and algorithm models created by hundreds of data scientists. In addition, it provides various security algorithms and decision engines, as well as security APIs based on the public cloud. These have a 95% accuracy in tracking hackers. This layer has a regulatory application layer jointly built by Tencent and ecosystem partners.

Small WeChat programs will help create a new pattern of universal co-supervision. Based on fusion engine WeCity2.0 support,

---

[11] *Ibid.*

the public can use a simple program to: (i) complete commodity inspection, (ii) inspect goods efficiently, (iii) do market research, (iv) manage complaints, and (v) complete reports. Combined with geographical position, regulatory issues can be flagged and other outside information can be seen immediately. The system will accurately flag regulatory information according to user characteristics.

(3) Improving decision-making ability

In terms of insight, WeCity2.0 fully combines IoT, big data, and AI technologies to continuously improve the level of application. With the continuous improvement of visual range and accuracy of urban perception, WeCity2.0 is able to perceive micro-events that are difficult to understand. Simply put, it can explore the connections and influences among hundreds of events occurring simultaneously. When the dots are connected, similar situations and expected outcomes can be found through similar algorithms.

In terms of decision-making power, WeCity2.0 can deepen and optimize the important role of intelligent analysis in decision-making. When an event occurs, the system will automatically correlate all decision elements within the default range and automatically analyze the influence range and potential harm from an event. It then generates different decision schemes and tasking according to the knowledge map. Pre-programmed plans and a rule engine offer additional help, thus rapidly improving the decision-making.

(4) Improving governance[12]

WeCity2.0's future community solutions effectively connect owners, properties, streets, and towns. They combine the applications of "city code" to integrate online and offline community services and reach users efficiently. These apps include quick repair service, property management, community announcements, epidemic prevention station, and consulting advice.

---

[12] *Ibid.*

Furthermore, in WeCity2.0, public abilities such as IoT perception and AI are widely used. For example, community disputes can be resolved through unified city codes and connected to micro-courts and micro-mediation platforms. This kind of governance can reach the masses in an efficient and convenient way.

Tencent Cloud Future Community provides multi-scene and full-dimensional capabilities and services by connecting the roles of government, property, partners, and businesses, forming a new intelligent community ecology.

(5) **Improving industrial ability**[13]

"Future Park" to create a new paradigm of integration between industry and city. In recent years, China has had problems with the integration of industry and city. For example, "there is industry but no urban," "there is urban but no industry" or "urban and industry are on top of each other." Tencent has successfully built a "future park" solution (WePark). It proposed a "new park" — "new industry" — "new towns" development paradigm. There is radical experimentation going on with regard to creating an environment where work and home can be seamlessly integrated. Why should humans spend 1–3 hours each day in uncomfortable and/or confined transit to work?

6.3.   WeCity Applications

6.3.1.   *Guiyang future city*

In the process of urban digital development, Tencent is developing Guiyang. This is located in central China, south of Chongqing. In June of 2020, Tencent launched "Digital Intelligence Guiyang Future City" Phase 1. This is a collection, processing, and algorithm creation for municipal government data, expanding urban services, urban governance, and other applications. It possesses a $1 + 1 + 1 + 8$ main structure.

---

[13] *Ibid.*

One city entrance: Digital intelligence Guiyang small program;

One urban operation center: Urban Block Data Center;

One city center: Block data integrated service platform (application center, data center, AI center, digital twin center);

Nine smart applications: Smart market supervision, digital urban spatial database (natural planning), public security smart livelihood government affairs service system, smart municipal (IoT), private economy comprehensive service platform, Smart education comprehensive platform, Smart Travel Guiyang management service platform, Guiyang Digital Museum, and Digital Tax.

6.3.2. *Jiangmen talent island: New model of WeCity's city of the future*

To expedite the construction of Guangdong–Hong Kong–Macao Greater Bay Area, Jiangmen City has cooperated with Tencent to create WeCity's "City of the Future." It aims to build a "2 + 2 + 2" "wisdom city" innovation mode, which includes two centers, two platforms, and two applications. It first starts with the infrastructure layer, which consists of a data center and operations center. As the hardware base for Talent Island, Jiangmen Talent Island International Talent Data Center has adopted a Tencent T-Block data system including deployment, security, reliability, and green efficiency. With 99.9% reliability in the data center (annual average failure time less than 1.6 hours), it provides 5,000 CPU resources and 500 TB storage resources of cloud computing service ability. It carries the IoT platform named "wisdom literature brigade," as well as intelligent community, intelligent transportation, education, and wisdom city operation monitoring (Figure 6.5).

The next platform is the support layer. This consists of an "urban platform" and IoT platform. The urban platform adopts the technology Tencent independently researched and developed. Its big data processing capacity once broke the record of Computing Olympics. In the Jiangmen Talent Island project, it cleaned and analyzed the IoT data and application data to provide reliable data support for urban decision-making. The IoT platform gathers the

Figure 6.5.   Jiangmen Talent Island.

data collected by sensors and adds attributes such as time. After the data is cleaned and processed by the data center, it provides indicators of the operation monitoring system as well as daily monitoring and management for transportation, municipal administration, city appearance, community, environmental protection, and security for Talent Island.

Third, there is the intelligent application layer. This is the urban integrated service platform and urban operation monitoring platform. WeChat's program is a comprehensive urban service application on the mobile phone network. In turn, this connects commercial, community, education, medical, government, and other services on the island to each person's mobile phone. This provides both residents and visitors with comprehensive services.

Based on the above framework, the WeCity's City of the Future in Jiangmen hopes to form a full closed-loop support for intelligent cultural, travel, education, medical treatment, transportation, architecture, and community within the island. This is the foundation — the tilled and fertilized soil — for the harvest of proptech.

6.3.3. *Zhengzhou fuze gate community: Blockchain + community*[14]

"Sloppy management and helpless owners" has always been the pain point of community property management. The management of property is not transparent. Therefore, owners cannot participate in decision-making. The maintenance fund of houses is hard to use. To solve this problem, Tencent Cloud Future Community partnered with WeBank to develop a voting system for all owners and a funding decision system for owners' representatives. This is based on the FISCO BCOS platform. FISCO BCOS is the underlying technology for open-source blockchain developed by the Open Source Working Group of the financial Blockchain Cooperation Alliance.

The first goal is to lower the threshold for voting. The blockchain-based voting system actually replaced the paper voting method of the original owners' assembly. If there is no online voting to accommodate the owners' assembly, the owners need to apply to the owners' committee first, and then go to the street authority after a vote. The authorities will send a commissioner to supervise the process. The owners who participate in the voting need to provide real estate proof to obtain voting rights. In the owner's voting system based on blockchain, all parties are connected. The owners need to use facial recognition and compare the public security information to determine identity. This would decide the voting weight; then the owner can vote. During the voting process, all voting information of the business will be linked up and synchronized to each node. The intelligent contract on the chain will specify the execution conditions

---

[14]https://www.sohu.com/a/326497399_99902056.

such as time, minimum turnout rate, passing rate, etc. After the voting, results will be automatically calculated and publicized to all the owners. All decisions are directly transmitted to government departments, which can serve as the basis for government affairs.

The second purpose is to jointly manage funds. The funding and spending decision system for the residential committee is a bit like the custodian mechanism of traditional finance, which solves the pain point that the supervisor cannot manage his own money. This system uses the name of the property company to open an account in any cooperative bank, introduces the bank as the supervisor, and each property payment request needs to be approved by the industry committee (or voted by the owner) to prevent the funds from being misappropriated. The whole process of payment request, approval, and subsequent fund use is recorded on the blockchain, which can be seen by and approved by owners.

The change of property, account, and committee makeup will not affect the recording and tracing of information. At present, the funding decision system uses the structure of one community and one chain, which has been set up in the Fuze Gate Community of Zhengzhou, The chain includes banks, property companies, Tencent Future Community (a property system provider), and industry committees. In the future, arbitration and the Housing Authority are expected to be introduced. If businesses have disputes with property companies, they can directly initiate judicial arbitration. The voting system is ideal for "one chain per city" to leverage economies of scale. The feature is being agreed with several urban housing authorities and will be released in the future.

6.3.4.   *Taiyuan: Government + new community network*

As of mid-2020, the Tencent future community platform have been launched in 1,255 communities in Yingze District of Taiyuan city, covering a population of 600,000. The back-end connects community service, government affairs, epidemic prevention, and so on, forming the "Internet + Community" solution.

(1) The first is an integrated service that connects community and government. It covers 18 application scenarios of community services, including quick repair report, complaints, and suggestions; online rumor refuting; and electronic access codes. It also covers street applications such as community interaction, garbage classification, and smart voting, as well as COVID-19 maps, return registration, and application for old age cards.

(2) The second is to provide strong technical support and core application tools for the community platform. The future community platform will use cloud computing, big data, AI, and other technologies in order to:

   (i) connect property, residents, government, media, and community service providers,

   (ii) give play to its ability to connect all products of the community, and

   (iii) improve the service ability and efficiency of the community.

At the same time, it connects relevant data interfaces of government affairs and provides the core application tool for government management at the community level. A new communication mechanism between the government and the community will be established to improve the efficiency of government information, services and reduce the cost of social management in communities.

(3) Third, four modules are created that comprises a "Yingze mode," namely Waste Classification, Safe Community, Smart Contracts, and Community and Mutual Assistance. This would constantly enhance the management and service ability of Yingze district government.

Figure 6.6.   Smart community.

Shenzhen will be the first true smart city in the world — everything will be tokenized and digitalized (Figure 6.6). Here we will discuss another company located in Shenzhen, which also provides electronic devices for proptech.

Shenzhen ZNV manufactures many of the devices necessary to digitize physical assets. These include sensors, cameras, coders, and surveillance platforms for requirements like battery supply, utility output, environmental monitoring, and telecom equipment quality (Figure 6.7).

The equipment can be used in education, railroad, energy, finance, and civic activity. It can link multiple video networks. It works in crowd control, easing traffic congestion, and early wearing for emergencies. More than 100 million people travel during Chinese New Year. This technology can ease bottlenecks. Most important, this technology learns space–time integration among and between people, houses, objects, and networks. One node can monitor millions of people to anticipate emergencies, police activity, accident prevention, and debottlenecking.

Shenzhen ZNV Technology Co – Electronic Security Devices (1/4)

What do they do	Who is their boss	New Technology	How do they make money
Electronic Security Devices:	• Own company	**IoT Products**	• Shenzhen ZNV Technology serves:

• Shenzhen ZNV Technology Co., Ltd. produces electronic security devices. The Company offers cameras, sensors, coders, decoders, supervision modules, surveillance platform hardware, and related software products.		1. **ZNV IMP1500** – Intelligent micro-station power supply specialised for outdoor, reduced construction costs by 80% and equipment costs by 50% by intelligently monitoring power status and battery capacity
		
		2. **ZNV IG2000 V3** – Smart gateway for dynamic environment monitoring of communication for telecom operators
			• Telecom,
			   • Government,
			   • Public security,
			   • Railway,
			   • Military,
			   • Environment,
			   • Energy,
			   • Finance, and
			   • Education sectors
			by supplying electronic security devices to them.

Source: http://www.znv.com.cn/

Shenzhen ZNV Technology Co – Electronic Security Devices (2/4)

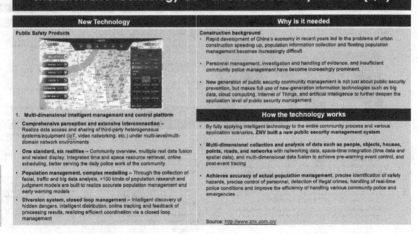

Figure 6.7.   Shenzhen technology security devices.
Source: Schulte Research.

Shenzhen ZNV Technology Co – Electronic Security Devices (3/4)

New Technology	Why is it needed
Public Safety Products	**Urban population flow management**

2. Big Data Facial Recognition System

- **Powerful platform access and integration capabilities** – Fully supports docking with third-party platforms, access and standardized processing of devices such as HD cameras and face capture machines from various manufacturers, and can be deeply integrated with video platforms.
- **First-class recognition algorithm** – Cooperate with first-class algorithm manufacturers to support multi-feature (gender, age, glasses, mask, etc.) and multi-scene (variable illumination, multi-angle, occlusion, blur, etc.) recognition and feature extraction of human faces through deep learning technology.
- **Face recognition rate up to 99%** – securing the safety of the community (analysis of strangers, elderly, children out alone, suspicious public behaviour)
- **Big data technology application** – System has the ability to search for data and retrieve billions of data in seconds, and supports online expansion of the system, guaranteeing reliability

- Population flow has increased rapidly and population composition has become increasingly complex, insecurity factors have also increased.
- Cities in China have completed the coverage of HD video, using AI to improve the use efficiency and application value of massive surveillance video
- Achieving predictive intelligent prevention, timely disposal during an event, traceability of the process post event to benefit the people are important requirements for the construction of a prevention and control system for public safety

How the technology works

- **Real-time acquisition:** detection and recognition based on real-time video stream or captured pictures, accurate capture and recognition of complex scenes, real-time display of time axis;
- **Face de-duplication:** multiple real-time pictures of the same person in the same scene, presenting an optimal feature picture;
- **Real-time deployment and control:** a single-node list of millions of key personnel, multiple deployment and control methods, and second-level alarms;
- **Search face by face:** single image and multi-image combined search, feature compound search, tens of billions of data, second-level search
- **Feature retrieval:** second-level retrieval of any combination of facial features (age, gender, glasses, mask, etc.)
- **Combination of personal identification:** real-time capture of portrait pictures and identification information check and comparison, display other detailed information
- **Peer analysis:** peer analysis and detailed information presentation of the target person (geographical location information, image information)
- **Wandering analysis:** quickly check the residence time and wandering frequency of the target person in a certain area
- **Trajectory route:** key personnel deployed and controlled, according to the deployment control alarm time, presents the trajectory route
- **Data statistics:** multi-dimensional data statistics and multi-type report presentation: people flow statistics, control alarm statistics, related case event statistics, etc.

Source: http://www.znv.com.cn/

Shenzhen ZNV Technology Co – Electronic Security Devices (4/4)

New Technology	Why is it needed
Public Safety Products	**Public security interrogation improvement**

3. Emotion Recognition and Intelligent Interrogation System

- **Facilitates positive interrogation** – The AI utilizes a non-confrontational dialogue served to placate the dignity of the interrogated; concurrently, the system supports multi-dimensional restoration of the interrogation scene, ensuring fairness and transparency of the interrogation result.
- **Iterative evaluation system** – Improve the level of intelligence and digitization of interrogation by combining research results from multiple instances and fields to alter the original interrogation mode,
- **Multi-approach** – provides a series of functions such as electronic interrogation, smart digital interrogation, intelligent analysis, etc.

- How to combine the latest artificial intelligence technology, information technology, big data technology, etc., to realize the transition from ordinary interrogation to electronic interrogation, and even smart digital interrogation is a top priority
- Demand is derived from how to reduce the burden on interrogators and improve interrogation efficiency and accuracy, how to ensure productive and civilized interrogation questions

Application(s)
- Public security, judicial organs, national security and other powerful national agencies interrogation sites
- Border inspections, customs, airport/railway security inspections and other places that require in-depth identification of quarantined persons

How the technology works

- **Combines research results in multiple fields** of artificial intelligence and is applied to public security interrogations and other scenarios.
- **Integrates cutting-edge psychology, biophysiology, image recognition technology, and machine learning technology** to detect the physiological indicators, micro expressions, micro movements and skin resistance of the interrogated person when answering questions
- **Collected data are analysed through an expert intelligent evaluation system** to then determine the emotional abnormality of the interrogated person, whether he or she is lying, the level of truthful information behind the lie, and finally lock the direction of the case for the interrogator and narrow the scope of hypothesis.
- **Provides a scientific and important reference basis** for the final judgment of whether the suspect has committed a crime.

Source: http://www.znv.com.cn/

Figure 6.7.   (*Continued*)

6.4.   Conclusion

As this book goes to press, we see an Ant Group decimated by a government which saw its authority — and the fabric of the Five Year Plan — challenged at the core. It is hard to know what is going on with Ant, but the general consensus is that Alibaba and its subsidiaries are, for the time being, in the regulatory doghouse. It is being investigated for antitrust violations and predatory lending. Much of Ant will need to be dismantled. However, this does not take away from a superbly built infrastructure. We think Ding Talk is one of the most undervalued of the many services that Alibaba has going for it. SME lending is a top priority for the government, and Ding Talk is the nerve center for tens of millions of SMEs.

The company that most impressed us in this book is Tencent. No company is doing more to experiment, innovate, and invest in smart cities and the digitization of all parts of the Chinese economy than Tencent. The past few years belonged to Alibaba. The next few years belongs to Tencent. It is turning Shenzhen into a showcase city of the future.

Ping An is also one to watch. It will use a new digitized infrastructure to define healthcare globally. It is by far the most digitally advanced healthcare company globally. Peter Ma has relentless energy, passion, and hunger for innovative technologies and pays up front for it. He has gone from strength to strength. Watch this space.

Section 3

The Potential

In the previous two sections, we have laid the foundation of the technologies China has developed to get to the next level. 5G connects with robotics, sensors, and edge technology to integrate data — from anywhere in the country and from any building. Artificial intelligence (AI) processes the data and creates new industries via the private sector super apps owned by Ping An, Tencent, and Alibaba. Of these three, Tencent is in the lead in proptech. These super apps are only now moving into the world of smart cities, homes, buildings, and logistics. They are collecting hundreds of millions of digitized data sets, which correspond to the movement of people, places, and things, bringing them to life and creating new businesses. These data sets can be tokenized and can run on a new set of rails via BSN. In Section 3, we will focus on both the up and coming giants like JD as well as smaller companies which are moving ahead quickly to solve new and unique problems in the area of proptech.

Some of these smaller companies will grow to be new household names. Some will fail and some will be acquired by the Big Three. In the meantime, we see companies like JD.com, Yitu, Bytedance, Huawei, and Baidu getting involved. The larger companies may acquire the smaller ones to gain access to their technology but most likely their teams, or they may shelve the technology to prevent competition. For example, Ping An has been cooperating with — and investing in — four companies: Xkool, Hongwa, Qizhi, and PAL MAP, to further participate in each of these respective markets (Figure 7.1). Peter Ma has a relentless appetite for new technologies... and is willing to eagerly pay for it.

Figure 7.1.   Ping An city digitization services.

In this section, we divide the smaller companies into three categories according to their function: the development; deployment; and construction of office, home, and warehouse spaces. We have gotten an inside look into their strategy and technology through conversations with the CEOs of these companies.

In addition, we highlight some medium-sized firms that are more diversified but are moving into proptech. They are unicorns in their own right already. However, some of them want to expand their product line and are using existing technology to expand into the untapped area of proptech. These include YITU, JD, and Shenzhen ZNV. Among them, for example, YITU has extraordinary capabilities in the area of R&D in chips and AI, so they are integrating their own chip technology and algorithms into smart city projects. In addition, JD has become a giant in logistics and e-commerce. It has a rich and diverse set of data which it owns and can harvest for wide-ranging applications in proptech.

Chapter 7

Established Challengers

7.1. YITU

7.1.1. *YITU — A company devoted to public welfare*

In early 2020, a burgeoning disaster made its appearance in the form of COVID-19. The potency of this new threat was initially underrated. As time went by, the world recognized the severity of this nightmare. Millions of people were killed by the virus, and the world's economy stagnated as a result.

China serves as an example for how to deal with this epidemic. When the virus began to spread at an alarming rate in February 2020, the Chinese government implemented a series of swift and immediate measures to prevent its spread and attempted to diagnose the disease as soon as possible. The entire country was on a severe and unrelenting lockdown for 55 days. In the process, some Chinese companies reformulated their technology to help treat patients and curtail the pandemic. YITU Tech is one such company. In July 2020, YITU developed an epidemic prevention system comprising breakthroughs in the following technologies:

- New coronary pneumonia diagnosis system via a new form of intelligent CT scan.
- New coronary pneumonia prevention digital doctor — Xiaoyi.
- Regional infectious disease intelligent prevention and control solutions.

The new CT diagnosis system is the first artificial intelligence (AI) imaging product for intelligent assessment of new coronavirus pneumonia in the medical industry. AI conducts a quantitative analysis of the entire human lung to provide clinical experts with CT imaging of new coronavirus lesions. It can complete this analysis in 2–3 seconds, a far cry from traditional radiology, which can take up to 15 minutes.

To help quickly obtain a comprehensive knowledge of the epidemic, and conduct a timely self-health assessment, YITU developed the pneumonia specialist doctor — Xiaoyi. The tool helped outpatients automatically order imaging examinations or laboratory tests based on their chief complaints. Thus, outpatients could get examined or tested before they went to see the doctor, fueling access to medical institutions by reducing medical wait time, especially for those in key epidemic areas. The system has since been used in more than 200 medical institutions, Internet medical platforms, and government agencies worldwide.

7.1.2. *Management team*

The epidemic revealed a powerful side of YITU — smart medication and hospital technology. However, its business and ambition extends far beyond this. As an AI company, fundamental research in AI remains its chief focus. Learning from YITU's CEO, we dive deeper into its tech-driven foundations.

Dr. Zhu Long received a Ph.D. in Statistics from UCLA in 2008, under the tutelage of Professor Alan Yuille, the founder of Computer Vision (IEEE Fellow and Master of Physics), to learn how to understand and portray the world. From 2008 to 2010, he worked as a postdoctoral researcher in the AI Laboratory of MIT. From 2010 to 2012, he worked as a researcher at the Courant Institute of Mathematics at NYU. When working with Prof. Yann LeCun, who laid the foundation for neural networks, he led the NYU team to win the International Computer Vision algorithm competition.

His team also includes Lin Chenxi, senior expert and former technical director of Alibaba Cloud. From 2008 to 2012, he organized and led a team of more than 100 outstanding engineers

Dr. Zhu Long
Source: Baidu

and built the largest distributed cloud computing operating system with independent intellectual property rights in China — Feitian Technologies.

Dr. Zhu Long is a world-renowned AI scientist. In 2012, he founded YITU Technology in China. With a team including several prominent scientists from MIT, Oxford, Cambridge, and Chicago, YITU's R&D capabilities are evident.

7.1.3. *YITU's development process*

Founded in 2012, YITU focused mainly on AI technology facial recognition. In 2015, YITU had already cooperated with China Merchant Bank to promote its facial recognition technology to 1,500 branches. In 2015, it also cooperated with Alibaba Cloud to build a big data platform to help Guizhou traffic police in real time.

In 2016, YITU further collaborated with China Merchant Bank to launch the first no-card ATM in China. Furthermore, the intelligent CT diagnosis system was invented by YITU and put to use in several hospitals in China.

From 2018, YITU launched an audio recognition platform and won several awards pertaining to AI technology, including Face Recognition Vendor Test (FRVT), Face Recognition Prize Challenge (FRPC), and the globally prestigious Super Artificial Intelligence Leader (SAIL).

In 2019, YITU participated in constructing Shanghai's AI Innovation Center and accelerated industry innovation and development. It was also rated by MIT as part of "the Top 50 smartest companies" in the world. Collaborating with China UnionPay, YITU successfully managed to apply face recognition in payment processing.

From 2020, it began preparing for its IPO. The main challenge was profit. The company faced nearly CNY 7 billion worth of losses in the last three years, primarily due to its massive R&D investment. YITU Technology has consistently argued that the company is in the startup phase, and extensive resources are used for research, innovation, and market development. It should be expected that, in the next few years, the company may continue to lose money. However, we think its investment has already shown significant results.

In this listing, YITU Technology plans to raise CNY 7.5 billion, and 70% of the raised funds (approximately CNY 5 billion) will be used for project research and development. These include a new generation of AI Intellectual Property (IP) and high-performance System-on-Chip (SoC) projects, a visual inference-based edge computing system, a new generation of AI computing system, a high-end visual intelligent computing system, and a new-generation speech semantic capability platform.

7.1.4. *YITU's products*

7.1.4.1. *AI solutions*

(1) Intelligent public service solutions

(i) Urban visual center solution

Facing the business needs of city managers at different levels, YITU provides high-performance and precision algorithm platforms to solve problems in urban traffic dispatch, emergency command, and residential areas (Figure 7.2). Functional

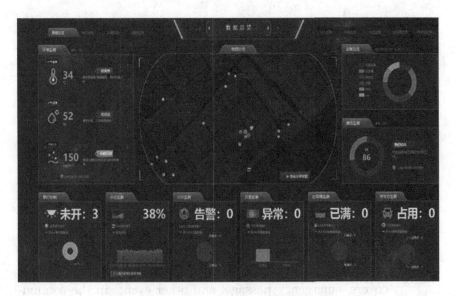

Figure 7.2.   YITU city management platform.

applications in different scenarios such as security and public facilities management include:

(a) Urban vision central platform: Integrating computer vision technologies such as object detection, object recognition, and pedestrian recognition with voiceprint recognition, speech recognition, and natural language processing to automatically aggregate and analyze information.

(b) Urban management scenario application: Through the urban visual hub platform, YITU improves traffic management, emergency command, residential area protection, and public facility management.

(ii) Smart community solution

(a) Personnel access management: Tracks the registration and passage of owners, visitors, etc., and automatically understand the relationship between visitors and owners.

(b) Vehicle management: Monitoring vehicle license plates, non-motor vehicle owner recognition, etc., and fully track all vehicles entering and leaving the community.

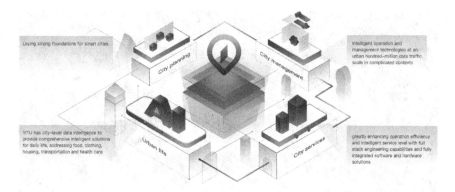

Figure 7.3.   Yitu's smart city matrix.

(c) Event management: Using smart sensing equipment to automatically identify high-altitude throwing, loss of manhole covers, emergency passage, and other events in the community, reminding relevant personnel to deal with them in a timely manner.

(2) Intelligent business solutions

(i) General Personnel Access Control (PAC)

(a) Employee attendance management: Indoors and outdoors facial recognition, preventing employees or non-registered personnel from entering the office without permission, and protecting company property and information security.

(b) Visitor reception management: Establish a self-service front desk system for self-registration and VIP customer pre-registration, to improve traffic efficiency and enhance visitor experience.

(c) Parking lot management: Unified identification of people and vehicles to prevent car theft and fraud.

(d) Meeting management: Automatically login to register meetings through the identification terminal, improving efficiency of meeting recordings through intelligent voice hardware.

(e) Building epidemic prevention management: Utilizing the integration of computer vision and sensor technology, the

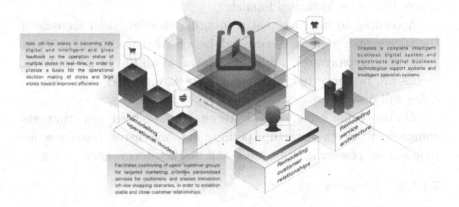

Figure 7.4. Yitu's retail matrix.

identity and temperature information of people entering and leaving the building are automatically correlated.

(ii) "One face travels the city" solution

    (a) Traffic Facial Recognition: Recognition of faces on public transportation such as subways, buses, and MRTs in provincial capital cities and achieve a gate speed of 45 people/minute.

    (b) Secret-free payment: Meet financial security standards to allow for facial ID transactions.

Red Date, the co-founder of Blockchain Service Network (BSN), also focuses on city traffic. It relies on a traffic card to access different transportations. These traffic cards are linked by blockchain to then ensure that confidentiality and privacy is guaranteed.

7.1.5. *YITU's financial statistics and analysis*

7.1.5.1. *Profit*

According to the prospectus, as of June 30, 2020, YITU Technology has accumulated a loss of 7.2 billion yuan. In this regard, YITU Technology stated that the company's accumulated losses were mainly due to the book losses caused by the fair value of the preferred shares issued by historical financing.

According to international accounting standards, an increase in the fair value of preferred shares will be recorded as a company's loss. After the company goes public, it claims that all the issued preferred stocks will be converted into common stock, and the losses from fair value will disappear.

At the same time, YITU Technology pointed out that the company is in the startup period, and extensive resources are required for research, innovation, and market development.

7.1.5.2. *Investors*

Most of YITU's operating funds come from external financing. YITU Technology has gone through nine rounds of financing since its establishment.

YITU Technology's accumulated financing exceeded 2.567 billion CNY. Many well-known investment institutions including Zhen Fund, Hillhouse Capital, Yunfeng Fund, Sequoia Capital China, ICBC International, and SPDB International are all investors of YITU Technology.

We also noticed that YITU Technology's financing frequency has increased in recent years. In the initial stage of its establishment, YITU Technology carried out financing once every two years on average. Later it became once a year. This shows that YITU Technology has gradually increased its demand for funds in recent years.

7.1.5.3. *Wages*

From 2017 to June 2020, YITU's annual R&D expenses were 101 million yuan, 291 million yuan, 557 million yuan, and 381 million yuan, respectively, accounting for 146.94%, 95.77%, 91.69%, and 100.1% of the company's total revenue. The company's R&D expenses continue to expand, and the R&D expense ratio is basically consistent with the industry average.

Among them, the salary of R&D personnel accounts for a larger proportion of total R&D expenses. From 2017 to June 2020, the company's annual R&D staff's salary was 84 million yuan, 214 million yuan, 431 million yuan, and 250 million yuan, accounting for 83.09%, 73.34%, 65.53%, and 65.52%, respectively, of the total R&D expenses.

YITU Technology's sales expense ratio is higher than comparable companies. The prospectus shows that from 2017 to June 2020, YITU Technology's sales expense ratios were 79.66%, 92.81%, 58.31%, and 41.66%, which were compared with the average sales expense ratios of comparable companies in the industry, at 13.33%, 10.76%, 9.97 %, and 12.42%.

In this regard, YITU Technology said that the company's higher sales expense ratio is mainly due to the expansion of marketing staff. As of June 30, 2020, YITU Technology has 385 marketing personnel, second only to the number of R&D personnel.

From 2017 to June 2020, YITU Technology's annual net operating cash flow was −235 million, −677 million, −119 million, and −581 million, respectively. The company's liquidity is insufficient as well.

7.2. JD

7.2.1. *An overview of JD*

If you ask a Chinese citizen, "What apps do you use when you go shopping online?" Aside from Taobao, which is the sub-brand of Alibaba, most people's second answer will be JD.

JD also specializes in logistics in a way that few other companies in China do. In 2017, the firm established the department to provide solutions for supply chain management. This is vital to understanding just how central a role that JD could eventually play in the world of prop tech. The data it owns in all parts of the supply chain of everything that moves in China could be one of the most valuable assets of any company globally. It comprises both the intentioned merchandise data as well as the unintentioned movement of goods and people, both domestically and internationally. Again, it owns all of this data, so its capacity to digitize and tokenize most of the economic activity and place it on the new digital rails that is BSN is virtually limitless.

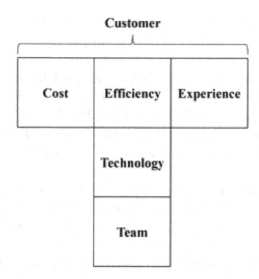

Figure 7.5.   JD business model.

In 2018, JD founded JD Property. The department supports the logistics operation by managing and developing facilities and hard property.

In 2018, JD Health was founded to build a comprehensive "Internet + healthcare" ecosystem. It focuses on virtual healthcare services from the convenience of your home (Figure 7.5).

(1) Technology is the key for maintaining their competitive advantage. Upgrading core technologies can effectively reduce cost, improve operating efficiency, and deliver best-in-class customer experience. In order to achieve sustainable growth, they have been heavily investing in technology and will continue to do so.

(2) Their technology strategy focuses on three key areas, namely:
    (i) AI
    (ii) Big data
    (iii) Cloud computing.

(3) By adopting a middle platform model and compartmentalizing the IT components and standard APIs in their IT architecture, they have greatly enhanced R&D efficiency, and accelerated business innovation. More importantly, this has enabled them

to offer more value-added technology services to their clients across a wide spectrum of industries. Moreover, the company is in a prime position to digitize and tokenize all of these following services, i.e. logistics, health, property, and warehouses. This could be even more valuable than anything either Tencent or Ping An has.[1]

7.2.2. *JD iCity*

7.2.2.1. *JD iCity: Introduction*

JD Intelligent Cities (iCity) focus on empowering smart cities with AI and big data. Marking a fresh start for the company's urban computing business, JD iCity is the company's intelligent city brand, which provides complete intelligent solutions for China's urban development. These solutions cover seven major areas, including: (1) planning, (2) transportation, (3) energy, (4) environmental protection, (5) urban credit, (6) public safety, and (7) e-government services.

Lying at the heart of JD iCity is its pioneering operating system for cities, which helps to solve the key challenges faced in intelligent urban development. This operating system aims to empower cities and their public services to go online and become highly digitized. At present, JD iCity has deployed its system in Beijing, Shanghai, Guangzhou, Nanjing, Chengdu, and Suqian as well as other cities.

7.2.2.2. *JD iCity Research*

JD iCity Research is a top research institute consisting of data service lab, AI lab, industry application institute, business model lab, technical industrialization department, and multiple branches in Beijing, Nanjing, Chengdu, and Guilin. Gathering hundreds of postgraduate and Ph.D. talents, it explores new patterns of building intelligent cities in China and leads the trend of developing intelligent cities in the world.

---

[1]www.JD.com.

JD iCity has been working closely with over 20 top universities and research institutes by resolving major research projects, offering collaborative courses, creating new subjects and degrees together, and jointly training graduate students. It pushes the application of AI and big data technologies on Industry–University–Research (IUR) integration in the field of urban computing, and trains a number of compound top talents for intelligent city industry.

As of now, JD iCity Research has published 24 articles in world's top journals and conferences, been granted over 30 invention patents, hosted and sponsored plenty of world-class major academic activities, and played an important role in many national conferences. It has been widely recognized in both academia and industry.

7.2.2.3.   *JD iCity's products*

(1) **Urban credit**

JD iCity has gathered JD's resources and advantages, along with data from the government, corporations, and the Internet, to develop AI algorithms to rate credit holders and forecast, correlate, and provide urban solution plans for individuals, businesses, and governments.

(2) **Intelligent transportation**

With deep fusion of multisource, spatio-temporal data and elaborate model analysis, JD iCity provides intelligent travel services for residents and optimized operational guidance for government and traffic control agencies.

(3) **Intelligent public security**

JD iCity uses big data and AI technology to predict crime rates across districts in a city and design appropriate inspection routes, predict fire and accident probability, troubleshoot hidden dangers, and decrease accident rates.

(4) **Intelligent energy**

Through data acquisition from energy distribution chains and application of techniques including multi-source heterogeneous data

Figure 7.6. JD iCity map.
Source: JD Corporate Report.

analysis, deep reinforcement learning, and data-driven optimization, productivity improvement and energy saving can be achieved. This leads to the building of a low-carbon, clean, safe, and efficient intelligent energy system.

(5) **Intelligent environment**

JD iCity constructs intelligent environment protection systems from aspects of data sensing, real-time monitoring, future prediction, history tracing, and dispatch optimization to effectively promote sustainable environment development.

7.2.2.4. *JD iCity's founder*

Dr. Yu Zheng is a Vice President of JD and the Chief Data Scientist of JD Digits. He also leads the Intelligent Cities Business Unit as the president and serves as the managing director of JD Intelligent Cities Research. His research interests include big data analytics, spatio-temporal data mining, machine learning, and AI.

Dr. Zheng Yu

Before joining JD Digits, he was a senior research manager at Microsoft Research. Zheng currently serves as the Editor-in-Chief of *ACM Transactions on Intelligent Systems and Technology* and a member of Editorial Advisory Board of *IEEE Spectrum*. He is also an Editorial Board Member of *GeoInformatica* and *IEEE Transactions on Big Data*, and the founding Secretary of SIGKDD China Chapter.

7.2.2.5. *JD iCity project: Nantong City*

With the strong technical support of JD iCity, Nantong (Jiangsu Province) established the country's first modernized command center for municipal governance in 2020, becoming an example of scientific government decision-making, precise municipal governance, and efficient public services. Zheng Yu elaborated on the four major construction highlights of the command center.

The first is urban operation and unified perception. In the construction of urban governance, through sensor-centered perception and human-centered perception, a unified perception of the rhythm and pulse of urban operation is realized.

The second is global convergence and secure sharing. The command center breaks data islands and gathers billions of data from 64 departments and 10 counties in Nantong City.

The third is data fusion and thematic integration. With the help of the city operating system, which is a solid foundation for smart cities, JD Digital has developed an overall situational map and 16 thematic maps. The traffic operation, public safety, and environmental pollution in Nantong are all presented on a large screen in real time.

The fourth is intelligent analysis and decision-making, and digging into the value of data. Nantong has many large chemical engineering industries. The command center has opened up the data of 18 business systems in 9 commissions and 3 chemical parks, effectively reducing blind spots in the supervision of hazardous chemicals.

7.2.3. Case study: Ming Yuan Cloud

The multifarious nature of innovative smart city systems such as JD will revolutionize the way property development is planned. It will, we believe, disrupt the real estate industry end to end. This will give JD the ability to track property data to unify the following areas:

(1) urban life,
(2) converge secured data sharing,
(3) monitor traffic,
(4) public safety, and
(5) environmental pollution.

This can all happen in real time and make strategic decisions led to its eventual rise in the Cloud market, more specifically, Software as a Service (SaaS).

Ming Yuan Cloud is one such example that gained prominence due to the multiplier effect that proptech has brought to the real estate industry. It offers enterprise-grade resource planning solutions and other related SaaS products (Figure 7.7). This pioneering software-based Chinese firm is the first proptech to list on the Hong Kong Stock Exchange. It captures the entire value chain of property development — from smart construction projects to cross-departmental collaboration to resource reuse optimization to property transaction and ultimately maintenance, all on the cloud. It has been a great performer as this book goes to print.

Figure 7.7.   Ming Yuan Cloud.

7.3.   Dahua

Zhejiang Dahua Technology Co., Ltd. (Dahua Technology) specializes in smart video-centric IoT (Figure 7.8). The firm focuses on city operations, commercial real estate, and individual consumers. It is currently being used in more than 180 countries. It is hoping to expand to robotics, video conferencing, and drones.

Fu Liquan, main founder and President of Dahua, obtained his Executive MBA in Zhejiang University. He is a member of the Digital City Professional Committee of the China Urban Science Research Association, an expert of the Expert Committee of the China Security Products Industry Association, and a communications member of the National Security Alarm System Standardization Technical Committee.

Dahua has mature solutions of proptech in several industries, such as Government, Building, Transportation, Retail, Banking & Finance, Infrastructure, and Warehousing & Logistics. We take three examples to illustrate how it uses IoT technology to make money.

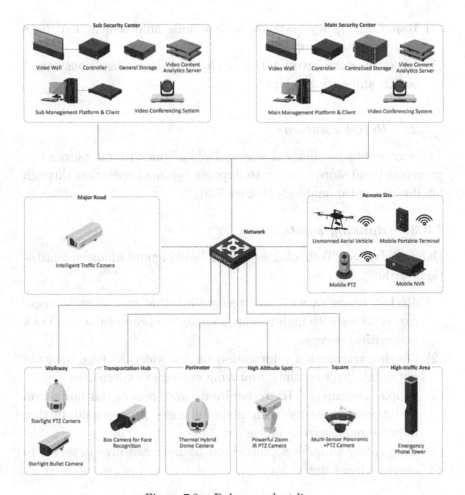

Figure 7.8. Dahua product lines.

7.3.1. *Safe city solutions*

(1) Smart threat detection via Face Recognition and License Plate Recognition (LPR).
(2) Better coverage and more details with ultra-zoom and panoramic view.
(3) Powerful target sensing with thermal detection.

(4) Rapid emergency response with mobile enforcement and integrated management.

(5) Effective crime investigation with the help of suspicious target search and path tracking.

7.3.2. *Retail solutions*

The way we buy is quickly changing. Dahua Smart Retain tackles loss prevention and store security to improve business operation through intelligence video analytics (Figure 7.9).

7.3.3. *Banking solutions*

Dahua Advanced Technologies secures banking and financial institutions with:

(1) 4K UHD camera with face recognition that can identify suspicious objects with high-resolution image to prevent potential risk and critical events.

(2) Overlay transaction information on the video footage to avoid potential disputes, thus improving customer experience.

(3) People counting, VIP recognition, and remote authorization to integrate security with main business process and further improve management efficiency.

(4) Data safety through sophisticated backup measures in server to secure critical data.[2]

7.3.4. *Case Study: Huawei*

At the end of this section, we would like to mention Huawei, while not a specialized proptech company, has also contributed significantly to this area.

Huawei, for better or worse, has become a symbol of China. Starting from a phone manufacturer (PBX), it has now become a

---

[2] *Ibid.*

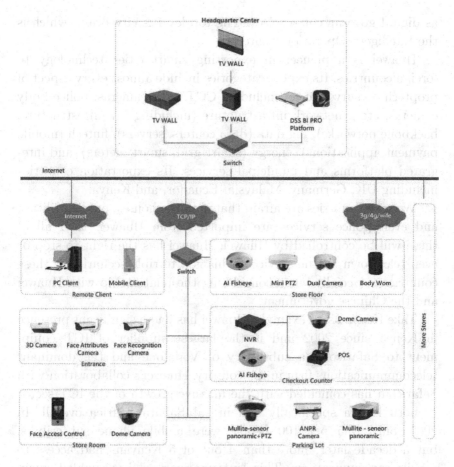

Figure 7.9. Huawei product line.

leading global provider of information communications technology (ICT) infrastructure and smart devices. It has more than 194,000 employees and operates in more than 170 countries.

Huawei has a vision for future cities named "Maslow Model for Smart City," inspired by Abraham Maslow's tiered psychology concept of human needs. The bottom level is fundamental infrastructures, i.e. Cloud, IoT, Data Center, etc. The second level is security protection. The third level is city service digitalization, such as digital government services. The top level is city brain, which is the Intelligent Operation Center.

Huawei is a pioneer in exporting smart cities technology to foreign countries. Its export categories include almost every aspect of proptech — surveillance (including CCTV, IP cameras, police body cameras, etc.), network infrastructure (including 5G infrastructure, backbone networks), big data (data centers, servers), fintech (mobile payment applications), energy (smart grid, smart meters), and integrated platforms and municipal services. Its exportation countries including UK, Germany, Malaysia, Ecuador, and Kenya.

Western countries are afraid that if all the houses, public utilities, and even police services are imported from Huawei, then all of these will be controlled by Huawei. Huawei has the right to stop or even tear down all the services. This is a terrible scenario for these countries, especially when considering the relationship with Huawei and the Chinese government.

Take Kenya as an example. Huawei has had a significant presence in Kenya since 2002 and is the largest supplier of ICT equipment to Safaricom, a subsidiary of Vodafone and the dominant telecommunications firm in the country. Huawei's collaboration with Safaricom has coincided with the massive growth of the ICT sector in both Kenya specifically and in sub-Saharan Africa overall. In 2005, only 13.5 per 100 people were mobile phone subscribers, but a decade later, more than 4 out of 5 Kenyans had access to mobile communications. This "informatization" has enabled smart city technologies to grow in a country many may not think of as a driver of technology innovation, and Chinese technology firms have been deeply involved in that evolution.[3]

A perfect example of the rapid deployment of information technologies in Kenya is the growth of mobile payments technology. In 2007, Safaricom established the M-PESA system, a mobile money

---

[3]Katherine Atha, "Research Report Prepared on Behalf of the U.S.-China Economic and Security Review Commission," January 2020.

system that allows people to transfer money or pay bills using their cell phones. By 2017, more than 58% of Kenyans used a mobile payment system to transfer money and there were 40 times more M-PESA agents in Kenya than ATMs.[4]

---

[4] *Ibid.*

Chapter 8

Emerging Innovators

The key value of the smaller companies covered in this chapter is niche technology and rapid innovation. Some of them have only 30–50 people, but they still managed to cooperate with Chinese property giants and thrive in the industry. They possess and develop cutting-edge technologies that giants like Alibaba and Baidu have not yet developed and command the heights in niche markets. They all manage to seek ways to develop unique products to manage, design, develop, and monetize data in the area of space: commercial, residential, and warehouse. We break the chapter down into three sections:

(1) **Space development.** These companies focus on the acquisition of data from the outside world which surrounds buildings, homes, malls, and factories. This includes both geographic and commercial data. The customers of these companies can easily make plans about their location, size, and development of the space and formulate right decisions based on the data they provide.

(2) **Space deployment.** These focus on the artificial intelligence (AI) technology and virtual reality (VR) application to analyze and forecast the development of space before building even begins. Some of these companies can further provide platforms that can help users foresee what they project should look like to prevent costly mistakes. Environmental projections will be central to predicting the resilience of a building 100 years out.

189

Data-backed decisions for location of offices and shops is vital. Knowing areas of saturation is key.

(3) **Space construction.** This focuses on the actual construction of proptech, such as smart office size and the way in which Internet of Things (IoT) fits into the new working environment. They help make the building smarter and create a better working and living environment.

We are living in the world of big data. About 2.5 quintillion bytes are generated every day. This is 2.5 followed by 18 zeros. Yet, so little of the physical world has been digitized. The number of IoT-connected devices is estimated to increase three fold (to almost 50 billion) by 2023. We should fully expect the amount of data we need to process to grow by more than three times its current level within three to four years. Proptech should be smack in the middle of these developments since the digitization of physical space is the next frontier after the digitization of finance, insurance, and health.

"Space development" proptech companies are a good starting point. They acquire data from the outside world and visualize them, turning them into valuable assets. Some provide further applications or platforms from this data, so that customers can manage their flows more easily. Imagine that if you want to make a plan for a building. With a single click, you can see all the relevant information from the surrounding environment. What is the soil and geographical situation? What is the population flow nearby? What products do customers prefer to buy? This data is precious to space developers.

Space deployment is another problem for real estate developers. How should they construct the building? What should the building look like? In order to answer these questions, real estate developers would pour huge sums toward engineers and planners. With proptech, however, time and money can be saved. For example, with the assistance of AI, developers can easily complete the diagram or a building, a neighborhood, or a vast complex without much human labor. The planners can focus on the larger vision while letting the technology focus on the laborious details! Moreover, virtual reality tech is able to simulate a real house and let users see and feel the home in 3D. These technologies are transforming this industry and lowering the cost of deployment.

The third element of proptech we will explore lies in construction. This is closest to the customer and has two main pillars: Insurtech and IoT. Property insurance will get a much-needed boost, since it had arguably changed very little in the past few decades. Blockchain and AI make this process more easy and reliable. Smart contracts powered by blockchain could provide customers and insurers with the means to manage claims in a transparent, responsive and irrefutable manner. As to IoT, it can make our life much more convenient. Tasks you have to remind yourself of every day — turn off the oven, switch off all the lights as you leave the house, manage the heaters and air con, turn off gas, make sure the pipes do not burst — could be virtually forgotten as they become automated.

Case Study: Panda Electronics

We include an example of Panda Electronics to introduce the relationship between IoT and proptech more clearly. Panda is a truly integrated IoT and AI company, which installs fail-safe systems for smart buildings, smart cities, and smart homes (Figure 8.1). This is a company at the heart of proptech in China. The company uses 5G, audio, and video technology to integrate automation, IoT and cloud to produce a vast array of products. Few hardware companies will be in a better position to take advantage of the coming explosion in proptech.

8.1. GISUNI

8.1.1. *Introduction*

GISUNI is lean and small, but it has already developed cutting-edge technologies and has built a solid reputation in several industries. The company has platforms, data management technologies, an array of tools to manage data, as well as comprehensive solutions. These are widely used in more than 20 industries such as smart cities, governments, finance, real estate, retail, automotive, logistics, media, and education (Figure 8.2).

Panda Electronics – EMS Provider

PANDA 熊猫电子

What do they do	Who is their boss	New Technology	How do they make money
• Focusing on intelligent manufacturing, modern digital cities, smart cities and electronics manufacturing service (EMS), it has greatly developed core equipment of intelligent manufacturing and system integration services. • These services include development plans for smart plants, together with four keys for smart city businesses which include intelligent transportation, safety within city public facilities, intelligent buildings and information network devices.	• Panda Electronics Group Co., Ltd. was sponsored by China Electronics Corporation and Nanjing Municipal People's Government. • China Electronics Corporation is Central Government-led Enterprise. Now, Panda Electronics Group Co., Ltd. has registered capital of RMB 3.448 billion Yuan, 70% of which comes from China Electronics.	• 5G mobile communication systems and satellite mobile • developed smart communities and smart home services based on digital video and audio transmission coverage as a technical means • integrates intelligence, automation, Internet of Things, cloud computing and other technical means	• Its proptech products mainly focuses on three aspects: • Safe City • Information Network Equipment • Smart Buildings

Panda Electronics – EMS Provider

Safe City	Information Network Equipment	Smart Buildings
• For safe city, it gives full play to the company's advantages in the field of military-civilian integrated communications. • It strives to cultivate a new generation of information technology, 5G mobile communication systems and satellite mobile R&D. Panda also provides satellite mobile and television wireless coverage, and communications application systems for other industries.	• For Information Network Equipment, it has developed smart communities and smart home services based on digital video and audio transmission coverage as a technical means, with a smart central platform as the control center. • It also constructs an efficient management system for residential facilities and family schedule affairs, improve home safety and convenience and realize an environmentally friendly and energy-saving living environment. • At the same time, the use of satellite communications, shortwave communications, mobile communications systems and other information network technologies and terminal equipment to establish a number of projects that benefit the people, such as village-to-village and household-to-house communication.	• Panda uses architecture as its platform and computer network as its core. • It integrates intelligence, automation, Internet of Things, cloud computing and other technical means to integrate security, fire alarm, building automation, integrated wiring, computer networks, HVAC, and Power distribution. • It aims to create a safer, more comfortable, fast and convenient, energy-saving and environmentally friendly living and working environment.

Figure 8.1.   Panda Electronics.

8.1.2.   *Products*

First, it provides solutions around the field of spatial information. All of its services are based on GPS. Their products include two aspects.

The first is for specialized geographical information users, like city planners, traffic departments, and communications. It provides for management, building, and maintaining equipment of buildings.

The second is for commercial users, such as developers. It helps to provide a better understanding of the locations where projects are to be built by providing special and customized data.

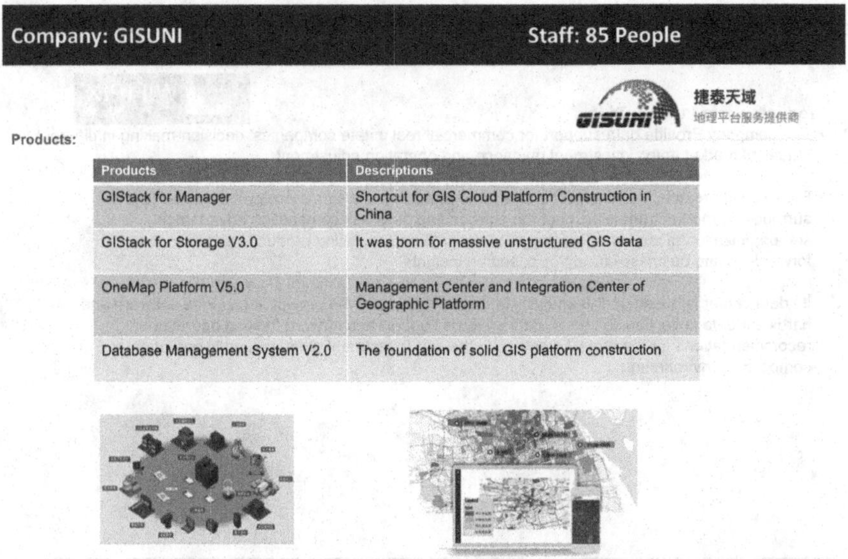

Company: GISUNI	Staff: 85 People

捷泰天域
GISUNI
地理平台服务提供商

Products:

Products	Descriptions
GIStack for Manager	Shortcut for GIS Cloud Platform Construction in China
GIStack for Storage V3.0	It was born for massive unstructured GIS data
OneMap Platform V5.0	Management Center and Integration Center of Geographic Platform
Database Management System V2.0	The foundation of solid GIS platform construction

Figure 8.2. GISUNI.

8.1.3. *Technology*

For database technology: GISUNI provides thorough geographical information where database users can implement different machine learning algorithms.

For AI technology: GISUNI combines the industry and locations, activating location-based industry analytics capabilities to assist in decision-making.

8.2. WIFIPIX

8.2.1. *Introduction*

While GISUNI focuses mainly on geographic data, WIFIPIX provides commercial data, including real estate and retail data. Founded in 2013, it focuses on data mining of behaviors of mobile users using both merchandise activity as well as movement and location (Figure 8.3).

It has 10 major business lines, including commercial real estate, retail brands, cultural tourism, car lots, advertising, and marketing.

Company: WIFIPIX	Staff: 27 People

Products related to PropTech
- The company Provide data support for commercial real estate companies' decision-making in different stages of market entry, investment guidance and operation adjustment.

- For existing projects, they support and test the matching of their services with the needs of the surrounding market from aspects of the surrounding business competition environment, self-organization of customer groups, and research on competing products, and formulate forward-looking business strategies based on insights.

- Its data center is based on the analysis of the crowd around the project. It provides software and hardware data collection solutions, data analysis support and forward-looking operational recommendations for the project's entry into the city, investment guidance, daily operation and competitive environment.

Company: WIFIPIX	Staff: 27 People

How do they implement the technology?
-     Big data technology. They use SaaS to collect data, then Use big data analysis to obtain offline visit trajectories and online crowd portrait analysis results, helping companies to more accurately mine potential customer groups
- Data center and AI.
   Based on the analysis of the crowd around the project, AI can help provides software and hardware data collection solutions, data analysis support and forward-looking operational recommendations for the project's entry into the city, investment guidance, daily operation and competitive environment.

How do they make money?
For the retail brands, it helps them better understand their customers by providing SaaS service.
For the real estates, it provides the data to help them make decisions about the locations and make assessments about the estate plan.

Figure 8.3.   WIFIPIX.

It absorbs more than 3 billion data sets on a regular basis. It has recently established a domestic commercial real estate big data alliance with Gaode, RET, and other founders.

It provides more than data. It also provides Software as a Service (SaaS) for shops and companies to acquire data about their customers. With this data, WIFIPIX can help retail brands perform complete analyses of corporate functions, thereby increasing potential customers and expanding operations.

8.2.2. *Products*

It provides one-on-one special services for customers in different regions.

For retail brands, it helps them better understand their customers by providing SaaS service.

For the real estate developers, it provides the data to help them make decisions about the location and make assessments about the estate plan.

8.2.3. *Technologies*

In the area of big data, they use SaaS to analyze offline traffic to get a better picture of online activity. They can figure out the disconnect between shoppers and buyers to accurately mine potential customer groups.

For data center and AI activity, they look at the behavior of crowd traffic around offices or mall developments. AI can help to create forward-looking recommendations for the project as it pertains to location, size, product, and manpower.

8.3. GeoHey

Different from GISUNI and WIFIPIX, GeoHey focuses on the geographic big data platforms (Figure 8.4).

The company has only 33 people, but it has managed to get decent funding from investors. Moreover, it cooperates with some of the well-known Chinese and overseas companies like Longhu Real Estate, Chinese Academy of Standards, McDonalds, Moovit, and Xad.

How do they get to achieve such incredible accomplishments with so few people? Their product line tells a lot about how so few people can produce so many different products.

Figure 8.4.   GeoHey.

8.3.1.   *Products*

Proptech: GeoHey City Map is a thematic map of the information flow from urban real estate. It can provide strategic guidance for real estate plot layout, customer positioning, environmental adaptation, differentiated housing products, and precise marketing. It can also provide efficient and low-cost solutions for land acquisition, design, and sales.

Smart City: GeoHey Platform provides multi-source spatial data, visualization, and analysis services and solves the needs of government planning, transportation, and other departments for geospatial and big data platform construction in one-stop. They provide insight into cities through hundreds of millions of multi-source big data analytics to provide platform support and data support for smart cities.

8.4. Xkool

Different from companies we mentioned before, which are more focused on space development and big data analysis, Xkool takes advantage of AI technology to help with city planning, urban design, and architectural plans.

Xkool is an industry leader in the vertical application of AI in real estate and construction. It focuses on the vertical application of AI and cutting-edge technology in the construction and real estate industry.

8.4.1. *Profile: He Wanyu, Founder of Xkool*

He Wanyu, Founder and CEO of XKool Technology, is a highly successful entrepreneur. She is an adjunct assistant professor of the Hong Kong University Architecture School. She graduated from Berlage Institution Delft University of Technology. She was a protégé of Rem Koolhas, who won the coveted Pritzker Prize in 2000 and recognized in the top 100 of The World's Most Influential People by *Time* magazine. From 2009 to 2016, He Wanyu served as project architect of the world's top architectural firm OMA. During that period, she was involved in several projects including the CCTV building, the Shenzhen Stock Exchange, and the Rotterdam City Hall. She is also a Sci-Fi writer, as she says, "Writing a Sci-Fi is as same as designing an architecture scheme, both are the same as creating a great tech based startup."

He Wanyu, Founder of Xkool

We had an interview with Wanyu, and she updated us with the latest real estate situation. "Under the effect of several factors, such as COVID-19 and government policy, China's traditional real estate industry has stagnated. They are seeking changes and breakthroughs. Some of them resort to traditional methods such as improving management and bargaining for cheaper land, while others turn to explore the benefit of science and technology. Indeed, now, many real estate companies are introducing Chief Investment Officer to their business structure, reporting directly to CEOs," Wanyu said. This can help with making investments in new industries.

What distinguishes Xkool from other similar companies? As Wanyu said "We are the pioneers of this industry. We focus on exploiting the Artificial Intelligence building design." Xkool possesses the self-developed AI design engine based on AI-Driven Beam on Cloud (ABC). This AI engine is specially designed for urban planning and architecture design. Capable of generating complex designs automatically, this engine differentiates itself from conventional tasks that requires a lot of human labor.

Xkool also adopts stringent policy to ensure data privacy. It stores data in three different cloud platforms — Ali Cloud, Tencent Cloud, and Azure.

8.4.2. *Products*

Xkool's main product — an AI architectural design cloud platform — is the world's first cloud-based AI architectural design application. Designs no longer involve just drawing; the tool will create scientific solutions based on data analysis and optimize the solution with the assistance of intelligent interaction. Iterative learning is involved in this process, and efficient communication and collaboration methods have been established between project partners.

It includes six characteristics:

(1) Query of data around the plot.
(2) Artificial intelligence-assisted design.
(3) Real-time feedback of modification results.

(4) Linked accounting indicator data.

(5) Collaborative project interactive editing.

(6) Users only need to input the building type parameters and the house type parameters to directly generate the building blueprint.

8.5. 51VR

Similar to Xkool, 51VR uses AI to make breakthroughs in the real estate industry as well. Their key distinction is the addition of VR technology to contribute to the transformation. More interestingly, they also use 5G+AI technology to realize real time cloud rendering of architectures.

51VR achieved great operational success — its clients include over 400,000 users and 500 partners in 124 countries. The company has already worked with hundreds of corporate customers at home and abroad, including BMW, Daimler, Auto House, Weimar Automobile, Vanke, Contemporary, Country Garden, China Resources, JQZ Group, FAW Pentium, Alibaba, Mercedes-Benz, China Mobile, China Railway Construction, and National Intelligent Networked Automobile (Shanghai) Pilot Demonstration Zone, amongst other well-known enterprises and institutions.

51VR's products cover four areas (Table 8.1)

We can see that these four areas focus on the most important aspects in proptech. 51 City OS is the most impressive product, which creates a brand new city management system to help city

Table 8.1.   51VR products.

Product Area	Products
Smart Cities	51 City OS
Automobiles	Virtual Automobile
Real Estate	VR Housing, Housing Finance
5G	51 Cloud 5G Real-time Cloud rendering platform

Company: 51VR   **Staff: 92 People**

The essence of the company

How do they implement the technology?
- They implement the technology in different aspects:
- In Intelligence Vehicle Department, they use visualization to simulate cars and roads and real driving scenery, for one thing it can provide road situations to city management, for another it can be implement in cars retailing.
- In the Digital City Group, they create simulation of real estate, help estate companies to provide with their clients plans and VR experience. The clients can experience the real sense of the house without actually being there.
- Through 5G, they can better and quicker implement the real-time rendering process.

How do they make money?
- As mentioned above, by selling these plans, solutions and simulations they offer, they make money. Its main clients including city plan departments, real estate companies and technology giants.

Figure 8.5.   51VR: An overview.

planners and managers improve efficiency. It is used to simulate several scenarios including:

(1) monitoring collective driving to various destinations;
(2) movement of traffic to housing complex in order to simulate urban–suburban movement, and
(3) helping businesses and individuals experience the world more efficiently, safely and realistically (Figure 8.5).

8.6.   My Dream+

Having explored the space development and space deployment companies, we now shift our focus to space construction companies. The former two contribute to architecture, i.e. where a structure should be built and how it should be built, etc. The "space construction" part of proptech creates the world that we see up close every day. My Dream+ is one such company that provides such services.

My Dream+ is currently in its fourth round of financing. It has recently raised about 350 million RMB for its development, and has become one of China's most popular office brands. My Dream+ provides office customization services to enterprises of different sizes and types, such as SF Express, Longhu Real Estate, Tencent Zhongchuang Space, and Yiqixiu, with an output area of nearly 300,000 square meters (Figure 8.6).

Its technology specializations relate to IoT and AI. The Office as a Service (OaaS) system created by My Dream+ was officially released in 2017. This system upgrades the office from a single physical space to a composite service. It provides the service of connecting almost everything in the office together, including computer, air conditioner, seats, WIFI, lights, etc.

Users only need a WeChat ID to quickly and easily complete daily tasks such as attendance check-in and guest invitations, which improves user office efficiency and experience (Figure 8.7).

Figure 8.6. Longfor Properties and My Dream+ partner to launch new shared office.

Company: My Dream+	Registered Capital: 1,900,000

Products

- Dream plus smart office system, with intelligent linkage, non-sense experience of smart office scenarios greatly improve venue management, corporate management and daily office efficiency. Dream+ became the first co-working office brand in Asia to obtain WELL certification in May 2019, creating a more healthy office environment for customers with highly standardized space products.

Welcome to the Dream Factory

Figure 8.7.　My Dream+: An overview.

8.7.　9am

Intelligent office AI IoT solution leader 9am is another unicorn in this industry. 9am has established solid collaboration with Microsoft in the provision of office services and has set off a new trend of smart offices in more than 1,000 locations in 29 cities and 9 countries around the world. This ranges from world-class co-working spaces such as WeWork, TEC, and Atlas, to Fortune 500 companies such as Bosch, Siemens, BMW, and HNA Group to Internet technology giants such as Baidu, Xiaomi, and Megvii.

The way 9am entered the industry boasts an interesting story. At the early stage, 9am had a deep insight into two pain points that hindered the popularity of the lift desk market. The first is posture and back pain caused by poor posture, and the second is the low utilization rate. For this reason, 9am has developed the world's first intelligent cloud lift table. With the addition of an original smart hand control panel, the lift table can actively remind users to stand up and work, and the utilization rate of the lift table has been improved by 60%.

Thereafter, it sought to maximize the value of workstations beyond that of tables. 9am innovatively combined self-developed sensors with smart desks to collect real-time data so that employees can develop a better sense of the work cycle and cultivate good habits of healthy work. Enterprises will also use this data to better understand the working status of employees, and then optimize resource management and improve human efficiency.

The products 9am developed are more humanized compared to products we mentioned before (Figure 8.8). They are working with Microsoft in this area, focusing on optimizing health and work efficiency for its employees.

Company: 9AM	Staff: 35 People

Products:

Products	Descriptions
The bar provided by 9AM	Users can interact with standing desks via Bluetooth
Visualized Workspace Management	It provides a distinctive workplace layout, a clear overview of each division and space and accurate indoor location to each desk.
Solely developed cross platform Cloud solution	It allows smooth synchronization between Web, desktop and mobile. All data will be instantly synced cross platforms and needless local deployment that occupy IT personnel and resources.

Figure 8.8.   9am — An overview

8.8.   ZiFiSense

Li Zhouqun, the CEO of ZifiSense, has a Ph.D. in Mobile Computing from Plymouth University and a post-doctorate degree in Wireless Sensor and Mobile Ad-hoc Networks from Imperial College. He spent 14 years in the UK, working as a senior systems engineer in Motorola, where he mainly focused on System Architecture Design. In PA Consulting Group, he provided technical consulting for the ICT industry. In 2016, he came back to China and launched ZiFiSense.

ZiFiSense is an IoT technology provider offering end-to-end IoT solutions to customers based on three innovative technologies — ZETA LPWAN, Edge AIoT, and ZETag.

ZETA LPWAN is a low-power, wide-area wireless communication standard technology. What makes it distinctive is that it is combined with 5G and can form a complete ecosystem of any industrial solution. This means the entire digitalized transformation of the IoT industry and the construction of new fundamental infrastructure of China.

ZETA AIoT is an online store providing IoT hardware and software. This makes it more convenient for customers to purchase items they like and easier to connect them into an IoT ecosystem.

ZETag is a sensor label based on LPWAN technology. This can be widely used in item tracking and management, identification, and special event reporting. It has an extremely low price (half of existing products) and long covering distance (2–10 km).

The company has strong R&D capabilities and expertise in telecommunication hardware, server platform, wireless protocol as well as AI algorithms. Now it adds AI to IoT — instead of using people to do the examination and inspection, machines can automatically complete it. This has given rise to a new area termed "new property management" and lowers the cost of building management.

The company aims to build itself as a top three communication standard across all industries — and it certainly possesses the ability to do so. With ZETA, which is the world's first LPWAN communication standard that supports distributed networking, by using the underlying protocols from communication chips to smart hardware and cloud platforms, it takes an active role in constructing an ecosystem.

Products and solutions have provided services to many countries and regions such as Japan, the UK (Cambridge), the Middle East, and South America. ZiFiSense also cooperates with ZTE Microelectronics, China Tower, CLP Public Facilities Operation Company, UK Trade Agency (UKTI), John Lang Lasalle (JLL), and other units established strategic cooperation. Among these partners, China Tower collaborate with ZiFiSense in deploying an electronic seal system for community epidemic prevention and control using ZETA.

JLL is cooperating with ZiFiSense to create the building "Intelligent Command Center." It provides real estate owners and users of 200+ commercial buildings managed by JLL with advanced technology for management of data collection, analysis and operation, and real-time and remote monitoring of the performance of buildings and facilities (Figure 8.9).

Company: ZiFiSense	Registered Capital: 4.3Million

Awards

• ZiFisense team won the PropTech Award at the Angel Hacker 2018 Global Hackathon Shanghai Station. From a business perspective, using this technology in combination with a full range of AI + IoT (artificial intelligence + Internet of Things) technology to trigger work orders, engineers grab orders and realize shared properties. This new business model has won the PropTech sponsored by JLL Jones Lang LaSalle.

Figure 8.9.   ZiFiSense: An overview.

8.8.1. *Profile: Li Zhuoqun, CEO of ZiFiSense*

"Proptech is truly booming in China nowadays," according to Li Zhuoqun, CEO of ZiFiSense, "and ZiFiSense is playing a vital role in it." "The difficulty exists though", as Li said, "The IoT is a comprehensive technology which requires the collaboration of the entire supply chain. However, the supply chain is not complete and perfect in China." For example, from the terminals, sensors, antennas, to electromagnetic partners and IoT cloud platforms, all of these require reliable providers and partners, which is rather difficult to find. Also, he mentions that the payoff of investment in technology is hard to calculate, because the period would be much longer than normal companies.

As a leading technology supplier in the LPWAN industry, ZiFiSense has formed three major business sectors, namely smart lighting, smart cities, and smart communities. As for smart cities in particular, Li mentioned that this industry is increasing greatly in demand, though it is not expected to be as fast as the Internet boom, because this industry relies on inventory and equipment and needs time to accumulate. "The smart cities can develop relatively fast in China's eastern area, because of government support and completed city infrastructures," he concluded.

8.9. Conclusion

In both the large and small companies, we see some common characteristics. The teams are staffed at the very top by scientists with impeccable credentials from US, UK, European, and Chinese universities, and most have earned their Ph.D. degrees. Their R&D budgets are, in most cases, the largest expense, and they are willing to run into losses to keep investing in further R&D.

They are also in a great position because they have solid national infrastructure to work with. 5G has been rolled out nationally. Edge computing is widely available. Cloud computing is also widely available. Lastly, the rollout of the Blockchain Service Network (BSN) — happening as this book goes to print — will cause prices for cloud services, contracts, coding, and other corporate services to fall by 80%–90%. These companies will have the opportunity to digitize and tokenize virtually anything that moves or stands in China: buildings, warehouses, homes, cars, and carbon emissions. This entire phenomenon would be impossible if the government did not begin planning for this in 2014.

Chapter 9

Biden Administration's Response to China's Technological Advances in Smart Cities

This book began with a foreword by luminary and blockchain expert David Lee. He has delved in depth about the revolutionary way in which physical assets — buildings, homes, ports, etc. — would be wedded to digitized tokens along new rails and connected to the PBOC's Central Bank Coin (DC/EP) and run along Blockchain Service Network (BSN). He calls this the "Internet of Everything," or IoE. Much of the book is precisely about this, i.e. the way in which buildings, homes, and warehouses are digitized, tokenized, and welded on to the financial system. However, he also warned that countries in the midst of civil strife brought about by inequality can cause the body politic to miss the boat when it comes to innovation and technological leaps. His warning applies to the US.

Cold civil wars — and certainly hot civil wars — can lead to long periods of stagnation and decline. Just consider China on this. It was in the midst of foreign occupation and civil war for more than a century from 1820 to 1949. As a result, it missed the first and second industrial revolutions from the early 1800s to the 1940s. It was a lost century. As a result of what it calls "The Century of Humiliation," China currently vows never to let this happen again. US, on the other hand, is feeling the tremors of civil strife all over.

Bridgewater Founder Ray Dalio made a profoundly simple point about the US: when inequality gets too extreme, people start fighting. This is true in too many countries now, but especially in the US. Dalio points out that capitalism has broken down in the US and has stopped working for most of its people. He calls this economic crisis a "national emergency." Americans' confidence in a better future has been shattered. This sentence explains the phenomenon of Donald Trump.

"There will need to be a new resolve of the system to work for the majority of the people — one in which there is productivity. . . . This can be obtained in a bipartisan way or it will come by greater conflict," Dalio says. He concludes that large wealth gaps during an economic downturn produces a political toxic brew of "conflict and vulnerability."

A simple measure of the inequality between rich and poor is the Gini coefficient. It is a measure of how much concentration of wealth there is in certain segments of the population. 0 represents perfect equality (everyone has the same) and 1 represents perfect inequality (a small group has everything). The higher the number, the greater the likelihood of violence. It is that simple.

The overall US Gini coefficient in the US is about 0.4, which is equivalent to Turkey. If we look at individual cities, however, many cities in the South have a Gini coefficient similar to many developing countries. These include Atlanta and New Orleans. Cities in the Rust Belt like Cleveland and Cincinnati are also suffering from massive inequality. The Gini coefficient applies equally to both countries and cities.

9.1.   The American Century of Trouble

This accelerating tension between the rich and poor causes the body politic to seek out a bogeyman, preferably a foreign one. In 2016, it found China. Fareed Zakaria said that, "the US has managed to turn China into the Soviet Union of the 1960s–1980s. This is the most ominous sign of where we are going. Democrats can't be seen to be outflanked by the right. This was true in Vietnam and Iraq. I wonder if this dynamic may be true with China today."[1] In other words, even if the Biden Administration wanted to cool down the nasty rhetoric, it could not, due to severe attacks by the right accusing them of being "soft on communism."

Fred Feldkamp, author of *Financial Stability: Fraud, Confidence and the Wealth of Nations*, makes the point that the road to reducing this inequality within the US has little to do with the way the US and China trade. The solution lies within the US: massive infrastructure investment led by the government to help re-educate and retrain people to adjust to rapid technological progress that has disrupted the workforce. This investment is tantamount to an "increase in the capital stock" — whether it be physical, technological, or intellectual stock. Tax cuts and stock buybacks are great for the stock market and for the wealthy, but they are not good for retraining a workforce and easing the shocks of sudden technological advances.

Feldkamp continues by saying that as this wealth gap widens — due to rich people having access to credit to buy leveraged assets such as property and stocks — the middle class is left without enough income to buy the things that are produced by the rich. This leads to sluggish growth and anemic consumption. It builds resentment and makes the middle class see themselves as victims of an unfair system. It robs them of the dignity of work. It is bad for everyone and leads to civil strife.

What is the evidence for this? Table 9.1 shows the increases in prices for basic household goods versus the increase in wages during the same time. The average increase for a basket of goods for Americans since 1970 has been 663%. The average increase in income has been 233%, almost exactly in line with the minimum wage. A careful look at the individual items for these shows that only the prices of eggs and coffee have kept up with wages. Everything else, particularly cars and houses, are way out of reach for most Americans.

---

[1]Fareed Zakaria, *Ten Lessons for a Pandemic World* (S.l.: Penguin Books, 2021).

Table 9.1.   Cost of living comparison (1970 vs 2020).

Category	1970	2020	% Change
New House	$23,450	$329,000	+1303
New Car	$3,450	$40,107	+1063
Movie Ticket	$1.6	$11	+588
Gasoline	$0.36/gal.	$3/gal.	+733
Postage Stamp	$0.06	$0.55	+817
Sugar	$0.39/5lbs	$3.6/5lbs	+823
Milk	$0.62/gal.	$3.5/gal.	+465
Coffee	$1.9/lb	$4.5/lb	+137
Eggs	$0.59/doz.	$1.5/doz.	+154
Bread	$0.23	$1.5	+552
Average			+663
Average Income	$9,400	$31,300	+233
Minimum Wage	$2.1/hour	$7.25/hour	+245

Source: U.S. Bureau of Labor Statistics, Edmunds.

Why? The minimum wage has been stagnant and has not kept up with the cost of living. At US$7.50 per hour, it has been the same for more than a decade. Our calculation of the minimum wage required merely to keep up with this basket of goods is US$16.10. Not only does this create greater inequality and bitterness of the aggrieved "have nots," it is also bad economics because they simply can no longer afford the goods and services produced by the companies in the Fortune 500.

Table 9.1 does not include the cost of college education, which has increased in the same period by about 10x, from roughly US$2,200 to about US$25,000 per year. A college education for a family who is making only 2.5x more in that same period is out of luck. Furthermore, even if both parents worked full time, they would still come up short. In addition, healthcare costs in 1970 were US$355 and skyrocketed to more than $11,300 by 2019. Again, this is a 30-fold increase, according to Balance.com. These increases in healthcare spending are occurring at a time when life expectancy has been falling in the US for several years in a row. This fall in the purchasing power of the middle class needs to be redressed politically. This is not China's fault.

9.2. Did All the China-Bashing Work?

It is said that the US is a rich country with poor people. Who is to blame for this? The past four years have been an exercise in misdirection. China has been painted as the source of all of US' ails. If blame cannot be apportioned internally, it helps to have an outside bogeyman. The bashing of China is also an attempt to slow China down while the US finds a way to catch up to her advances in transport, ecommerce, super apps, blockchain, a digital currency, fintech, quantum communications, digital insurance, proptech, and many other fields.

The methods to contain and possibly undermine China have been as pointed as they have been multifarious. These include tariffs, sanctions, targeted restraints on particular listings, de-listings, export controls, restrictions on university cooperation, active counter-espionage investigations, and aggressive pressure on allies to alienate China. They have included publicly stated policies to foment marginal chaos in Hong Kong (which incidentally is experiencing a similar phenomenon as the US, only in a city-state of nine million people). The list goes on.

Let us step back and see what the past four years of China-bashing has achieved. Before the dispute with China began in 2016, 23% of all US imports came from the PRC, about as much as Canada and Mexico combined. In the following two years, the US trade deficit with China actually rose and reached a record US$419 billion in 2018. It shrank a bit in 2019, but the overall deficit was similar.

Of course, China sent goods to America and received paper in return — US bonds to finance the US deficit. China MUST buy US dollar assets with its US dollar surpluses, so it is a win for the US. The US gets goods and services. China gets paper. Every dollar of deficit China creates must be deployed back into the US economy in the form of government securities to fund the deficit and keep the lending rates in the US about 200 bps lower than they would otherwise be. The US got cheap goods to beautify their homes and much cheaper finance to buy homes. These are undisputed facts.

Furthermore, China did what all countries do when their goods are blocked by tariffs. They divert trade flows to other countries like Vietnam, Malaysia, Taiwan, and Mexico. This is exactly what Japan did in the 1980s when it had tariffs imposed on it. When the US blocked exports from Japan, it picked up entire industries and moved them to Southeast Asia.

There is another way in which the measures imposed on China not only failed but also backfired. Chinese exporters did not lower prices to keep the price for US consumers the same as pre-tariff prices. It turns out that the price increase was paid for by US companies and consumers. On top of this, Beijing's ambitious plans to import US$170 billion worth of goods fell apart with the Boeing engineering problems of its new aircraft. Two crashes of the Boeing 737 MAX caused China (and all countries) to halt purchases until engineering malfunctions were fixed.

In addition, during this entire time, investment by US companies inside China was actually UP from 2016 to 2019. This is according to the Rhodium Group. In addition, a 2019 survey of more than 200 US manufacturing companies showed that more than 75% would not move production out of China. Lastly, the newest numbers for 2020 show that, for the first time, net investment in China was greater than in the US.

The US also blocked much of the semiconductor production from Taiwan to China. So, China did two things. It doubled down on capital expenditure in its own semiconductor capacity and vowed never again to get caught being dependent on foreign technology. Second, when the US restricted Taiwan's semiconductor exports to China, countries quickly came in to fill the void: Japan and South Korea stepped in and increased exports of semiconductors to China. Sumitomo Electric made a commitment to reduce its 5G base station semiconductors to 50% of production but over a period of five years — hardly a painful blow.

In addition, Samsung and other South Korean companies have decidedly stepped up exports of semiconductors and other equipment to China. In fact, the prohibitions on Taiwan exports likely brought South Korea and China closer together. This is another unintended outcome, since South Korea is one of US' closest allies in Asia, with more than 50,000 US troops based there.

In conclusion, many pundits have compared the measures of the US to constrain China as kneecapping a rising power to maintain a tight grip. China's successes have led to more successes, and it is gathering even more internal political momentum given the perceived existential threat to its survival. This renewed domestic unity against a common threat can and should allow it to hold to its promise to maintain autonomy, ensure domestic peace, and seek out regional stability. It is simply not in a mood to be dictated to and has the strategic patience to work around most sanctions. Lastly, in an interview with Fred Feldkamp, we asked a simple question, "Tell me an instance when kneecapping actually worked to actually win a race." This all begs a vital question that went unanswered for four years: what was being done **inside the US** to retrain, re-educate, and upgrade the American workforce while these ineffective sanctions were taking up valuable time and space that could have otherwise been used for rebuilding the US' domestic infrastructure?

9.3. How Did China Get So Much Right in Such a Short Time — Right Under US' Nose?

Since 2014, China's national policies on economic development have had a singular focus on infrastructure investment and technology to achieve growth. It knows its population is aging and that robotics is the only viable solution. It knows environmental technology is vital to keep China from devolving into a toxic mess on land, sea, and air. It knows that blockchain technology is vital to create an external alternative to dependence on the dollar. It knows that eliminating corruption in both the military and its own domestic FBI is vital to maintaining internal and external security, and it knows that super apps are a way to implement a digital currency and chip away at money laundering, tax evasion, and capital flight. It has made these pronouncements loud and clear through its Five-Year Programs. The private sector has taken cues from the programs and invested accordingly. All US policymakers had to do to create countermeasures to China was to read the FYPs in 2010 and 2015. It was there for all to see.

What is poorly understood is just where China got these rather ingenious ideas over the past two decades to allow public–private partnerships to flourish in order to upgrade all of these technologies: environmental, blockchain, military, smart city, robotics, autonomous cars, etc. A report from the Center for a New American Security called "Myths and Realities of China's Military-Civil Fusion (MCF) Strategy" makes a bold claim that MCF is hardly an invention of China or Xi Jinping.[2]

The report smartly points out that:

> "MCF as a strategy is uniquely expansive and ambitious in China today. But there are distinct parallels in aspects of the relationship between American companies, universities, and the government. In fact, American approaches to using commercial technologies have been closely studied in China as models for its own MCF efforts."[3]

China has looked with great admiration on how the US created the Atomic Bomb project with the help of the University of Chicago, MIT, Berkeley, and CalTech. The same goes for the development of the Apollo project, the Internet, and ARPA (Stanford played a central role in many of the Apollo projects of the 1960s). The same is true for the interstate highway system and many other massive infrastructure projects (Intercontinental Ballistic missiles (ICBM), Strategic Defense Initiative (SDI), drones, precision-guided missiles) that required federal government leadership at the level of the Pentagon to coordinate among and between universities, military contractors, private companies, and the intelligence community. The study is pretty clear. China got its ideas about military–civilian cooperation from the US.

---

[2]Elsa B. Kania and Lorand Laskai, "A Sharper Approach to China's Military-Civil Fusion Strategy Begins by Dispelling Myths," *Defense One*, February 4, 2021.

[3]*Ibid.*

The conclusion of our book is that all countries are building a new infrastructure, only it is a digital one. There is a new Apollo program to go to space, only it is digital and quantum, not physical. It involves cloud technology and digital rails — not cement, aluminium, or phosphates. There is a new global telecommunications system being laid, but it is not undersea cable — it is above-ground edge computing in the cloud. There is a new currency system being created, only it is not through the World Bank or the IMF run out of DC buildings. It is through a new set of blockchain rails using tokenized assets and traded via cryptocurrencies, including central bank coins. China has the BSN network for a new digital currency. BUNA is the new digital rails for the Middle East. The Euro zone is working on its own system while the US seems to be throwing the dice with Facebook's Diem (formerly Libra).

China is years ahead of the curve on all of these new systems at the moment precisely because it has borrowed the "Apollo project" mentality of the 1960s from the US — and began building out this new infrastructure starting in 2014. It also borrowed some of the ideas from post-war Germany and how it funded the rebuilding of a country devastated by war. Indeed, in the 1980s, China was just emerging from decades of civil war, invasion, and political chaos. Germany's emergence from the chaos and destruction of World War II was an apt model as well.

9.4. The Drive of China's Technology Today

Every country has a different path to success. Here we outline the views of Asia's experts on China and technology. We have taken stock of the evolution of the US–China relationship with George Yeo, the *eminence grise* of the Singapore diplomatic community in public commentary over the years. We also consider informed opinions from former Prime Minister Goh Chok Tong, and recent conversations with Gao Xiqing, former Wing Hang OCBC co-CEO Frank Wang, Dr. David Lee in Singapore, Charles Liu, Fred Feldkamp, Jim Stent, Gao Xiqing, Amit Rajpal of Marshall Wace, Adam Levinson of GAMA, Tian Chong Ng of HP, Simon Ogus, David Halpert, Dede Nickerson, Rob Jesudason of Serendipity, Gary Ang of Temasek,

Danny Lee of Blue Pool, Richard Margolis and many other world-class thinkers throughout the Far East. (We suggest paying attention to senior thinkers and diplomats in Singapore — they possess unique insights into China that cannot be gleaned in other Asian capitals. Singapore and Beijing have a very close and very discreet relationship). We commingle these views together below and keep them general to maintain confidentiality.

These luminaries have all shed critical light on how China has developed, so we have incorporated their collective views into nine basic ideas that make modern China what it is. (Another excellent book to understand China very well is Peter Frankopan's *The Silk Roads*, which describes 2,500 years of empires and nations trying to gain the upper hand along the trade routes from Beijing to Chengdu to Jerusalem and then to Rome and London).

First, along with Persia, China is among the oldest civilizations in the world. It has been ruled from an imperial center for more than 2,000 years. It has great strategic patience and sticks to long-term programs "no matter what" once they are laid down through consensus. As has been the case through multiple kingdoms, highly educated mandarins at the center rule from the center. There is not now — and there never has been — a federal system of democratic representation. To expect a sudden move to federalized democracy is naïve.

Second, China is now churning out more STEM graduates than the entire OECD (37 countries) combined — almost 5 million annually! This is in comparison to about 500,000 in the US. There is great momentum behind its technological advancement. This is not going to change any time soon.

Third, China took no action against Apple inside China when Huawei's US business was destroyed. Inside the US, dozens of Chinese companies were put on an "enemies list" and others were delisted. Huawei's business was closed. Again, China has great patience and showed restraint. It could have destroyed Apple's business in China in one day, but it did not.

Fourth, the last thing China wants is a war. They lived with devastating wars for 120 years from 1820 to 1949. China's current diplomatic thinking is driven by a famous adage of Sun Tzu: If you have war, you have failed in your policies. Fred Feldkamp reminds us to consider that *five* of the top ten deadliest wars in human history have occurred in China. There is little appetite for war in Beijing right now. As part of its move into modernity in the 1990s, China's had a clear policy of making peace with its neighbors. It has not had a single international skirmish since 1979, when it had a conflict with Vietnam.

Fifth, Westerners must pay attention to China's dual-circulation system. This is laid out carefully in Chapters 1–3. The internal system will have a singular focus on upgrading the technical functionality of the economy, promoting domestic consumption, building out smart cities, and advancing technologically on all fronts at flank speed. The external system facing the outside world will continue working with the international system as much as possible. However, it will prioritize a China that is autonomous technologically, financially, and monetarily. In other words, China will create autonomous backup systems that can be called up and rolled out quickly if external sanctions arise in any area — whether it be trade, finance, technology, or equipment. China reserves the right to "go it alone" in any area if it is sanctioned for any reason. It will have a "rip cord" to parachute out of the SWIFT-based global banking and monetary system at any time within 12–24 months.

Sixth, despite the dual-circulation system, China very much wants to keep the global economic engine running — and well oiled. A slowdown in the global economy now means a slowdown in China's economy. China is now more than 50% of emerging market indices. It does not seek at all to upturn the status quo. It very much wants a status quo and a global partnership with the US where it can make it happen. This is very clear in the Chinese diplomatic corps.

Seventh, the purge in Alibaba/Ant group today is very similar to antitrust momentum both in the US and Europe. It is a fact that major players like Ant, Tencent, JD, Ping An, and Baidu are private sector entities, but the government is coming after them in the same way that Senator Amy Klobuchar is coming after the tech companies with new antitrust laws. This is part of a global phenomenon. Our extensive outside research on Ant leads us to this conclusion as well. Ant went too far in its ambitions, just as Facebook and Google have done. The US and Euro authorities are beating the antitrust war drums when it comes to big tech. Ant is a taste of things to come.

Eighth, China's girth can no longer allow it to remain unnoticed. It is a major power and will very likely remain so. It is not going away and attempts to throw it off balance have failed to work so far — and are unlikely to work. The key to the region is to keep the Malacca Straits open with peaceful cooperation. China is asserting its authority and will tend to do beneficial things for the region from a position of strength. Both sides are deeply sensitive to criticism when it comes to the Malacca Straits and the South China Sea. Countries like Singapore will need to become experts at diplomacy to manage the two navies in the busiest sea lanes in the world — right on Singapore's doorstep.

Ninth, it is in the interest of Asia to have healthy competition between China and the US. This offers choices and keeps the parties honest. No one wants to be forced to take sides. Shigenobu Nagamori, Chairman and CEO of automobile EV maker NIDEC put it well: "As a business owner, I don't have any country I like or don't like. My company operates in 43 countries."

9.5. The Biden Administration's Approach

Now, let us look at the plan of the US to counter China's "peaceful rise." Many leaders in Asia are confident that the US could and should emerge from this tumultuous time as a stronger and renewed economy just as it always has done during previous emergencies. However, the advent of the Biden Administration is showing a hardening of the lines between right and left, which could be an omen of deepening civil strife. Trump's impeachment trial in the Senate is a prime example of this. Countries in a period of deep civil strife cannot focus on renewal, re-education, skills upgrading, and technological progress. This is deeply worrying to many diplomats and business leaders in the Far East. Many Asian political and business leaders, including in China, do really want to see the US succeed. However, the civil strife in the US is becoming more divisive, violent, and organized than at any time since the civil war of 1861–1865.

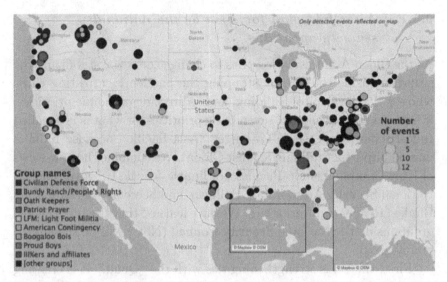

Figure 9.1.   Activity of militias and armed groups in the US (May 24–October 17, 2020).

Source: Hampton Stall, Roudabesh Kishi, and Clionadh Raleigh, "Standing By: Right-Wing Militia Groups & the US Election," ACLED, February 11, 2021, https://acleddata.com/2020/10/21/standing-by-militias-election/.

Figure 9.1 shows the major armed militia groups throughout the US. Essentially, they are everywhere. The Oathkeepers, Boogaloo Boys, and the "III Percenters" are the largest and best organized groups. The Proud Boys are concentrated in Oregon and Washington State. The major congregation of these other groups lies in Indiana, Kentucky, Tennessee, North Carolina, and South Carolina. After the storming of the Capitol Building on January 6, 2021, the FBI started an unprecedented national manhunt for people in these groups. Canada declared Proud Boys to be a terrorist organization.

The history of counterinsurgency suggests it will take a decade to quash these groups. In only a few weeks since the troubles in the Capitol, the FBI has arrested more than 500 men and women but has received more than 140,000 videos and photos of the events of January 6. The FBI warned in early February 2021 that the dragnet would be wide and far. Hundreds of trials have already begun and pressure will be applied to break up these groups by arresting the leaders.

9.5.1.   *A six-fold plan for Asia by the national security apparatus*

As the Biden Administration tries to change course by stabilizing the situation inside the US, by stopping the pandemic, arresting those who sacked the Capitol Building, and redirecting economic priorities, it has also rapidly laid out seven basic priorities for what is now called Indo-Pacific policy. (It is no longer "Asia-Pacific" because India is now an important fulcrum against China). We combine the new views of Kurt Campbell (Indo-Pacific coordinator for the US government), National Security Advisor Jake Sullivan, and Secretary of State Tony Blinken to offer eight priorities. We have learned that the Indo-Pacific group inside the National Security Council (NSC) will be the largest of any group.

First, the US is strengthening ties with the "Quad." It is creating a much deeper alliance among and between Japan, India, and Australia. Detail on this would require an entire book, but we should suffice it to say that the deepening ties with India — as well as ongoing Alliances with Japan and Australia — will continue. India is a huge beneficiary of the recent US munificence. But bear in mind that no country did a better job of playing the US and Soviet Union off each other during the Cold War than India. It got both F16s and MIGs. The Quad has been solidified since the first summit and it seems the Biden Administration will continue. The policy of trying to isolate China via traditional Cold War alliances.

Countries will — and should — shop around for better deals on technology, funding, perks, and political favors in the new "Great Game" for control of the Silk Road. The phrase "Great Game" is nothing new. The British coined it when their Empire was vying for the Silk Road against Russia in the 1800s. (See Frankopan's *The Silk Roads* for an excellent review of how countries and empires are constantly positioning for power, gold and land — and will often say and do anything for all three). This is as true now as it was during the Roman Empire and its attempt to control Jerusalem in the first century.

It appears that the endgame here for the US is to create a D10 (Democracy10) to counter China — an upgrade from the G7. The additions would be Australia, India, and South Korea. There is even talk about including Japan in the "five eyes." Making it six eyes would mean that Japan would be privy to all intelligence from the US, UK, Australia, Canada, and New Zealand, and vice versa. This is not as easy as it sounds, as Japan is opposed to both India and South Korea in the G7 as it morphs into the D10.

Second, the plan is to spread out the military forces throughout the Pacific and away from concentrated areas like South Korea and Japan. The idea is that missiles, drones, and submarines would be dispersed to more and smaller facilities. One idea is to deploy part of the Pacific Fleet to Southeast Asia as a permanent base, possibly in Singapore (This came as a complete surprise to Singapore, by the way!). So far, this plan is merely in its infancy and may still seem incoherent.

Third, a strong divergence from Trump's policies. The Biden Administration is looking to establish an ad hoc, multilateral approach to specific problems in Asia to solve practical problems rather than constantly attacking the Chinese government. These ad hoc working groups would focus on individual problems. Examples of this include issues surrounding trade, environment, technology, supply chains, and standards. Standard setting in Asia, for example, is an important issue and will include the International Telecom-munications Union (ITU) standards and the IGF negotiations for pollution emissions from ships. Essentially, there are many individual areas where there is vast room for cooperation with China and the US. Chief among them is the environment, where China has a commanding lead in the mass rollout of new technologies. At the same time, America has rejoined the Paris Climate Agreement. If there is any one big issue that the US and China can agree on, it is investing in the environment to reduce greenhouse gases.

Fourth, there is a vital need to begin negotiations for zero-hour "weapons of mass destruction." China and the US (and many other nations) have hidden technological weapons (digital time bombs), which are kill switches for vital infrastructure within each other's countries. This could end up being a new set of arm control talks similar to the ones held in Helsinki for reducing nuclear arsenals in the 1980s. These talks are likely to be held in secret because, unlike nuclear weapons, the very fact of showing that they work (like public nuclear testing) undermines the very fact of their secret installation. Therefore, they cannot act as a mutually assured destruction argument because their effectiveness is guaranteed only by keeping their location and function secret. This is the new form of war — zero-hour bots to disable steering systems of ships, turn off airport control towers, stop electricity generation, shut down fresh water pumps, etc. We will see how this ties into prop tech below.

Fifth, National Security Advisor Jake Sullivan makes a valid point that the current struggle between the US and China is a battle of ideas about who is better at offering a superior competing message of peace, liberty, and prosperity. Which side has a more compelling way to offer a "chicken in every pot?" Sullivan advocates a consistent "chorus of voices" from the G7 to push back against China in a "great-power competition of ideas." It is interesting to note that China is still learning the art of soft power, as the country only achieved independence in 1949. Therefore, its articulation of a message of prosperity for the Silk Road occasionally sounds tinny, hollow, or ham-fisted. Soft power is a vital part of the "Great Game." Both sides are definitely ramping up and finding their footing.

Sixth, America's fear of China — and a central theme of this book — lies in China's Smart Cities Development. China sees the use of digital technology to collect and share data to:

(1) Improve efficiency.
(2) Optimise logistics.
(3) Automate manufacturing capacity.
(4) Reduce burdensome bureaucracy.
(5) Use robotics to perform tedious tasks both in the public and private spheres.

China is leading urban, rural, logistical, and commercial digital development. China clearly intends to tie these digital signals to its digital currency (and super apps) in order to allow its private sector companies like Alibaba, Tencent, JD, and Ping An to become more competitive and more efficient as they expand into the Silk Road.

The US sees this as a mortal threat for the reasons stated in the fourth initiative above. Are Chinese super apps benign? Is this new set of digital rails via the BSN a threat to US interests from Hong Kong to Singapore to Istanbul? Can BSN and its connections to logistics and working capital for small and medium enterprises (SMEs) eliminate dollar funding? The current US view is there are too many endpoints of business, government, and consumption throughout capitals in developing countries that could be compromised with a "Chinese kill switch." Technologies that capture and synthesize massive amounts of live data from buildings and homes can jeopardize national security because the systems that control the technology have a potentially very powerful tool: to turn off vital infrastructure and to shut down one's political allies or popularize one's political enemies. This is true for both sides. Sri Lanka and Myanmar have both silenced Facebook for political reasons in the past few years, for instance.

We conclude that the bottom line is as follows: The US sees a fully self-contained and digitized BSN system owned and operated by China as a mortal threat. Why? Chinese industrial, economic, consumer, and lifestyle activity would all occur on a brand new Chinese-owned "digital rail" currency system using untraceable quantum communications. The US has enjoyed unchecked "dollar diplomacy" and naval hegemony for seven decades. Can the US give up dollar dominance to the CNY and can it cede some naval supremacy to the Chinese Navy? Let us see.

Seventh, Secretary of State Antony Blinken comes from West Exec Advisors, a high-powered Democratic consulting firm. Five of the principals are currently serving in the Biden Administration. West Exec is a very hands-on policy advisor which focuses on issues such as cybersecurity, data privacy, trade, and finance. This approach is ideal for the ad hoc approach to solving problems with strategic competitors. In essence, West Exec is a firm that focuses on technology and the way new technologies interact between the private sector, the defense community, and diplomats. Whether this experience is an opportunity or a bane for the Biden administration is yet to be seen.

Eighth, the US is taking two approaches:

(1) Enacting national legislation to protect critical infrastructure internally; and
(2) Considering legislation about how it will compete on the Belt and Road Initiative (BRI) with better products at lower prices.

In essence, the US will review its aid programs as a way to "win hearts and minds."

China is doing exactly what the US did in the 1950s to 1990s with the World Bank, the IMF, the Ex-Im Bank, and OPIC. China is spending US$1.1 trillion on BRI programs, in part to export excess capacity since its own domestic infrastructure buildout is finished. These projects are being implemented in transport, public services, safety, education, healthcare, and the environment. On the technological side, major private companies like Alibaba, Tencent, JD, Baidu, and Huawei are installing integrated IoT, cloud, mobile, and big data analysis in smart cities and smart homes. These programs have *already* been implemented in 106 countries.

In conclusion, the vital differences between the Trump and Biden administrations is that:

(1) The Biden Administration will take a more practical and multi-lateral approach to solving ad hoc issues.
(2) Cooperation on environment is front and center.
(3) Russia is now recognized as far more of a clear and present danger than China.

However, what is needed to secure the US role as a leader of the 21st century is a renewed focus on technological modernization inside the country. Putting international intrigue on hold while *internal renewal* in both human and technological terms seems very wise.

9.6. US' Digital Marshall Plan for the 21st Century

Don Tapscott runs the Blockchain Research Institute. He is a global authority on blockchain technology and released in mid-February

2021 an extensive report which has offered advice to the Biden Administration on what is needed now to maintain competitiveness globally.[4] The bottom line is that it calls for nothing short of a domestic digital Marshall Plan coordinated at the federal, state, and local levels to upgrade America's digital infrastructure.

The extensive report of Tapscott recommends a fresh new approach about the digital age in the economy, in political life, and in society. This must come from the top. It requires breaking down departmental silos across the Federal Government and to support innovation and modernization. It must be devoid of partisanship and cannot be short-sighted or half-hearted.

The recommendations fall into five areas. Prior to the recommendations, the authors adjust expectations by acknowledging that the Biden Administration is facing a host of challenges: a global pandemic, a crushing recession, economic hardship, mushrooming debt, right-wing extremism, and a divided country. That being said, only a focus on innovation and modernization will offer the US a solid footing to compete with China globally.

First, Russian hackers entered the servers of several agencies and wandered around undetected for several months. This breach calls for a coordinated secure technology supply chain that recognizes that the information of citizens are protected and where each citizen's data is, in essence, a sovereign digital identity. This will work to reduce the digital divide.

Second, the US system should embrace a digital dollar. China is years ahead on this score and systems like Facebook's Diem and Coinbase's digital dollar make great sense. Regulatory guidance on digital tokens is needed quickly. Blockchain-based technology makes the most sense in these situations for purposes of tracking, provenance, reporting, and taxation.

Third, leaders at the federal level need to introduce technology that can break through departmental silos. Collaboration is critical.

---

[4]Don Tapscott and Anthony Williams, "New Directions for Government in the Second Era of the Digital Age," Blockchain Research Institute, February 2021.

There is a need to reinvent the government as a digital entity for a new era.

Fourth, these technologies can help to rebuild trust in democracy. Technology can be utilized personally by President Biden and VP Harris to reach out to a far more diverse network of citizens and communities. The new president can use new technologies to create confidence.

Fifth, there is a key need to use technology to aid small businesses. Publicly funded incubators and accelerators need to be improved. There are many gaps in the startup infrastructure that needs fixing. There is a profound need to increase education in technology at the high school and technical college level. This is the only way to inspire a new and diverse set of entrepreneurs and representatives. The US needs business owners and politicians that resemble it and are able to give back to their communities. Aggressive and sweeping policies are needed to overcome decades of inequality and discrimination.

If this sounds familiar, it is because this is exactly what China has done in the past decade.

9.7.   Ongoing Initiatives of the Pentagon and the Private Sector

If we look at specific attempts by the public sector (Pentagon) to connect directly the bottom-up approach with a top-down approach, we should start with the Pentagon's Joint AI Center launched in 2019. This center is focused on the following areas:

(1) Deploy AI in back office in HR legal security budgets contracts logistics.
(2) Train staff to be AI literate: acquisitions, practices and standards.
(3) Lead the understanding of AI talent hubs in Silicon Valley and exchanges with foreign military labs.
(4) Be a focal point for interagency and intelligence sharing.
(5) Make Big Bets via national labs with Pentagon funding, but tackle hard problems by itself.
(6) Advance machine learning where it is practical.

(7) Scale AI implementation throughout academia and technology.
(8) Integrate all systems within Department of Defense. US needs to become top down as well.
(9) Have a regional approach to smart cities.
(10) Prevent foreign investment inside the US where national security could be threatened.

For a more detailed treatment of the strategies that the US could and should employ to kickstart a technological revolution INSIDE the US, please see our book: Austin Groves and Paul S. Schulte (2020). *The Race for 5G Supremacy: Why China is Surging, Where Millennials Struggle and How America Can Prevail* (Singapore: World Scientific).

9.8. Where Does the Private Sector Ends and Government Begins?

It is said China is going through a top-down technological innovator phase while the US is a bottom-up one. This is somewhat of a myth since, for both countries, it is a little of both. Alibaba and Tencent are private companies but do a lot of heavy lifting to advance the FYPs. On the other hand, companies like GE, IBM, and Intel also have very close relationships with the federal government. For the purposes of this chapter, however, let us look at Figure 9.2 to see what is happening in the US with the private companies.

While there is much sound and fury in Washington DC on the political front, there is real progress occurring in California and Washington State with private companies. In particular, we hear of Google and Amazon's progress in smart cities and smart homes. In a more general way, we are quickly learning about the secretive implementation of the IoE, which is to say they are both integrating finance and insurance into the physical world. A different word for this, according to Serendipity founder Rob Jesudason, is "embedded finance." This is another sturdy concept along with proptech.

We also note that Apple is on a tear in this area, although they, too, are deeply secretive about their plans. On the other hand, Microsoft and Facebook are lagging.

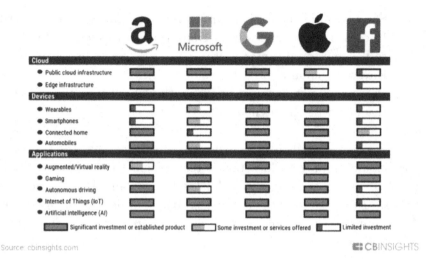

Figure 9.2.   Comparison of the Big 5 as they move further into cloud, devices and apps.

Facebook is, instead, focusing on Libra — now called Diem. This may end up being a competitor to BSN, although it is not yet clear about the intentions and agenda of Facebook. Do not count them out yet!

Amazon has expressed similar commitments to smart cities. In some off-the-record comments with Amazon Web Services (AWS), we came away impressed with the scope and depth of the smart cities initiative. Amazon sees the smart city in similar tones to Tencent. AWS imagines a seamless technology that increases efficiency and uses it for transport, public safety, civic activity, energy efficiency, and economic development. It creates safer and healthier communities.

All of this relies on data and the way in which it can be shared but also kept confidential and the way it can be tokenized and traded. The smart city arrangement that Amazon envisages is built around citizens, infrastructure, and objectives. It is all about four pillars: environment, education, security, and living.

It is trying to use this integrated digitized data pool to:

(1) create sustainable growth and reduce environmental damage;
(2) improve education by virtual learning tools;

(3) fight crime and protect the public; and

(4) enhance daily life.

It is a bold vision and is still in its early stages. It requires a long game, which is difficult with the current fractured US political system. It requires new comprehensive laws and policies to determine what is private and what is public when it comes to the digitized world. Like China, however, the key to all of this lies in the effective use and monitoring of the cloud services.

The problem with the implementation of smart city initiatives in North America is that there are literally billions of data sets all over the place but they are in silo locations belonging to individual private companies, all of which have their own limited apps. Facebook has

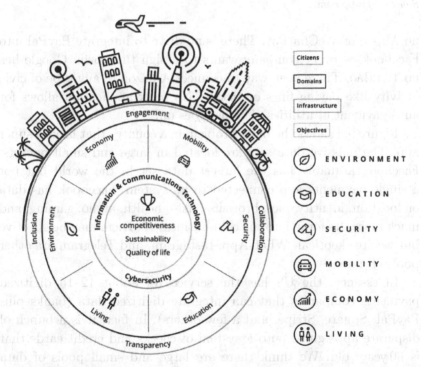

Figure 9.3. The heart of the smart city: economics, security, education, transport, living, environment. It is truly the Internet of Everything (IoE).

Source: Rana Sen and Mark Price, "Smart Cities and the Journey to the 'Cloud'," Deloitte, 2020.

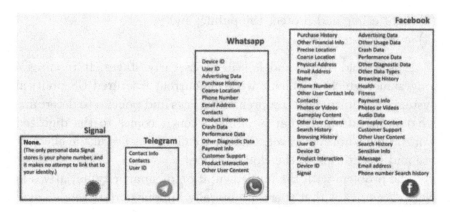

Figure 9.4.   Signal vs Telegram, WhatsApp Facebook Messenger: What data does each app collect from your phone?

Source: Setapp.com.

no Alipay or WeChatPay. There is no drive to integrate PayPal into Facebook — every company wants to design their own. Google has no Tao Bao. There is no way to connect Amazon to any type of civic activity like paying fines or tickets. No bank application allows for auto-payment of utilities. The list goes on.

Figure 9.4 shows the basic problem in a country that lacks a super app. The massive data sets are located in large and small pockets. Facebook arguably has the largest data set in the world but not a single payments app connected to its system. Facebook has data on location, identity, pics, browsing, likes, health, audio, gaming, and much more. Its foray into the coin business via Diem may be effective but we are skeptical. WhatsApp, Instagram, and Telegram are other pools of data.

In essence, the US has the services of about 12–15 digitized payments companies that can integrate digitized data (banks plus PayPal, Square, Stripe, and a few others). In fact, it is a bunch of disparate apps glued onto a system of checks and credit cards that is 60 years old. We think there are large and small pools of data that do not share any data with each other for the simple reason that no super app has yet become powerful enough to swallow up large and disparate data sets. Moreover, the US' fear of monopolies will probably guarantee it will remain so. Our bet is on Visa and MasterCard to reverse engineer and "branch out" to other touch points of credit card users and digitize in that way. It is really a vertical integration from the plastic credit card to a fully digitized business. They are very quietly doing this, and their stock prices reflect the long-term vision. They have both outperformed the banks by a wide margin.

9.9. Case Studies of Innovative Companies in Proptech in the US

In the last section of this chapter, we want to focus on four companies that have developed fascinating ventures in the area of proptech. Prologis may be one of the most interesting (Figure 9.5). We believe

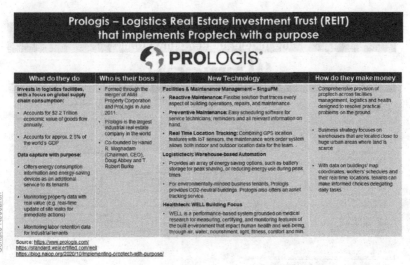

Figure 9.5.   Prologis — An overview.

that the lesson of China is that the integration of 5G, blockchain, finance, and insurance is of the greatest benefit to SMEs and logistics. It is great for personal finance, but the world of the warehouse, port, working capital, production, insurance and distribution is really where these complex systems can reduce or eliminate chronic and debilitating bottlenecks. Prologis is such a company. The following tables shows details of the companies. It focuses on global supply chain management and on operations and maintenance. It includes software solutions, and it looks to solve practical problems on the ground, whether it involves health, environment, logistics, or facilities.

Details on Tricon are elucidated in Figure 9.6. Tricon focuses on several key efforts of proptech: ease of listings, maintenance apps for homes, mapping for new homes, drone spotting for new home listings, end-to-end property rental, and many other features. This company was brought to our attention by property expert Joshua Varghese of CI Signature Investments.

Figure 9.6.   Tricon — An overview.

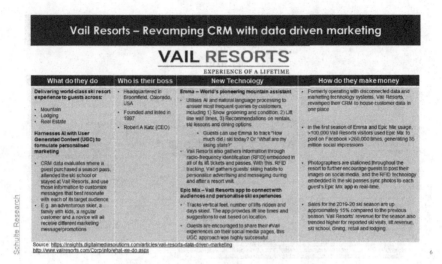

Figure 9.7.   Vail Resorts — An overview.

Vail Resorts has an interesting technology that utilizes AI to deal with every type of skier: family, individual, novice, or experienced (Figure 9.7). It monitors snow conditions, wait times, rental options, lessons, and dining options for skiing. It has gone viral with 55 million hits. In addition, technology embedded in ski passes sync photos to the guest Epic Mix in real time. This helps to turn an event of skiing into an experience of skiing. The skier becomes involved in the experience of camaraderie, dining, learning, and having fun in new ways with like-minded people. Families can interact with other families. Experienced skiers can find other experts. Learners can have fun with other learners.

Lastly, Hilton is blazing trails with AI in the hospitality business (Figure 9.8). It is using data to translate insights into discreet services. It connects hotel reservations to flights. It connects the experience of the hotel to all dining facilities. It connects the interests of the customer to local hangouts. It has taken a long time for hotels to get their act together to offer coordinated and synthesized services

Figure 9.8.   Hilton — An overview.

for a total experience. It is finally happening, but many are asking "Why did this take so long?"

9.10.   The Small Companies in Proptech That Need Careful Consideration

In this section, we describe and analyse many proptech companies in the West that have made great strides in the implementation of technology to harness large amounts of data to more efficiently manage cities, housing estates and commercial real estate. As with the sections focusing on Chinese companies earlier in the book, we also want to highlight below some of the smaller proptech companies that are employing very intriguing technologies to harness the use of data to improve the lives of workers and consumers and make money for shareholders.

We highlight six companies below. The first is Pavegen, based in London (Figure 9.9). It is a joint venture (JV) with the Hinduja Group and is involved in energy and power. It employs kinetic energy of human footsteps on tiles and then uses data from foot traffic to discover consumption patterns and redeploy foot traffic to avoid

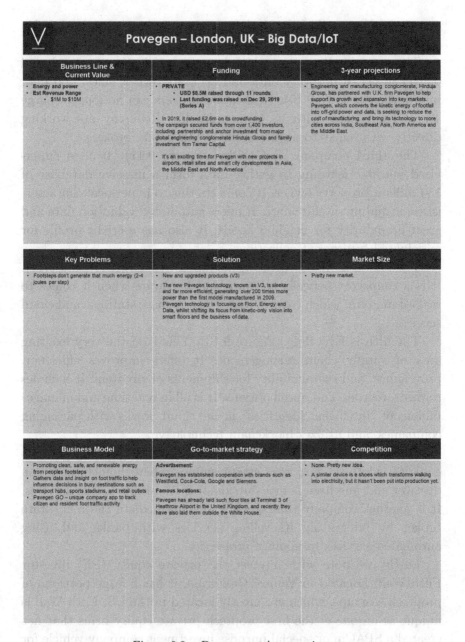

Figure 9.9.   Pavegen — An overview.

crowds and jams. This is ideal for venues such as transport hubs, sports stadiums, and retail outlets.

The second is Reonomy, which is a web application to search and deliver in-depth property data and accurate owner, sales, and debt information (Figure 9.10). Real estate brokers can no longer charge 4% and get away with it. Companies like Reonomy are working directly with banks to disintermediate real estate brokers.

The third company is GeoPhy (Figure 9.11). It uses supervised machine learning to gather data form a massive database of 150 million property owner. It connects this to hyperlocal characteristics, including satellite data. It offers automated valuation data and great granularity for neighborhoods. It also has a credit profile for anticipated future rent collections.

The fourth is Neul, which was acquired by Huawei (Figure 9.12). It is a connector between software and hardware when it comes to real estate data, which travels from chip sets, base stations, and cloud services.

The fifth is Evrythng (Figure 9.13). This is in the very exciting area of supply chain management. It offers improves efficiency, provenance, and sustainability for shipments of any item. It includes rewards, reorder, and upsell options. It is all in real time and manages billions of "intelligent identities" in the cloud, works with packaging companies, and utilizes blockchain technology.

The last is REX, based in Austin, Texas (Figure 9.14). It is a digital platform and real estate service where homeowners can discover and purchase homes outside of the multiple listing services. It is another company that seeks to disintermediate the real estate broker by integrating its selling services with banks and using automated services to manage properties.

Lastly, we note with interest the private equity (PE) investor Fifth Wall. Located in Venice, California, it has a large portfolio of proptech startups, which are mostly located in the US. Fifth Wall is unique as on one of the first proptech private equity firms that has created a SPACm or special purpose investment company vehicle for future investments. This is one to watch.

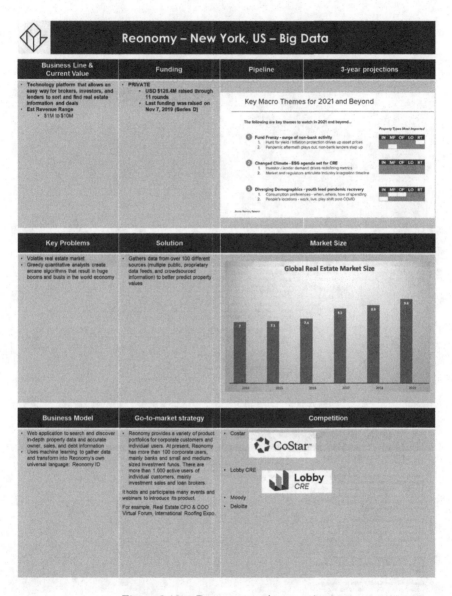

Figure 9.10.   Reonomy — An overview.

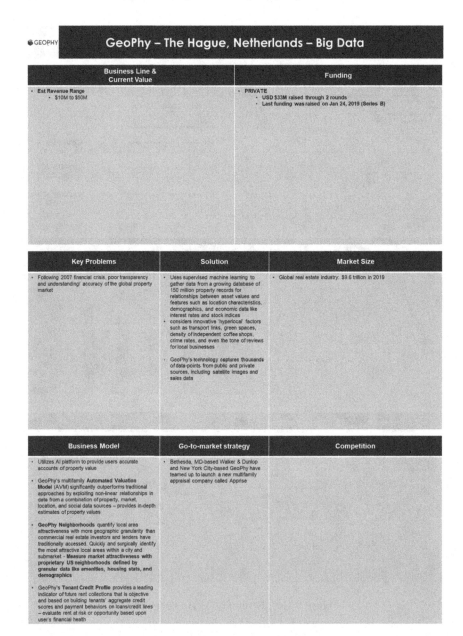

Figure 9.11.   GeoPhy — An overview.

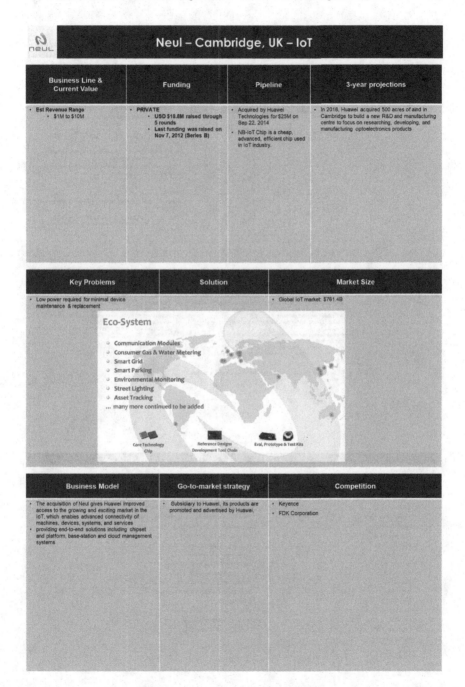

Figure 9.12.   Neul — An overview.

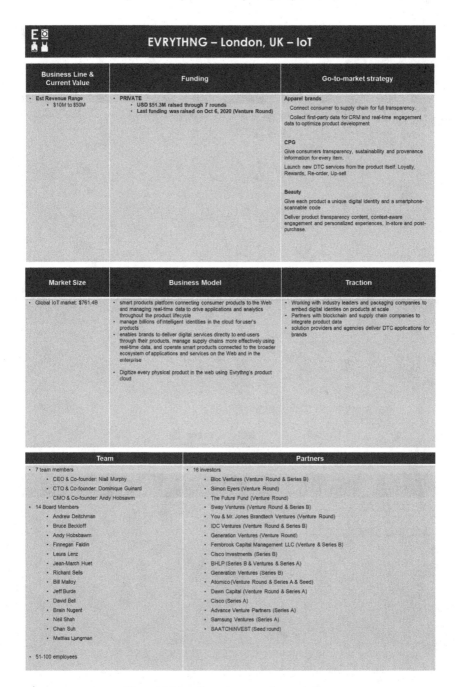

Figure 9.13.   Evrythng — An overview.

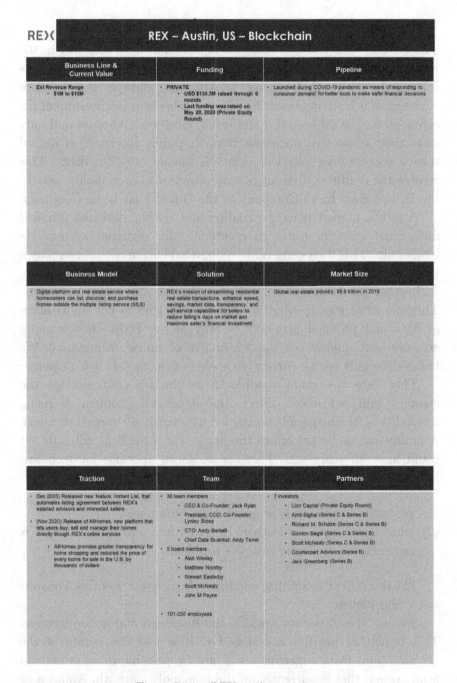

Figure 9.14.   REX — An overview.

9.11.   Conclusion

The US has both political and ideological challenges standing in the way of a fully digitized economy where physical assets can become tokenized and tradable currency. After all, data is the ultimate currency. If it is sitting inside Excel spreadsheets or in government file cabinets, it is worthless. If it sits inside Google or Amazon and only suits their respective purposes, then a "public Internet" of digital tokens representing physical assets is usable only by them. This creates the digital equivalent of state-sanctioned monopolies akin to the British East India Company or the Dutch East India Company.

A public market place for trading and valuing digitized physical data must exist in order to create a fully digitized system via blockchain. This then can lead to a digitized currency that can play a vital role in the outside world and includes some ease of functionality with other blockchain-based cryptocurrencies and smart contracts. This is a vital way to counter China's vast lead in the digitization of data and physical property by way of the BSN. Only a rapid advancement guarantees the possibility of dollar ascendancy. We believe the only entity currently capable of doing this is Coinbase.

There are two main roadblocks as the US contemplates the strategy laid out above. First, the structural problem of rising inequality is leaving people poorer in an increasingly expensive world. A family can no longer afford the house, car, or college education it could have 40 years ago. There is no social appetite for technical integration of property when:

(1) property ownership is at generational lows, and
(2) when this inequality leads to mistrust in a government which is not seen to be solving people's problems.

The discontent is spilling out through corrosive politics, conspiracies, and violence.

Second, the corporate world is too dispersed and uncooperative. This is neither positive nor negative; it is just the reality of the US situation. Data supremacy will not be possible in an American legal system that is currently on the monopoly warpath. Amazon or

Google cannot integrate enough data to capture civic, urban, and private property without the Department of Justice's watchful eye. The only time monopolies in the US were allowed to flourish with bipartisan support is during times of extreme international tension. Must China be made into a much more imminent threat for Amazon, Apple, and Google to gain the control they want?

At the end of the day, the digital integration of property is a fight for the New Silk Road. Central Asia, Africa, and Eastern Europe have massive swathes of undeveloped land, exploding populations, and weak property rights. The Washington Consensus tried and failed to bring development in this area of the world. Are we entering an era of the Beijing Consensus? Is it their turn to take a crack at it? So far, the Beijing Consensus has far fewer political and economic constraints, and more infrastructure and technical support.

If China is able to quickly build the area between Xinjiang, Kyiv, and Lagos, it will win hearts, minds, and most importantly, customers. Since the US cannot currently compete on digital property, it has resorted to kneecapping China and vilifying it enough to build up domestic support for a seamless integration of Silicon Valley and the Pentagon. The US partnership is trying to create its own digital Silk Road, perhaps with unwitting allies like Facebook (Let us never forget Crypto AG. The country that was using technology to spy on more than 120 countries for the past 60 years was not China).

Both countries are filled with incredibly bright, talented, and globally minded people. Friendly competition between the two has the potential to push global technology forward, bring billions of people out of poverty, and solve seemingly intractable global problems (climate change, inequality, etc.). However, competition must come from within. It requires an honest acknowledgment of your own and your competitor's achievements, potential, and flaws. It requires goal setting, national planning, and a vision for the world a hundred years from now, not just two or four. Losing ought not to become a spark for violent conflict. It should be a wakeup call, not a clarion call.

A multipolar world is always better than a unipolar one. One co-author of this book is an American citizen of Ukrainian descent who knows the pain of a country in civil war — he and his mother fled an incipient civil war and a collapsed USSR to become US citizens. Another co-author of this book has two parents who met in Asia during war and has a few siblings who are part of the US nightmare of opioid addiction. A third is from Hangzhou, China, who has been raised in the shadow of Alibaba and its astonishing cutting-edge progress. However, his ancestors came from a China that only 70 years ago was embroiled in a chaotic civil war. As the eerie saying goes, "Do not look for war. It will always look for you."

All peoples are acutely aware of both the hypocrisy and the hope of national leadership. All are proud of the breakthroughs and innovations of entrepreneurs. Everyone acknowledges the dark implications their missteps can produce especially if the digitization of physical assets turns into a tokenized Orwellian bazaar. In the midst of all of this, all peoples require dignity. If nothing else, this book is a call to action. The times call for leaders on both sides of the Pacific to learn from each other, find new room for collaboration and, above all, offer each side a modicum of human dignity. We want to make sure this is a century of building smart cities and wealthy nations instead of destroying them only to leave behind ignorance and poverty.

Acknowledgments

I am thankful to friends all over the world. In Hong Kong and China, I am thankful for people with great knowledge and insight like David Courtney, Frank Wang, Kyu Ho, Danny Lee, Maaike Steinbach, Gorlen Zhou, Danny McLellan, Boris Burgess, Suraj Sajnani, Ben Shenglin, Charles Liu, Dede Nickerson, Christian Ng, Tony Verb, Simon Carland, Terry Sun, Daniel Tu, and Gino Yu.

Joshua Varghese from CI and Rafiq Jumabhoy are original thinkers in the area of proptech and I have bounced many ideas in the book off them.

My wonderful interns over the years have taught me more than they know: Jason Kang, Andrew Ho, Philipp Hultsch, Ben Printz, Matt Zayco, Desai Chu, Will Stuart, Mirza Mohammed, Jasper Swaak, and Nik Lemeshko.

The US and Canada folks who have helped me along the way include the wonderful and brilliant Fred Feldkamp, Todd Tibbetts, Peter Early, Tom Eslinger, Austin Groves, Michael Del Castillo, Craig Asano, and Drummond Brodeur.

My friends in Singapore who have been guides and friends cover the past three years are the very smart Rob Jesudason, Gary Ang, Melissa Guzy, David Lee (who penned the foreword), Dan Liebau, David Dredge, Malcolm Bone, Chia Hock Lai, John Fowler, Greg Li, David Toh, Yinglan Tan, my agent Andrew Vine, Zhan Qing, and Taiyang Zhang.

Important guiding lights for me from points East and West include David Halpert, Scott Sleyster, Jim Stent, Lawson Emanuel, Paul Guthrie, Brian Ganson, James Brackenbury, Pamela Berkowsky, Annabel Betz, Fr. Bill Fulco, SJ., Barbara Thole, my brothers Chris and Dan, Mixo Das, Kevin Tang, and my birth twin Jorge Sebastiao. Lastly, we had a great deal of help along the way with boundless energy and editing of JY Phuang and great help from Dillon Hunter and Connor Lee. Special thanks to Jiang Yulin at World Scientific.

Paul Schulte

I am thankful to my parents, Sun Xiaoming and Zhang Jiali, who accompany me through all the hard times of life and support all my decisions. Thank you to my cousin, Song Zizhang, hope you are well in the UK, and his parents, who took care of me when I was away from home. Special thanks to my best friend, Xu Yuan, for the companion though the whole university life and the friendship, forever and always. I am very thankful to Jiang Xubeier for your emotional support; Cui Jing, for the fancy times we had together and your life advice; Wangwei, for being affectionate and encouraging during the hardest times; Ye Shuyuan, for the pleasure and time we enjoy together. I am also thankful to my friends, Zhai Yonghao, Xu Chenyao, Zhu Yuqi, Zhang Qihang, and Pang Ningjing.

I owe a lot to my professors, Prof. Ben Shenglin, for all the help he provided for this Book, and Prof. Zhu Yanjian, Prof. Liu Xiaobin, Prof. Zeng Tao, and Prof. Li Shenghong for imparting their knowledge on science as well as of life.

I am very thankful to my coworkers, Desai, Andrew, Dillion, JY, Roman, Lingjie, Taotao and Xiaoqian, for the skills they taught me and work experience we have shared together. I am most thankful to Paul Schulte, who is not only my employer but also my life mentor.

I would like to give special thanks to Dr. Li Zhuoqun and Mrs. He Wanyu, who are the CEO of ZiFiSense and Xkool Technology, respectively, for doing the best interviews with us.

Last of all, thank you to all the heroes who impact my thinking on science and life: Elon Musk, Tim Cook, Barack Obama, Albert Einstein, Vincent Van Gogh, Chu Kochen, and Michael Artin.

Dean Sun

This book stands testament to the people who raised me intellectually, emotionally, and of course, physically.

First, thank you to my family: Yevgen, Liliana, Vitaliy, and Tatyana Shemakov. Special thanks to my sister Olga Melnyk, for putting up with my childhood antics.

Thank you to my closest and longest friends — Reed Orchinik for being the single most important reason I could attend a university; Ben Shindel for having the biggest impact on my personality; and Emma Hobbs for being the greatest source of confidence. Special thanks to each of their families who took me in and treated me like one of their one: Miles and Dana Orchinik, Matvey and Sharon Shindel, and Lisa Monheit.

Special thanks to Libby Hoffenberg, without whose brilliance and care this work would not have been possible. Especially, thanks to her parents, Peter Hoffenberg and Saundra Schwartz, for being an incredible intellectual support network, even without their knowledge.

Special thanks to Jonathan Kay, without whom nights would be shorter and days would be dimmer. Especially, thanks to his parents, Barbara and David Kay, whose sponsorship enables both our success and that of the broader northern California viticulture economy.

Thanks to the pedagogues who have been an indispensable source of support and knowledge in my life, and who manage to change the lives of their students through wisdom and patience, while also creating world-class research at the same time: Jose Vergara, Megan Brown, Catherine Sanger, Marjory Murphy, Ricardo Cardoso, Richard Glover, Tim Cornwell, Erin and Jack Kahn.

Thank you to the mentors in my life who have shown me what leadership looks like. David Kim, Valerie Jones, Jim Snipes, John

Phillips, David Foster, Paul and Pat Hsu, Andrew Afflerbach, Jaonne Hovis, Alla Soroka, Robert Gamble, Tony Verb, Jordan Kostelac, Karen Henry, and Dion Lewis. Special thanks to Li Ling for the invaluable lessons he has taught me on perseverance, fearlessness, and optimism in one's work . . . and humility in one's ping-pong skills.

Thank you to those who made 2020 manageable: Varya Nekhina, Alex Kuzmin, Kimi Mok, Andrew Locke, Beth Clarke, Chase Williams, Abby Diebold, Ruth Carolyn, Ethan Seletsky, Kai Golden, Kanhav Thakur, Ariel Chu, Halo Lahnert, Shivram Viswanathan, Saif Zihiri, and Annika Freudenberger as well as the entirety of the Luce 2020 cohort.

Thank you to the people who welcomed my family into the US and introduced us to the American Dream. Neal Horenstein, whose humor, intellect, and capacity to scare my mother is unmatched. Steve Pray, who opened his heart and his home. Alexander Oberhensley for having the greatest capacity for growth I have ever seen in anyone. Renai and Steve Oberhensley, for creating a beautiful family others can only strive for. Unfortunately, also one that is too large to even begin to list, nonetheless, thanks to every Oberhensley and De Jesus.

Thank you to all of the people I admire and whom I believe will craft the world in their brilliant image. David Pipkin, Jia Chern Teoh, Brandon Zunin, Gilbert Orbea, Cassandra Stone, Natasha Markov-Riss, Jigme Tobgyel, Al Lim, Grayson Mick, Ben Stern, Lily Fornof, Keton Kakkar, Minsoo Bae, Kendell Durkson, Daria Mateescu, Shreya Chattopadhyay, Egor Cherniuk, Francesco Massari, Galina Gagaeva, Heewon Park, Anastasia Vasilyeva, Simon Thibaud, Lu Min Lwin, Gus Burchell, Dany Kirilov, Galena Sardamova, Anastasia Varenytsya, Maria Ingersoll, Lexi Lampard, and Maisie Wills.

Thank you to those whose work I have deeply admired and who have influenced my thinking on technology, urban planning, and geopolitics: Benjamin Bratton, George Yin, Jili Chung, Sean Moss-Pultz, Wei Feng Lee, and Rafiq Jumabhoy.

Last, but not least, thank you to Paul Schulte. He has been a transformative support and guide in my life. Neither this project nor my personal development would have happened without his patience and guidance.

Roman Shemakov

Index

Singapore University of Social Sciences - World Scientific Future Economy Series

(Continued from page x)